THE ART OF LISTENING

W9-AWX-501

HARPER & ROW, PUBLISHERS

New York, Hagerstown, Philadelphia, San Francisco, London

THE ART OF LISTENING
Developing Musical Perception

Fourth Edition

JEANNE SHAPIRO BAMBERGER
Massachusetts Institute of Technology

HOWARD BROFSKY
Queens College, The City University of New York

With a foreword by **ROGER SESSIONS**

Sponsoring Editor: *Phillip Leininger*
Project Editor: *David Nickol*
Designer: *Frances Torbert Tilley*
Senior Production Manager: *Kewal K. Sharma*
Photo Researcher: *Myra Schachne*
Compositor: *Progressive Typographers, Inc.*

Sculpture for cover and part opening pages: *Miriam Brofsky*

THE ART OF LISTENING: *Developing Musical Perception,* Fourth Edition
Copyright © 1979 by Jeanne Shapiro Bamberger and Howard Brofsky

All rights reserved. Printed in the United States of America. No part of this book may be used or reproduced in any manner whatsoever without written permission except in the case of brief quotations embodied in critical articles and reviews. For information address Harper & Row, Publishers, Inc., 10 East 53rd Street, New York, N.Y. 10022.

Library of Congress Cataloging in Publication Data

Bamberger, Jeanne Shapiro.
  The art of listening.

  Includes indexes.
  1. Music—Analysis, appreciation. 2. Music—Instruction and study—Audio-visual aids. I. Brofsky, Howard, joint author. II. Title.
MT150.B25   1979   780'.15   78-20837
ISBN 0-06-040943-6

CONTENTS

PART TWO

Process and Design

PART THREE

Structure: Form and Function

PART FOUR
The Historical Context

FOREWORD *by Roger Sessions*

This book can be of great value to the student or layman who is attracted to music and who seeks to gain from it all that it has to offer him. To be sure, the reader will not be able to achieve his goal without effort; but it is not the authors of the book, but music itself, which demands this effort—an effort no greater and no less, after all, than that demanded by any of the other major arts.

The quotation from Stravinsky that begins the introduction should be pondered and kept constantly in mind as a kind of premise underlying all that the student can learn from the book. *The Art of Listening* is presented by its authors against a background of a general course in humanities at the University of Chicago; and the book's value derives from the authors' firm conviction that understanding of music, on any level whatever, is to be found only in music itself, and in a direct awareness of music rather than information about it. Much of the value of the book therefore stems to a large extent from its earlier portions, in which the reader is shown, through simple and effective steps, how such direct awareness can be cultivated. The authors have organized their material clearly and well, with a view to the reader's experience; they introduce each element first in its most immediately apprehensible form and follow this directly by illustrations of its application in a larger context. In doing so, material is drawn from a large variety of sources in such a manner, one would expect, as to stimulate the reader's curiosity and make him aware of the fact that the horizons of music are indeed very broad. The authors, by repeated emphasis, make clear the fact, often neglected, that these so-called elements of music must in no way be considered as independent of each other; they are facets of a whole that is indivisible by its very nature.

The authors also—without undue insistence but nevertheless very clearly—emphasize the importance of genuine involvement on the part of anyone who is drawn toward music, whatever the motive or the nature of this involvement may be. Such involvement is taken for granted by virtually everyone in literature and the visual arts, but is much less generally understood in music. No one could be very seriously regarded as a lover or connoisseur of poetry if his experience of poetry were limited to occasional cursory readings which did not include his lingering over the poem and savoring every detail to the full. The same quality of "savoring" is considered intrinsic to an appreciation of the visual arts. The problem with music, however, lies in the impermanence which constitutes its very nature. Far more than any art, its whole existence is in the realm of time, to which it gives shape and content. Like time, music passes, and its regulated flow is of the very essence. One cannot linger over music and enjoy its flavor to the full without, on the one hand, playing or singing it, or, on the other, listening to it attentively and repeatedly, and thus becoming aware of its movement in detail.

The authors (wisely, I believe) have left for the last chapters the section of the book whose function is solely to provide information of a historical nature. This information is provided in summary fashion, and ample indications are given as to where additional factual material can be found if desired. That such information should be offered is natural, if only to satisfy the curiosity of the reader. The reader will in the course of the book have become acquainted with a wide variety of music and may well have become curious as to the sources of and reasons for this variety. However, today probably as never before—and probably above all in colleges and universities—it needs to be tirelessly emphasized that music, like every other art, has existence and values of its own, quite distinct from its history, its ethnology, or its theory. It is these values which must be paramount if music is to be understood in any sense at all. The authors of *The Art of Listening* have, I believe, understood this point exceptionally well. Here too their aim is to stimulate the student's powers of observation and independent judgment. While starting with categorical distinctions of a conventional, and therefore convenient, nature, they quickly take pains to point out the looseness and inadequacy of these distinctions and the richness and variety and freedom of invention which lies beneath and ultimately remains quite independent of them.

PREFACE

In revising the book and records for the fourth edition we have made
major changes in nearly every chapter. The decision to do a major revi-
sion was initially motivated by a desire to economize through limiting the
number of examples, thus cutting down on the number of records and
the total cost of the set. This we have done (the set is now five records
instead of the original seven), but in the process we found it necessary to
rethink the whole course of the book.

A number of other factors have contributed to the major revisions
in this fourth edition. Our experience in using the book with our own
students, together with suggestions from our colleagues around the
country in a great variety of teaching institutions, have both been major
guiding forces. One of us (Bamberger) has, over the past four years,
been deeply involved in experimental studies in musical perception and
learning, particularly the cognitive aspects of musical development.
These studies have taken a practical form in some of the new approaches
to fundamental musical concepts—what might be called the "basic skills"
of musical understanding. The other (Brofsky) has "blown his cover" as
a long-time jazz trumpeter by applying his historical and analytic exper-
tise to this field. Thus, you will find in this new edition more jazz examples, a more thorough historical coverage of jazz, and also a perhaps
unique integration of the jazz idiom with that music usually associated
with the concert hall and with academic studies.

Other revisions can be summarized as follows:

1. The book has become a more integrated whole. Each chapter
explicitly integrates previous concepts with new ones. This includes not
only references to earlier examples but also new analyses of previously
heard works in the light of new considerations. For example, in the Additional Materials at the end of Chapter 2 we take a second look-listen at
a number of works initially used to illustrate aspects of texture, but now
from the point of view of rhythmic interest. In the Additional Materials
at the end of Chapter 5 we revisit a number of works initially used to
illustrate texture, rhythm, and melodic aspects, but now from the point
of view of harmony. Thus the book is truly cumulative; the student is
reminded of previous experience and this earlier experience is continuously updated.

2. Music notation has gained a new role. More actual printed music has been included in the book, but of even greater significance, the student is given progressive guidance on how to use the printed score effectively. The emphasis here is on helping students to make a productive connection between what they can hear and what they can see. In previous editions we shied away from notation because our experience suggested that students were unable to "map" their perceptions onto the particularities of the printed page. Sound and score remained at best two separate worlds; at worst the score was simply incomprehensible—useless. The guides we have incorporated take students from aspects of music they can hear to their "reflection" on the page; then, gradually, as their abilities to differentiate musical elements increase, these are made more explicit through their visible realization in notation. Thus, the score becomes a tool for increasing perception rather than merely a substitute for it.

3. Style and music history have gained a new role. While still reserving central focus on history for the final two chapters, all the chapters now include historical considerations. For example, at the outset we relate the "varieties of sound" to stylistic change, and in Chapter 2 we discuss and illustrate the uses of rhythmic complexity through a chronological "trip" over a period of 400 years. Similarly, the notion of an "intuitive model of a sensible tune" is related to its stylistic characteristics, harmony is viewed in the context of historical periods, and, finally, we make another historical sweep by illustrating continuous music over a wide range of periods and styles—including baroque and classical fugues.

4. Approximately 20 percent of the musical examples are new. In some cases new examples illustrate concepts that were not included previously (such as dramatic music), and in other cases we have substituted new examples that better make some point. And, as noted above, there are more jazz examples, including a short historical survey of jazz (in Chapter 8) based on the excerpts that occur throughout the book. Many of the recordings of previously included examples are new, but, as always, we have tried to be very particular in our selection of performers. Besides these general additions, Chapters 1 through 5 have all been reorganized with an eye to retaining what we believe to be their most effective aspects while at the same time compressing, expanding and rearranging where it seemed called for. Some distinctions which we felt

to be too particular or too detailed we have incorporated into more general distinctions. For example, a single heading, Rhythmic Complexities, now subsumes previously separate categories like syncopation, shifting meter and metric superimposition. The chapter on melody has been rewritten with a less fine-grained analysis and more appeal to the students' immediate perception.

The chapter on harmony, which seems to be the most difficult for students, has been made more accessible, keeping the major distinctions but dealing with them more globally, and including harmonic analysis (with score) of a whole Haydn minuet movement.

Finally, we have chosen new pictures and in general tried to create a book which is both attractive and practical. The aim of the book remains one of developing students' abilities to participate more actively in the musical process rather than one of learning how to talk *about* music. We have tried to achieve this goal by attending to what we believe to be an individual's natural course of musical growth while at the same time progressively developing students' awareness of those musical relations which, as directly experienced, create greatness in music.

Jeanne Shapiro Bamberger
Howard Brofsky

PICTURE CREDITS

We thank the individuals, organizations, and institutions for supplying the photographs that appear on the pages indicated.

Pages 2-3: The Cleveland Museum of Art, Gift from various donors by exchange

Page 13: Wide World

Page 14: Courtesy of Professor Stanley Backer and Dr. Stelios Arghyros, Fibers and Polymers Laboratories, M.I.T.

Page 39: Young, DPI

Page 40 (left): Johnson, DPI

Page 40 (right): Courtesy, Norlin

Page 44: Wide World

Page 45: Philadelphia Museum of Art, Louise and Walter Arensberg Collection

Page 48: India Consulate

Page 55: Courtesy RCA Records

Page 61: The Metropolitan Museum of Art, Museum Excavations, 1922–1923

Page 67: The New York Public Library Picture Collection

Page 72: The Juilliard School, photo by Gold

Page 79: Wide World

Page 94–95: Philadelphia Museum of Art, photo by A. J. Wyatt, Staff Photographer

Page 99: The Library of Congress, Washington, D.C. (purchased from the composer in 1934 with the help of funds presented by the "Friends of Music of the Library of Congress")

Page 112: Professor I. W. Bailey, Harvard University (from Gyorgy Kepes, *The New Landscape in Art and Science,* by permission of the author)

Page 114 (top): Professor Harold E. Edgerton, M.I.T.

Page 121: Yaeger, DPI

Page 125: Beckwith Studios

Page 127: Schreiber, DPI

Page 130: Wide World

Page 132: The Pierpont Morgan Library

Page 148: Bojilova, DPI

Page 149: The New York Public Library Picture Collection

Page 156 (left): The Metropolitan Museum of Art, Murch Collection, Gift of Helen Miller Gould, 1910

Page 156 (right): Peabody Museum, Harvard University, photograph by F. P. Orchard

Page 164: Hedrich-Blessing

Page 172: Victor Vasarely, *Oeta.* Number 4 from *Vasarely,* a portfolio of twelve serigraphs, 1959. Serigraph, $21^{13}/_{16}$ x $14\frac{1}{2}$". Collection, The Museum of Modern Art, New York. Gift of Madame Denise Rene.

Page 173: Louise and Walter Arensberg Collection, Philadelphia Museum of Art

Page 176: (top) Japan Information Service, (bottom) South African Consulate General

Page 185: (left) French Embassy Press Information, (right) Stock, Boston

Page 188: Ruiko, DPI

Page 215: Morty Yoss

Page 220: Martin, DPI

Page 232: Piet Mondrian, *Composition in Red, Blue, and Yellow,* 1937–42. Oil on canvas, $23\frac{3}{4}$ x $21\frac{7}{8}$". The Sidney and Harriet Janis Collection, Gift to the Museum of Modern Art, New York.

Page 233: Scala, EPA

Page 240: The New York Public Library Picture Collection

Page 244: Herwig, Stock, Boston

Page 260: The New York Public Library (presented as a gift in 1932 by the Bliss and Herter families)

Page 261: The Elizabeth Sprague Coolidge Foundation Collection, The Library of Congress, Washington, D.C.

Page 264: Vincent van Gogh, *The Starry Night,* 1889. Oil on canvas, 29 x $36\frac{1}{4}$". Collection, The Museum of Modern Art, New York. Acquired through the Lilliw P. Bliss Bequest.

Page 265: Professor J. C. Hunsaker (from Gyorgy Kepes, *The New Landscape in Art and Science,* by permission of the author)

Page 269: The New York Public Library Picture Collection

Page 270: Ministry of Information and Tourism, Madrid

Page 272: The Hispanic Society of America

Page 273: The New England Conservatory of Music, Boston, Mass. (presented by Mr. Eben D. Jordan)

Page 284: Spanish National Tourist Office

Page 285: Steer, DPI

Page 302: John Herrick Jackson Music Library, Yale University

Page 308: The Gertrude Clarke Whittall Foundation Collection, The Library of Congress, Washington, D.C.

Page 317: ARP Instruments

Page 326: The New York Public Library Picture Collection

Page 327: *Igor Stravinsky* by Pablo Picasso. Copyright © S.P.A.D.É.M. Paris, 1974.

INTRODUCTION

. . . verbal dialectic is powerless to define musical dialectic in its totality.
—Stravinsky[1]

This book grew from our desire to teach introductory music from an entirely new and radically different point of view. When we first developed the materials for this new approach, we were both teaching the introductory humanities course at the University of Chicago. There were no prerequisites for the course. Neither an ability to read music nor any extensive familiarity with it was required. Through encouraging an exchange among students and between students and instructor, we tried to discover the paths through which students become actively involved with music. We concluded that the primary emphasis in our classes should be on experience itself rather than on facts about music, terminology, or techniques.

We have taken the same approach now in this book. In every way possible, we have reinforced the principle of beginning with one's immediate response to a given piece of music rather than with "the acquisition of a vocabulary."

You, as a student using this book and its accompanying records, should first consider your own experience with a given example. Then try to determine what in the music has contributed to this experience. Having done so, you're ready to return once more to your own experience of the piece in the light of your more conscious awareness of what has stimulated it. The learning process must be an active one, one in which you are always personally involved, questioning, and critical.

Following the cue of our students, we begin with that aspect of music which seems most immediately accessible: its purely sensuous effect upon the listener. We examine a variety of possibilities for making and combining sounds in the works of different composers (Chapter 1). Having first isolated certain aspects of sound, we then show how these aspects are combined and interrelated in more complex fashions. Our

---

[1] Igor Stravinsky, *Poetics of Music,* Cambridge: Harvard University Press, 1947, p. 123.

analysis leads naturally into another aspect of music, rhythmic organization (Chapter 2).

You will discover, for instance, the notion of measured time—the beat and the grouping of beats into larger units of time. From here we go on to combine and interrelate other factors which contribute to a sense of organized time in music. You will consider the relative duration and motion of whole musical gestures and then hear how varying durations and rates of motion affect your experience of specific passages.

At this point, you will step back from these broader considerations once again to isolate elements, this time to consider *pitch* and how it can be organized to form *melody* (Chapter 3).

Next you will consider aspects of music that contribute to its larger scale structure (*return* and *variation* in Chapter 4, *harmony* in Chapter 5). Here you will naturally begin to move outward from the details of specific and rather isolated pitch and time relationships. Rhythmic, melodic, and harmonic aspects will eventually be heard not as isolated factors but as parts of an inseparable whole, combining and influencing one another to create the events, motion, and process of a unique work.

You will go on, then, to focus on the *functions* of passages within larger works (Chapters 6 and 7). In these chapters you will discover how the same melodic or rhythmic material can be dramatically transformed so as to create contrasts in the feelings they evoke (stability, instability, tension, repose) and also to create varying structural functions (statement, transition, development, ending) within a piece.

Having begun, then, with your response to an immediately perceptible aspect of music—its sound—our analysis becomes increasingly specific. Through a growing awareness of specific musical means we move toward more complete perception of, and response to, the total piece of music which those means generate. The excitement you feel in response to a significant detail in a small excerpt develops into the possibility for fuller participation in a complete work.

The process is paralleled in the recorded material itself. You will notice that the excerpts become longer as we move from isolated aspects of music toward the total experience of a work. For example, in the earlier portions of the chapters on texture, rhythmic relationships, or pitch relationships, you will find shorter excerpts chosen to focus your attention on one particular element. Later in these chapters (and especially when we deal with structure, function, or style), the excerpts will grow longer. Finally you are dealing with complete works.

In short, this organization reflects in a practical fashion the process which we described above: the movement from the perception of *isolated* aspects toward the perception of these aspects as an inseparable *whole*—a specific work with its unique emotional impact.

With the goal of developing active and full perception, we ask you from the beginning to listen carefully to each example, always with the appropriate section of the book in hand. Without the book the musical examples will seem a strange and often meaningless hodgepodge. The short excerpts (particularly in the early chapters of the book) demand a special and probably new mode of listening to music. You cannot expect simply to put on a record and listen straight through an entire side. Instead you will need to concentrate on each individual example, sometimes listening to it more than once. In many instances you will be asked to listen for very speific details which may not be immediately apparent. If you cannot hear in the excerpt what is described in the text, go back and listen again, since it may be just these new dimensions of a composition that will give the piece quite a different meaning for you. Notice, also, that each of the records is banded at organizational division points. Bands will help you to locate a particular example or group of examples which you might want to hear again.

While some parts of the demonstrations may require repeated listening, others may seem overly simple, particularly to those of you who play an instrument. However, even these rudimentary concepts are fundamental to later concerns. They provide a base upon which to build by putting forth in as functional a manner as we are able, the underlying, often unconscious foundations on which your musical experience is based. For the less experienced listener the more rudimentary demonstrations can serve as initial steps. For the more experienced listener they provide an opportunity to become aware of knowledge and listening skills that may already have been acquired but in a less organized and conscious fashion. In either case it is important that you not only understand the concepts discussed and the specific descriptions of excerpts but that you also hear in the music what is being described.

You will notice, too, that the examples in any one demonstration are chosen from widely different periods (we've included all known dates of composition). Thus, in addition to the specifically stated reason for including an example, the wide variety will also gradually develop your awareness of and sensitivity to a broad range of musical styles. In fact, one purpose of the book is to broaden your taste. By first helping you to become aware of those aspects of music that you already hear and take for granted as "making sense," we will then go on to develop these givens until you are able to hear new aspects which contribute to less familiar musical styles. In this way pieces that you may initially feel are dull or even incomprehensible, you can come to enjoy—your musical taste will be expanded to include more and different kinds of music.

You will notice that we do group examples by historical periods at times (in Chapters 2, 5 and 7, for instance), but it is only in the last section of the book (Chapters 8 and 9) that we consider the historical context of music directly. We have put off specifically discussing the significance of the historical moment in which a work is written for two reasons: (1) To grasp fully the characteristics of the style of a particular composer or group of composers writing contemporaneously requires all the listening skill that you have been acquiring before reaching this section. (2) Historical significance can be understood only against the background of experience with music of all periods. By the time you reach the final section, your increased perception, your broader musical experience, and your growing sensitivity to stylistic differences will help you gain a deeper understanding of specific musical styles.

We do not attempt to provide a short history of music or even a summary of all the features of different styles. Rather, we ask you to consider how an awareness of tradition and style influences your perception of individual works. We are concerned, then, with historical context as only *one* of the aspects contributing to your total involvement with a piece of music. The primary goal of the last section of the book is to encourage you to listen to each piece of music *on its own terms.* This kind of listening requires an awareness of the terms—that is, of the style of the music. Remember, however, that the identification of a style, period, or composer ought not to be a substitute for actually listening to the unique events of each work.

At the end of most chapters you will find a section entitled Additional Materials. These sections should not be considered as "extra"; they are an integral part of the book. Sometimes they present various kinds of exercises which encourage you to "perform" actively; but most important, they recommend further listening through which you can extend your newly acquired musical perception beyond the excerpts in the demonstrations to longer musical examples—in many cases, to whole pieces. We have tried with these Additional Materials to show how various aspects of music actually function within the context of whole works. You are strongly urged to find recordings of the works recommended or refer back to the examples discussed if they have already been included in a demonstration. In some chapters there is also a supplementary section called Ancillary Reading, which provides a number of definitions and other relevant information.

One of the greatest problems we have faced in preparing this book is that of the inevitable distortion which occurs when some aspect of a total organism is isolated—whether that organism be a living thing or a piece of music. An examination of any one aspect of music immediately distorts your hearing of those works we have chosen as illustrations, since we are asking you to listen only to that one facet of the music and to leave out others which also contribute to the total effect.

This problem cannot be entirely avoided. Still, we have tried to overcome it in two ways: (1) by choosing examples in which the particular aspect of music under consideration is a significant factor in the total experience, and (2) by trying to keep in mind all the facets of a given moment in a piece—such as rhythm, harmony, and melodic shape—as they influence the particular aspect which may be our temporary concern.

The problem of distortion is complicated in that any excerpt is only a moment in the total time span of the work. When we analyze the music, we are slicing it not only horizontally, so to speak, into its component parts but also vertically, into bits of time. That music takes place in time and not statically in space is a constant problem in trying to describe its effect. As soon as we stop it to look or listen closely, we are distorting the work as a total organism.

We feel a certain discomfort in fracturing this continuous, often immediate, emotional experience which one wishes kept inviolable. But a degree of analysis and objective scrutiny, both of the music and of the listener himself, will contribute, in time, to even more intense, and equally inviolable experiences.

One more type of distortion inevitably plagues an analysis such as this—the distortion introduced by the words used to describe musical phenomena. Just as we urge you to consider your own responses to a given example first, so we urge you to search for words which will appropriately describe both your own response and the attributes of the music which have stimulated it. We have attempted to avoid all terminology which has been derived only from the vague, often inaccurate, assumptions of traditional usage. To describe what is a complex intellectual, emotional, and highly personal experience generated by an equally complex set of phenomena is difficult. We feel, however, that the effort can be a most important way of exploring the manifold dimensions of music itself.

During the long hours devoted to selecting examples and to the actual writing of the text, each of us used the other as sounding board, critic, and mentor; and thus no part of the book is the sole effort of either one of us. We hope that you, in using the book, will learn as much from it as we learned in preparing it.

Remember, however, that the book itself *tells* you very little. Its value lies in what you can discover yourself by actively studying the musical examples, using the book as a guide. The facts we give *about* music are only important when they are transformed into your live experience—and that you must have alone. "The really 'understanding' listener takes the music into his consciousness, and remakes it, actually or in his imagination, for his own uses."[2]

J. S. B.
H. B.

---

[2] Roger Sessions, *The Musical Experience of Composer, Performer, Listener,* Princeton: Princeton University Press, 1950, p. 97.

PART ONE
Means and possibilities

Triumph of Eternity, Chaumont tapestry panel, France, 1500–1510

CHAPTER 1
Sound
and texture

Sound relationships and textures

The immediate sensory experience of sound itself is one of the most compelling dimensions of music. And music includes an enormous variety of sounds, limited only by the capabilities of the instruments (or voices) and by the imagination of the composer. The musical examples you will hear present a broad range of sounds, yet they provide only a small sample of the many possibilities. Nevertheless, as you listen to these examples, you can begin to expand your sensitivity to the different ways in which sounds can be combined and interrelated.

Demonstration 1-1

THE VARIETY OF SOUND (Side 1)

Since music of some kind is a part of everyone's experience, these first examples are certainly not an introduction to music. Instead, they serve as an exploration of exactly *how* you listen to music and what you *hear* (and comprehend). These examples are chosen to begin the discussion—to raise questions rather than answer them. Later you may find it useful to turn back to this first set of examples to compare your initial responses with your more "educated" ones.

Example	Composer, title	Date
1.1	Stravinsky, *Le Sacre du printemps* (*The Rite of Spring*), "Dance of the Adolescents"	1913
1.2	Bach, *Concerto in D Minor for Harpsichord and Orchestra,* first movement	c. 1730
1.3	*Veni Creator Spiritus* (Gregorian chant)	Middle Ages
1.4	*Music for the Rice Harvest* (West African)	

These four examples represent a wide range of music from very different times and places. As you listen, each excerpt will seem to create its own "sound world." It is unlikely that you would hear these four pieces one after the other except under the artificial circumstances of this book. But by listening to these unnatural neighbors in sequence, we can highlight the striking differences among them.

Finding words to express the differences you hear may be difficult, but certain aspects of each piece stand out right away. For example, the feeling of Example 1.1 is very different from the feeling of Example 1.2. But what in the music creates the differences? You may notice, for instance, that the sound of the orchestra is quite different in the two examples. This is due in part to the particular instruments that each composer has included in his score, as well as to what, and even how, the instruments are playing. For example, what are some of the differences in the kind of melody (or even lack of melody) that you hear, or the differences in rhythm, or the relationships among the various instruments? What other aspects of each piece do you think make the experience of listening to it unique?

Examples 1.3 and 1.4 are both music to accompany ceremonies. However, each creates a strikingly different ceremonial atmosphere. Notice that in the medieval chant, which is music for the Catholic service, all of the voices are singing the same tones at the same time. This is called singing in *unison*. (See p. 16 for further discussion of this term.) In contrast, the African ritual starts off slowly and spontaneously, seemingly out of a community gathering. First you hear one person singing, then more people join in, then drums, and finally a child's voice. Unlike the medieval chant, the participants do not all sing and play the same tones together. Instead, as each person joins in, he sings or plays his own individual part. The particular sounds of each part and their complex, interwoven relationships help to create the special quality of the piece.

Example	Composer, title	Date
1.5	Haydn, *Symphony 8*, first movement	c. 1701
1.6	Mahler, *Symphony 1*, fourth movement	1888
1.7	Debussy, *Rondes de printemps* (*Spring Rounds*)	1906–1909

Examples 1.5 and 1.6 are both orchestra pieces and yet, again, each has a distinctive sound and feeling. This is partly because Haydn has written for a smaller *number* of instruments and also for fewer *kinds* of instruments than Mahler. A glance at the Haydn and Mahler scores on pp. 7–8 will make this quite clear.

For example, look at the names of the participating instruments listed at the sides of the scores. Notice that the instruments are grouped (bracketed) according to families: from the top of the score there are woodwinds, brass, percussion (none in Haydn), and then strings. Haydn scores his piece for only three kinds of woodwinds: flute, oboe and bassoon (the bassoon plays with the cellos and basses, so it is written out with them at the bottom of the score). Mahler includes more *kinds* of woodwinds (piccolo and clarinet in addition to those above) as well as more of each kind (for example, four oboes and four clarinets). Haydn uses only one brass instrument, the French horn, while Mahler uses four different kinds of brass instruments, with more than one of each kind (and seven French horns!). Finally, Mahler has a large percussion section, while Haydn has none at all.

Listen to Example 1.5 again, this time trying to follow the score.[1] Think of the score as a kind of map which shows the simultaneous paths of each participating instrument through time. You may find it difficult to follow all the paths at once. Start by listening for the instrument that is playing the melody; then keep your eye and ear on just that part. (Notice that the score includes only the first portion of the recorded excerpt.) Mahler's much bigger orchestra makes it more difficult to follow his score, but it will be interesting to see how much of what you hear you can match with what is printed on the page. This is the last page of the Mahler score, and it is only the very end of the recorded excerpt. Because of Mahler's very large orchestra, a little musical time takes up a lot of space on a page.

---

[1] For a discussion of music notation, see Appendixes to Chapters 2 and 3. However, at this point it is better to use the score as a general map than as a note-to-note exact description.

Excerpt from *Symphony 8* by Franz Josef Haydn

Excerpt from *Symphony 1* by Gustav Mahler

Reprinted from Eulenberg Edition #570 by permission of the publisher.

A comparison of the Haydn excerpt with the Debussy (Example 1.7) will highlight another kind of difference in orchestral pieces, namely each composer's *use* of the orchestra. Haydn uses his orchestra to underline or reinforce other aspects of the musical design. Debussy, however, uses his orchestra actually to create the design of the piece through the interplay of the various sounds of the instruments themselves.

Look at the Haydn score as you listen once more to the example. You can hear and see that the violins start off the melody, but the lower strings (violas, cellos, and basses) finish the first little phrase. Haydn changes instruments to underline the melodic structure; the switch from violins to lower strings helps to define the beginnings and endings of the melody. A little later on, Haydn introduces a new figure (♩ ♫♫ ♪) played by the violins, but also by the flute, which is a new instrument that adds a new sound to the piece. Try to shift your listening focus to the flute, noticing how and when Haydn uses its characteristic figure to liven up the melody which is usually played by the violins.

Although a score is often helpful in illustrating or clarifying exactly what you have heard, it is always a good idea to listen first and then to look. You will need to practice coordinating what you hear with what you see in musical notation. Remember that looking cannot be a substitute for careful listening; you must believe first in what you hear.

Now listen to Example 1.7 again (no score is included here). Notice how Debussy uses the orchestra to create a kind of kaleidoscope of sounds, shifting your attention from one part of the orchestra to another, or sometimes combining instruments to create a unique sound. Unlike Haydn, Debussy uses contrasting sounds to shape the structure of the piece. He often repeats the same fragment of music several times using different instruments, one after the other. The change in tone color (*timbre*) gives a new impression to the same group of notes. The sensuous interplay of sounds might be compared with the patterns that are formed by color in a painting or by the play of light and shadow in nature. (You might refer to the Ancillary Reading at the back of this chapter for further discussion of the instruments of the orchestra. Also, you may want to listen to some of the many records available illustrating the instruments of the orchestra, as well as to Britten's *A Young Person's Guide to the Orchestra.*)

Changing Sound Environments

Example	Composer, title	Date
1.8	Sousa, *Semper Fidelis*	1888
1.9	Beethoven, *Symphony 9,* Op. 125, fourth movement	1823
1.10	Stravinsky, *Firebird Suite,* finale	1910
1.11	Bach, *Suite in B Minor,* overture	c. 1721

You have already heard a variety of means that composers and performers use to create contrasting sound worlds. Examples 1.8 to 1.11 illustrate means that composers can use to create contrast in sound *within* a piece. In each of these examples, a single melody is *embedded* in an ever-changing sound environment. While the melody itself always remains much the same, it seems transformed as the sound environment around it changes. This process can be part of creating *variations on a theme*. In each variation you hear the same melody but always with a slightly different effect.

For example, in the Sousa march (Example 1.8) each repetition of the melody defines a new section of the piece and a new variation on the theme. Since each includes one complete statement of the tune, all of the sections are of the same length. Notice also that the theme or principal melody is always played by the same instruments, the trumpets. But in each variation, other instruments playing new musical material are added to the basic sound environment.

Beethoven uses much the same general procedure (Example 1.9) as Sousa, but in a considerably more elaborate way. For in-a single melody is embedded in an ever-changing sound environment

stance, notice that each repetition of the theme is played by a new instrument. First we hear just the cellos and basses playing the theme in *unison*. Then, in the first variation, the violas and cellos play the theme, this time accompanied by the bassoon and double basses. Notice how different the melody sounds both as a result of the new instruments playing it and also because of the new sound environment in which it is embedded. In the next variation, Beethoven gives the theme to the violins. He surrounds the theme with more and still different instruments, creating another new environment for it. Interestingly, the theme moves higher and higher among the strings with each repetition. Finally, Beethoven gives the theme to the brass and woodwinds while the strings accompany it, weaving around the woodwinds and brass to disguise the repeated melody.

In the finale of the *Firebird Suite* (Example 1.10), Stravinsky also repeats a single melody and embeds it in changing sound environments, but the effect is rather different. This piece sounds more *continuous* than either the Sousa march or the Beethoven symphony excerpt. There are several reasons for this. The repetitions of the short theme (played first by the French horn) are not always literal, and therefore the lengths of the sections are not always the same. Also there is a more gradual increase in the kinds and number of instruments, which creates a continuous crescendo almost up to the end of the excerpt (and the piece). At the very end, the orchestra suddenly plays much softer in preparation for the grand climax (where's the theme?) with which the piece ends. In addition, the piece sounds more continuous because the beginning and ending of the repeated melody is itself less clearly defined, which tends to blur the boundaries between each new variation.

The excerpt from the Bach overture is also more continuous, but this time for still different reasons. You will notice that the

the texture grows increasingly more dense and more active*

participating instruments enter this sound world one by one, each playing the *same* melody. Each instrument *imitates* the one preceding it. Once a player is in, he continues to play but always something other than the "constant" melody which he gives over to another player. Notice, too, that the instruments (flute and strings) enter in a regular progression from high to low—violin 1 (*doubled* by flute), violin 2 (playing lower), viola, and cello (doubled by bass). Each successive statement of the melody is heard in a new

---

* The illustration shown above, and others like it throughout the book, are an artist's *graphic* expression of the *musical* relationships being discussed. The sketch is not limited to one particular work, nor is it the only drawing possible. For example, the drawing could apply to this Bach piece or to any piece which follows a similar procedure. The illustration tells you nothing which the text has not already discussed, but it may help fix the idea in your mind by projecting some of its relationships visually. Try making your own sketches as you listen to examples or read the text. How do yours compare with those scattered throughout the book?

Starting from the top rear and going clockwise: double basses, cellos, violins, and violas.

sound environment—one which grows more dense and more active as the instruments increasingly intertwine with one another.

Thus, while Examples 1.8–1.11 each have their own characteristic sound, all of them share a similar compositional procedure. In this sense, each of the examples illustrates the interplay of unity and variety which is so important to musical coherence. Each composer creates unity through the repetition of a single melody and variety by embedding this "constant" in new sound environments. And yet, each piece realizes this general procedure in a unique way. Learning to appreciate the interplay between unity and variety and between the defining limits of a procedure and its unique working out is an important aspect of the art of listening.

Demonstration 1-2

TEXTURE   (Sides 1–2)

In this demonstration you are asked to listen to an aspect of sound in music termed *texture*. The word *texture* is borrowed by analogy from another medium, as is often the case with musical technical terminology. Here, texture is borrowed from its more literal use in the description of woven fabric and its strands. In music the term refers to the particular way strands of *sound* intertwine and interweave with one another. Or, more specifically, the term refers to the way voices or instruments relate to one another. The word *voice* can refer to either instruments or singing voices as they weave together to form the particular texture of a composition. We can say, for example, that "the violin is the upper voice in the texture." We can describe the texture of a piece, or a particular moment in a piece, in terms of its *density* (how many parts are playing) or its *activity* (the relative degree of motion and contrasts in motion among the parts), or we can refer to the upper or lower strands, parts, or voices. Unlike its use in relation to fabric, however, texture, as used in music, does not refer to the sense of touch

Denim fabric (85X enlarged)

Texture: the particular way strands of sound intertwine and interweave with one another

or to the atmosphere or mood of a piece, although particular textural relations may contribute to the feelings which a piece evokes in the listener.

Before you listen to the examples which illustrate various kinds of textural relations, a word about the uses of descriptive or technical terms may be helpful. Words about music, as used here, serve two purposes: (1) they direct your attention to some particular aspect of music which we want to illustrate by a given example, and (2) they help you to grasp and make explicit what you can hear but what may be still quite elusive to you. Translating your perception into a verbal description helps to single out just what is contributing to your experience. Both uses are part of what is essentially an intermediary process between your initial impression of a work and your later, more complete experience of it. The process is one of learning how to find in your immediate sensory experience that set of features or relations to which a given term or verbal description applies or to search for a way of expressing this in words.

[handwritten margin note: hard to grasp mentally]

Keep in mind, then, that language about music can only be a guide or momentary pointer; it cannot substitute for careful listening. For example, no one term can capture the interplay of relations in various dimensions of a piece as it moves through time. Further, remember that the recorded examples are often short excerpts from larger works. Each excerpt has been carefully chosen to focus your listening on some particular aspect of the piece —for instance, the variety of possible sound relationships. But any large work will include many varieties of sound and texture within it; the particular moment we have chosen is just one part which contributes to the organization and *effect* of the whole. Listed at the end of the chapter are several short but complete works that will encourage you to listen to the variety of sound and texture within the framework of an entire piece.

Remember, then, that it is your increased ability to *hear*—to distinguish and interrelate—the various dimensions of the music itself which must teach you, and not merely the words about it.

Solo Playing or Singing

Example	Composer, title	Date
1.12	Varèse, *Density 21.5*	1936
1.13	Bach, *Partita 2 for Unaccompanied Violin*, gigue	c. 1720

Examples 1.12 and 1.13 can both be described as having a one-stranded texture since each is a solo played by one instrument alone. However, neither piece may strike you as being a melody in the sense of a popular tune or folk song. An important question, to which we will return in Chapter 3, is just how does each melody differ from your intuitive idea of what a tune is? However, it should be clear that the character of the melody is influenced by the fact that both Varèse and Bach, each in his own way, have skillfully "pushed the limits" of their respective instruments, giving each of the performers full opportunity to display virtuoso skill as a soloist. Varèse's focus on the instrument and its possibilities is reflected in the title of the piece, which alludes to the platinum flute of Georges Barrère, the flutist who commissioned Varèse to write the piece for him. 21.5 is the approximate density of platinum (21.37 grams per cubic centimeter).

Unison Playing

Example	Composer, title	Date
1.14	*Singing Game* (West African)	
1.15	Bach, *Concerto in D Minor for Harpsichord and Orchestra*, first movement	c. 1730

In the next two examples, there is again just one melody line, but now more than one instrument or voice is playing it. This is called singing or playing in *unison,* as in the medieval chant heard earlier (Example 1.3). The African *Singing Game* demonstrates in lively, playful fashion the contrast between solo and unison singing. You hear, first, one melody line with one person singing and then, in contrast, one melody line with several people singing. The piece sounds like a game of musical catch. The soloist is free to invent, since he is all alone, while the chorus, sometimes interrupting, always picks up and repeats the same beginning fragment of the soloist's tune—the opening motive.

Instruments rather than voices play in unison in the Bach excerpt (heard earlier as Example 1.2). Notice that unlike the African song, the melody line in this excerpt is played in different pitch areas, that is, all the instruments play the same pitches, but in different octaves—some higher (violins), some in the middle (violas), and some lower (cellos and basses).

Example	Composer, title	Date
1.16	Moussorgsky, *Pictures at an Exhibition,* "Promenade"	1874
1.17	*The Bird Has Come* (Bulgarian folk song)	

Examples 1.16 and 1.17 illustrate unison of a very different kind. Notice that in the excerpt from the Moussorgsky work, the trumpet first plays alone and then is joined by the other instruments. As the others join in, they all play nearly the same *rhythm* as the trumpet but not the same *pitches.* This we call playing in *rhythmic unison.*

Similarly, the Bulgarian folk song begins with all the women singing in unison, but then the group breaks up into two and then several parts. As in the Moussorgsky piece, all the women continue to sing the same rhythm, but not always the same set of pitches. So if the women instead of *singing* the pitches of their respective parts just *clapped* the rhythm, you would not hear any differences among them. Only pitch differentiates the various strands of sound. (does not include clapping)

Interestingly, the example also serves to demonstrate the two basic components of a tone and of a melody: pitch and duration. That is, while the *durations* of the notes are the same for all the performers throughout the excerpt, their pitches are sometimes the same (unison) and sometimes different (rhythmic unison). As a result of these changes from unison singing to rhythmic unison, you hear contrasts in sound and in the relations among the parts as the piece goes along. These contrasts create a sense of widening or deepening (as the pitches vary) and then again narrowing of the sound universe (as the pitches converge into unison). All the parts move along together, yet sometimes the top voice is reinforced and enriched as it becomes part of a deeper sound space.

Example	Composer, title	Date
1.18	Bach, *St. Matthew Passion,* chorale	1729

In the Bach example, all the voices generally move together in rhythmic unison. However, upon close listening you will hear that the lower parts sometimes move independently of the top part, creating a contrast with the prevailing rhythmic unison texture. At these moments both pitch and duration contribute to a somewhat more active texture. While Bach started with a preexistent melody (a chorale, or Lutheran hymn) which he gives to the sopranos at the top of the texture, he sets this melody off so that the three other voices (altos, tenors, basses) have a certain rhythmic and melodic independence. Note that in the Bulgarian folk song the lower voices at times diverge from the upper voice, but only in pitch, not rhythm. But in the Bach example, the lower voices of the texture at times begin to take on a life of their own as they diverge in rhythm as well as pitch.

Melody and Accompaniment

Example	Composer, title	Date
1.19	*Sourwood Mountain* (American folk song)	
1.20	Verdi, *La Traviata*, aria	1853
1.21	Haydn, *Concerto for Trumpet and Orchestra*, third movement	1796
1.22	Babbitt, *Philomel*	1966

The next four examples illustrate melody with a clearly subordinate accompaniment and yet one which has its own distinctive character. While the examples are clearly different from one another in feeling and in the kind of sound world they create, they

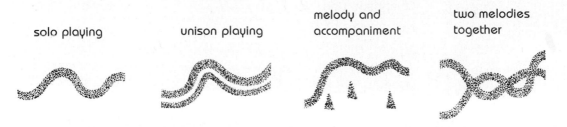

solo playing   unison playing   melody and accompaniment   two melodies together

are all similar in texture—they all present a foreground melody with a background accompaniment. In the American folk song *Sourwood Mountain,* notice that the accompaniment creates a steady beat and also hardly moves from its one sound (a single chord), while the melody line moves freely above it. *Sourwood Mountain* was recorded in Thomasville, North Carolina, in 1945; I. G. Greer, a native of Thomasville, is accompanied on the dulcimer by his wife.

1.19

1.20   The Verdi aria seems to epitomize the notion of melody with accompaniment. You hear the singer soaring over the oom-pah-pah accompaniment that is clearly subordinate and yet consistently and solidly present. The Haydn *Concerto for Trumpet and* 1.21 *Orchestra* similarly sets off soloist from background accompaniment, the soloist having ample opportunity to display his virtuosity while the orchestra provides a discrete sound setting for him. Compare this accompanied virtuoso solo with the unaccompanied solos of Examples 1.12 and 1.13.

1.22   Babbitt's accompaniment in *Philomel* is electronically synthesized and is "played" in performance by a tape recorder while Bethany Beardslee (for whom the piece was written) sings, live. Notice that as in Examples 1.19 and 1.20 the singer's voice clearly dominates this portion of the piece, while the accompaniment always remains in the background.

Two Melodies Played or Sung Together

Example	Composer, title	Date
1.23	Gibbons, *Fantasia a 2*	c. 1608
1.24	Mozart, *Duo for Violin and Viola*, K. 424,[2] second movement	1783
1.25	Gordon, Roberts, and Kaufman, *Me, Myself and I* (sung by Billie Holiday)	1938

Examples 1.19 to 1.22 involved pieces with more than one instrument or voice, but in each excerpt the upper part tended to predominate. There was a clear foreground-background relationship. Examples 1.23 to 1.25 illustrate music in which two instruments are of equal importance. This equality of the parts results in a more complex sound fabric with a more *active* texture. As a listener, you must follow not just one predominant part but rather shift your attention from one part to the other or sometimes attend to both as the two individual parts vie with one another for the foreground role.

1.23   In the Gibbons *Fantasia* you hear two recorders playing in

---

[2] K. 424 means the 424th work in a chronological arrangement of Mozart's music made by Ludwig von Köchel in the nineteenth century.

close *imitation*. That is, one instrument starts and the other follows right after with a melody that always begins in the same way as the first but then goes its own way. The result is a texture of much greater activity than you heard in the examples of melody with accompaniment. Each of the two instruments is playing a related but distinct melody which can stand on its own, has its own integrity. The ear, in a sense, must jump around to follow each part.

1.24   The Mozart *Duo* is particularly interesting because you hear, even in this short excerpt and with only two instruments, a variety of textural relations. First you hear an active texture with each instrument playing the same melody but "out of phase" with one another. That is, the violin begins and then the viola follows, imitating almost exactly what the violin started. Notice that while each part is thus self-sufficient, the melody is composed so that it "fits" when played against itself.[3] Then, as the piece progresses, one has a sense of decreasing activity and intensity as the texture moves from an active, imitative one to rhythmic unison and finally to a melody played by the violin with an accompaniment played by the viola. This is a good example of how textural contrast can contribute to changes in the feelings evoked—in this case from the sense of intensity resulting from the complex, active texture to relative calm resulting from the more homogeneous rhythmic unison and finally melody with accompaniment.

On first listening to *Me, Myself, and I* (Example 1.25) it may seem to you that Billie Holiday occupies the foreground role exclusively. But if you listen again more closely you can hear that Lester Young, playing tenor saxophone, is vying with her for the foreground role as he plays a different but equally important melody. This kind of perceptual "surfacing" of inner lines is the sort of experience that can change your appreciation of a piece. The rest of the group plays a rhythmic accompaniment which is subordinate to the voice and saxophone. Compare the texture of this

lower in rank

---

[3] You are probably familiar with this kind of procedure, called a *canon* or *round*, as in *Three Blind Mice* or *Row, Row, Row Your Boat*.

piece with the previous examples, noticing that it includes two voices of equal importance (but playing *different* melodies, not in imitation), as well as a subsidiary accompaniment.

Several Melodies Played Together

Example	Composer, title	Date
1.26	Gabrieli, *Ricercare*	c. 1580
1.27	*African Drums* (West African)	
1.28	Bach, *St. John Passion,* chorus	c. 1723

Examples 1.26–1.28 all involve several independent lines and a consistently active texture. This kind of activity among the parts —the opposite extreme from rhythmic unison—is often referred to as *polyphony* ("many-voiced"). But notice what differences there can be! In the Gabrieli *Ricercare,* for instance, the same short melodic fragment is tossed about among the brass instruments. In the African piece, on the other hand, each of the percussion instruments plays a different rhythmic figure, but not really a melody, which perhaps emphasizes the importance of rhythm in generating polyphony. While there are many differences between the two examples (instrumentation, kinds of rhythm, imitation and no imitation) the result in both is a highly complex and active texture.

rhythmic unison

active texture

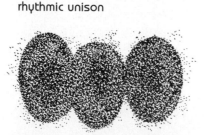

Following the score of the Gabrieli *Ricercare* may help you to shift your focus from one instrument to another as each picks up the same short melodic fragment. Notice that you need to shift

Gabrieli, *Ricercare*

your *visual* focus rapidly about within the "sound space." Now listen again without the score to hear how the voices interweave to create a single, complex, active sound.

You can also compare the Gabrieli *Ricercare* with the West African *Singing Game* (Example 1.14), which we described as a game of musical catch. Notice that in *Singing Game* the melody, sung by a single child, is picked up by the group, but the soloist and the group sing *one after the other* (in succession, not simultaneously) to create a single-stranded, inactive texture. In the *Ricercare,* on the other hand, you hear a single motive at first played against itself (as in the two-voiced Mozart *Duo* and Gibbons *Fantasia*) to form a many-layered, active texture. The *Ricercare* again illustrates what is technically called *imitation.* That is, a melody or melodic fragment (motive) is played in different strands of the texture but out of phase with itself. The motive moves about within the texture *embedded in itself* to generate this active, complex sound. *Singing Game,* in contrast, illustrates *successive* repetition—a single-line restatement of a melody or motive.

The chorus from Bach's *St. John Passion,* which occurs at a climactic moment in this monumental musical setting of the Crucifixion, shows you the dramatic effect of voices combining to create many actively moving lines.

Putting It All Together

Example	Composer, title	Date
1.29	Haydn, *Symphony 99,* minuet (first section)	1793
1.30	Stravinsky, *Four Études for Orchestra,* no. 2	1929
1.31	Handel, *Concerto Grosso,* Op. 6, no. 2, fourth movement	c. 1734

So far you have listened to various aspects of sound, but generally only in short, isolated excerpts. To conclude the demonstration, listen now to complete movements by Stravinsky and Handel and a complete section of a movement by Haydn. One of the goals in developing musical perception is the ability to appreciate the larger structure of a work. The composer's use of contrast in sound and texture often plays an important role in generating this overall design. Learning to hear and respond to these varieties of sound relations can thus help you to participate more fully and with more understanding in the process of a given work. These examples will give you the opportunity to use your increased perception to hear how each composer uses varying sound relationships within a work to create contrast which helps to shape the structure of the whole.

Listen first to the Haydn minuet (Example 1.29). Your increased sensitivity to changes in sound should help you to hear how rapidly the sound changes within this section. For example, the piece begins in unison, followed quickly by rhythmic unison which fills out the sound and reinforces the initial statement. Haydn then repeats this same contrast. Next he increases the *rate* of contrast by alternating between unison and rhythmic unison more quickly (in fact, twice as fast). At the same time Haydn also creates a thinner sound—fewer instruments are playing. This then leads into a more active texture with imitation between the upper and lower parts. This is followed by a more relaxed section of clear melody and accompaniment, with which the excerpt comes to a close.

Example 1.29. Haydn, *Symphony 99*, minuet*

* The symbol ‖: :‖ indicates that the music between the signs is to be played again.

The various contrasts in sound are striking, but you must listen actively in order to hear them. Once these changes in sound and texture become part of your listening experience, you will also become aware of the role they play in articulating or shaping the musical process. Specifically, you can enjoy the *function* of instrumentation and texture in creating the larger movement of the piece. Haydn uses the orchestra to reinforce events in other dimensions of the music, such as melody, rhythm, and harmony, much as he does in *Symphony 8* (Example 1.5). All these dimensions work together to create a dynamic movement between moments of relative stability and moments of relative tension, or what we will later describe as differing *structural functions*. Contrast in sound is an immediate way of approaching the perception of larger structural design. Others will emerge and become part of your listening experience as you move through the various demonstrations, culminating in their necessary integration when we examine the organization of large works in Chapters 6 and 7.

1.30   Stravinsky, in this *Étude* no. 2, displays a far wider variety of sounds in a relatively short period of time. When one compares this piece with Haydn's minuet, it becomes abundantly clear that sound is a primary building material for Stravinsky and thus necessarily of your listening focus. In this respect Stravinsky is much like Debussy (see discussion of Example 1.7). In the Stravinsky *Étude* you first hear the various instruments playing primarily in unison or in rhythmic unison. They are interrupted by the brass and piano, which, along with the strings and woodwinds, then predominate. This more active passage in turn quickly dissolves into a short oboe solo and another unison passage. Next you hear what seems like an accompaniment looking for a melody, and the melody finally materializes in the flute and piccolo solo. The *Étude* ends with a return to the opening material, now truncated and fragmented.

But to speak only of kinds of texture in describing this work clearly does it an injustice. The play of instrumental colors

—sometimes particular combinations of instruments, sometimes just the solitary special sound of one—appeals to that direct sensuous aspect of listening which is a large part of what this chapter is all about.

1.31   Finally, in the finale from the Handel *Concerto Grosso* you can hear two clearly opposed textures, each associated with its own melody. The first melody, presented in imitation (you hear four statements of the melody moving throughout the string section), is abruptly followed by a softer, more lyrical passage in which you hear a slower melody with a faster-moving accompaniment. As the piece progresses, these two "characters" in the drama (the faster-moving, more actively textured first section and the slower-moving melody with accompaniment) move closer and closer together. Contrast thus occurs more rapidly until finally you hear the melodies superimposed. The slower, more lyrical melody is sometimes heard below and sometimes above the more vigorous opening melody. Thus Handel creates rich varieties of sound and texture and also new embeddings for two persistently recurring melodic ideas. Near the end of the piece the opening melody is played in closer imitation as instruments enter virtually tumbling over one another, as if each can't wait for the other to finish out the tune.

You might like to go back and listen to the first four examples again. Do you hear more than you did initially? Can you now find just what aspects of each excerpt characterize its particular sound world?

Exercise 1-1

Sound and Texture   (Side 2)

The exercises in this book provide you with additional experience in listening within a particular framework. But they also have another purpose: to present self-correcting material through which you can discover how well you have learned to make distinctions. The exercises are a test only in the sense that they can help you to test your own perception.

At the beginning of each exercise you will find a description of the problem and blanks for answering the questions. In the chart following the examples (on a separate page) you will find the correct answers. We suggest the following procedure for each exercise:

1. Study the problem and the specific questions.

2. Do the first three questions and check the answers against the answer chart to see if you are doing better than guessing. If not, go back and do the three questions again.

3. Finish the exercise and check your answers. You may want to listen to the whole exercise again while checking. This procedure will give you a chance not only to correct yourself but to hear again a "demonstration" within the framework of the particular problem described.

Exercise 1-1 explores further the various kinds of sound relationships you have been hearing. In Examples 1.32 to 1.37 the instruments or voices play different roles in relation to one another. Match each excerpt with the correct statement below.

A. The texture is relatively *inactive*. For example, one instrument or voice plays a dominant role, or the parts play in unison or in rhythmic unison.

B. The texture is relatively *active*. The instruments or voices move independently of one another; all are of equal importance.

Example	A Inactive	B Active
1.32	✓	
1.33		✓
1.34	✓	
1.35		✓
1.36		✓
1.37	✓	

In examples 1.38 to 1.43 there is a *change* in the relative degree of textural activity. Match each excerpt with the correct statement below.

A. This excerpt moves (abruptly or gradually) from a relatively inactive texture to a more active texture.

B. This excerpt moves (abruptly or gradually) from a relatively active texture to a less active texture.

Example	A Inactive → active	B Active → inactive
1.38	✓	
1.39	✓	
1.40		✓
1.41	✓	
1.42		✓
1.43		✓

CORRECT ANSWERS

Example	A Inactive	B Active
1.32 Vivaldi, *Concerto*, Op. 3, no. 11, c.1712	X	
1.33 Beethoven *Quartet*, Op. 59, no. 3, fourth movement, 1806		X
1.34 Hindemith, *Mathis der Maler*, 1934	X	
1.35 Hindemith, *Mathis der Maler*, 1934		X
1.36 Morley, *Ho! Who comes here?* 1594		X
1.37 Milhaud, *La Création du monde*, 1923	X	

Example	A Inactive → active	B Active → inactive
1.38 Bach, *Cantata 31*, 1715[a]	X	
1.39 Bizet, *L'Arlésienne Suite 2*, 1872	X	
1.40 Mozart, *Quartet in G*, K. 387, fourth movement, 1782		X
1.41 Bach, *St. John Passion*, c.1723	X	
1.42 Haydn, *The Seasons*, "Summer," 1801		X
1.43 Beethoven, *Symphony 3*, Op. 55, second movement, 1803[b]		X

[a] The piece begins with only one melody line played in unison by all the instruments of the group.

[b] This excerpt has been included because it is such an extraordinary example of the dramatic effect of textural change. More "lifelike" than some of the earlier examples, it moves through several phases—from an active, complex texture generating tremendous tension to a gradual lessening of this tension through clarification and simplification of the texture.

ADDITIONAL MATERIALS

The examples suggested here[4] illustrate an additional aspect of sound relationships not included in the previous demonstrations and in some cases reemphasize the crucial role sound can play in creating musical structure.

I

Haydn, *Symphony 8,* first movement, c. 1761 (Example 1.5)
Debussy, *La Mer,* 1903–1905
Lully, *Armide,* overture, 1686
Gibbons, *Fantasia a 4,* c. 1608
Mahler, *Symphony 1*, first movement, 1888

Listen to the Haydn symphony and Debussy's *La Mer,* noting the striking difference in sound which results from different instrumental combinations and uses of these combinations. Notice that Debussy uses a much larger orchestra and a greater variety of instruments than Haydn (see the discussion of musical instruments in the Ancillary Reading, p. 37).

Haydn (as in Example 1.29) uses his orchestra to reinforce the musical design. His contrasts in instrumentation, for example, tend to coincide with and help to articulate such musical events as the advent of a new phrase or section. Debussy (like Stravinsky), on the other hand, uses his orchestra as an end in itself. In his sensuous *La Mer,* we hear how contrasting instrumental colors, contrasts in density of texture, and the extramusical associations of particular qualities of sound generate the events of the piece.

---

[4] Pieces discussed in the Additional Materials are primarily for outside listening and are not necessarily included in the accompanying recordings.

Which of these works would lose the most if transcribed for the piano?

The Lully and Gibbons pieces are both written for a group of strings, but Lully's orchestra, suited for a public performance, is large, while the Gibbons piece, scored for only four solo viols, sounds small and intimate. (Unfortunately, sometimes recordings distort this kind of difference, since the decibel level tends to be equalized for all records by sound engineers. Thus, the enormous difference between a live performance by 50 musicians and one by 4 musicians is often lost in a recording.)

The last example demonstrates how, with another large, varied orchestra, Mahler achieves an effect quite different from Debussy's, although the actual instruments present on the stage are nearly the same as those used in *La Mer.* In what ways is Mahler's use of the orchestra unlike Debussy's? In what ways is it similar to Haydn's?

II

> Stravinsky, *Firebird Suite,* finale, 1910 (Example 1.10)
> Moussorgsky, *Khovantchina,* prelude, 1873–1881
> Stravinsky, *Le Sacre du printemps,* "Rondes printanières," 1913
> Beethoven, *Symphony 3,* Op. 55, fourth movement, 1803
> Beethoven, *Trio,* Op. 11, third movement, 1798

These pieces, like Examples 1.29–1.31, illustrate the crucial role of texture and sonority in creating structure. In the finale of the *Firebird Suite,* notice how the effect is cumulative and climactic. We move from the opening solo horn statement to the full orchestra playing fortissimo at the conclusion. The Moussorgsky piece is similar to the *Firebird* in that the composer maneuvers the orchestra in relation to a melodic constant.

The excerpt from *Le Sacre du printemps,* however, is more complex. Listen carefully, noting the changes that occur in (1) timbre, (2) the range of instruments (high and low), (3) activity and density of texture, and (4) foreground-background relationships. These changes contribute significantly to the articulation of the four basic sections of the excerpt.

The Beethoven symphony movement is radically different from the preceding pieces, for it has fundamentally different goals. While in the first three examples the course of events depends on the manipulation of sound (as in Debussy's *La Mer*), in the Beethoven example sound tends rather to *reinforce* the course of events (as in Haydn's *Symphony 8*). Some of the dramatic changes in texture and sonority in this symphony were illustrated in Exercise 1-1. Listen to these and other striking changes in texture and sonority, now within the context of the whole movement.

The final movement of Beethoven's *Trio,* Op. 11, is less immediately striking in its sound contrasts, because the composer uses a smaller and less varied group of instruments. However, close listening will reveal a remarkable variety of sounds within the small ensemble of clarinet, cello, and piano. You will notice that a particular sonority or texture remains constant for relatively long periods, and this constancy helps to articulate the *larger* divisions of the structure.

For example, following a section in which all three instruments participate (the theme), there is a section for piano alone (variation 1), which is followed by a section for cello and clarinet alone (variation 2). Notice that there is also a change in the activity of the texture from the theme to variation 2; the single line with accompaniment in the theme changes to two equal parts played in imitation in variation 2. In variation 3 the piano plays an accompaniment, first to the clarinet and then to the cello. Then in variation 4 the piano sound alternates with the clarinet-cello sound.

Listen to the whole movement, noting as carefully as possible the characteristics of each change in texture and sonority. Then listen to it again just for the pure pleasure of savoring the marvelous play of sounds.

ANCILLARY READING

Acoustics[5]

Acoustics is the science of sound. Sound, in music, consists in the impact on the ear of air vibrations set in motion by (1) the vibration of some elastic material, (2) the vibration of an air column in a pipe, or (3) vibrations electrically produced or transmitted. The elastic material may be (*a*) a gut string or wire, set in motion by a bow (violin), or plucked with the fingers (harp) or a plectrum (mandolin) or a quill (harpischord), or hit with a metal tongue (clavichord) or a hammer (piano); (*b*) a reed or reeds set in motion by air pressure (oboe, clarinet); (*c*) a membrane set in motion by air pressure, such as the vocal cords (human voice) or the lips (brass instruments), or struck with a beater (drums); (*d*) a solid body, set in motion by striking (bells, triangle, xylophone).

The *intensity* of a note is determined by the amplitude of the vibration. Hence force is needed to produce a loud note.

The *pitch* of a note is determined by the frequency of the vibration. A low note vibrates slowly, a high one quickly. The frequency of the vibration may depend (1) on the length, thickness, tension, and density of the vibrating material, (2) on the length and density of the air column and the nature of the tube enclosing it, or (3) may be directly produced by electrical processes. Thus, other things being equal, a short string will produce a higher note than a long one, a taut string a higher note than one less taut. A short air column will produce a higher note than a long one: the piccolo is shorter than the flute and so higher in pitch. On the other hand, the clarinet, though approximately the same length as the flute and oboe, is much lower in pitch than either. This is because it has a cylindrical tube stopped at one end (the mouth-

---

[5] This entire section on acoustics is reprinted, with permission, from *New College Encyclopedia of Music,* ed. J. A. Westrup and F. L. Harrison (New York: Norton, 1960).

piece), whereas the flute, though cylindrical, is open at both ends and the tube of the oboe, though stopped at one end, is conical or expanding. String and wind instruments are differently affected by temperature. A rise in temperature causes strings to expand, so that their tension is relaxed and they drop in pitch; but the expansion of air decreases its density, so that the pitch of wind instruments rises, the expansion of their material not being sufficient to counteract this.

The *resonance* of a note depends on the presence of some auxiliary material or an air column that will vibrate either in sympathy or by direct contact with the original vibrations. Thus the violin owes its resonance to its belly, the oboe to the air column contained in its tube. There is, however, an important difference. In the violin the belly has to vibrate as the strings dictate. In the oboe (as in other wind instruments) the vibrating air column, being of a definite length, controls the vibrations of the reed; so that in this case the resonator determines the pitch.

The *quality* of a note depends on the complex character of the vibrations. A stretched string does not merely vibrate as a whole. It also vibrates simultaneously in sections, which are in an exact mathematical relationship to the length of the string. These sections are the halves, thirds, quarters, fifths, and so on. The halves produce a note an octave higher than the note sounded by the whole string, the thirds a note a twelfth higher, the quarters a note two octaves higher, and so on. The "overtones" sounded by the respective sections fall into a series known as the *harmonic series.* If the principal note or "fundamental" is the series will run as follows:

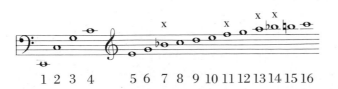

(The notes marked x are not in tune with our ordinary scale.)

The numbers of the series indicate exactly the mathematical relationship between the frequencies of the notes. Thus the ratio between:

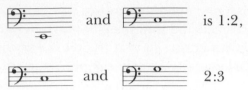

and so on. The sound of the overtones is very much fainter than that of the note produced by the whole string, but without them the note heard by the listener would lose its luster. The air column of a wind instrument or an organ pipe also vibrates in sections. If it is stopped at one end, as in some organ pipes, only alternate sections vibrate, so that a stopped pipe produces only Nos. 1, 3, 5, 7, etc. of the harmonic series. Much the same thing happens with the clarinet, with its cylindrical tube stopped at one end. The characteristic tone-quality of instruments is thus due to the extent to which the "upper partials" (the overtones of the harmonic series) are present or absent and to their relative intensity. This makes it possible, in electronic instruments like the Hammond organ, to imitate closely the sound of orchestral instruments by presenting an artificial selection of the appropriate upper partials and giving to each the necessary intensity. In some instruments the overtones do not fall into the harmonic series and are therefore "inharmonic." The result may be a confused but recognizable sound, as in a bell, or one of indeterminate pitch, as in most percussion instruments.

By touching a string lightly at a point halfway from the end the player can prevent the whole string from vibrating while leaving the two halves free to vibrate. A similar result can be achieved by touching the string at other sectional points. The notes so produced are known, for obvious reasons, as *harmonics*. In the same way a wind-player, by increased lip-tension (known technically as "overblowing"), can split the air column in his instrument into one of its component parts, so that instead of sounding No. 1 of the harmonic series it produces one of the upper partials as its principal note. This is done to a limited degree on woodwind instruments and extensively on brass instruments. The horn, for example, has a choice of upper partials from the 2nd to the 16th harmonic. This explains why horn-players sometimes seem uncertain about their notes. The higher harmonics lie very close together, so that the selection of the right one by lip-tension calls for considerable skill. The extent to which members of the harmonic series are available on brass instruments depends on the relation between the diameter of the tube and its length. Neither the horn nor the trumpet, being narrow-bored instruments, can sound No. 1 of the series.

Musical Instruments

As we have maintained throughout this book, it is your *experience* of music that is primary. Thus in learning about musical instruments, it is essential that you hear various instruments to find out what they sound like and what kinds of things they can do, separately and in combination. At this point, therefore, you should listen to a recording of the instruments of the orchestra. What follows is a list and brief discussion of musical instruments.

Look again at the final page of the score of *Symphony 1* (1881) by Gustav Mahler, which we have reproduced on page 8. Compare the Mahler score with the page from the score of Franz Josef Haydn's *Symphony 8* (c. 1761) on page 7.

The changes that occurred in the orchestra in a little over a century are apparent at a glance. The Haydn example illustrates the so-called classical orchestra, with its nucleus of strings and a few added winds. During the nineteenth century, more and different winds and percussion were added, and many more players were added on each part in the string section.

In the Mahler score the 29 staves of music are played by approximately 100 players constituting an orchestra similar in make-up, if not in sound, to that in Debussy's *La Mer* (see the Additional Materials section of this chapter). At the left of the page the names of the instruments are given, and braces divide the staves into four groupings. The traditional divisions of the symphony orchestra are *woodwinds, brasses, percussion,* and *strings.*[6]

Woodwinds

If we read down from the top of the Mahler score, we find the woodwinds listed as follows: first and second *piccolos;* first and second *flutes;* four *oboes;* three *clarinets* in C, the fourth in E-flat; and three *bassoons.* According to the method of sound production and other factors, we can divide the woodwinds into three families, arranged from high to low within each family, as follows:

> *Flute.* Piccolo; flute, alto flute, bass flute (rare).
> *Clarinet.* E-flat, B-flat, bass clarinet, double bass clarinet (rare);
>   saxophones: soprano, alto, tenor, baritone, bass.
> *Oboe.* Oboe; English horn; bassoon; contrabassoon.

The *flute,* though classed among the woodwinds, is today usually constructed of metal. The player blows across a hole near the end of the instrument, causing a column of air to vibrate inside the tube. (See Example 1.12.)

The *piccolo* (Italian for "small") is literally a small flute; it is approximately one-half the size of the flute and consequently one octave higher in pitch.

The *clarinet* has a single reed, which the player causes to vibrate against a slot in the pipe. Clarinets are known as "transpos-

---

[6] An all-encompassing scientific classification of instruments is as follows: *idiophones* (made of naturally sonorous material, such as cymbals and chimes), *membranophones* (made of stretched membrane, such as drums), *aerophones* (wind instruments), *chordophones* (strings), and *electrophones* (electronic instruments, such as the theremin and the electronic organ, or the electronic music synthesizer such as the Moog, RCA Mark II, etc.).

Full symphony orchestra

ing instruments"; except when they are in C, they do not sound as written. (See Examples 1.37 and 2.26.) In the Mahler score, the first three clarinets are in C and, like most other instruments, sound as written. The fourth clarinet, in E-flat, however, sounds a minor third higher than written.

The *saxophone* is a single-reed instrument and of much later invention (nineteenth century) than the other woodwinds. (See, for the alto sax, Examples 3.14 and 5.44; for the tenor, Examples 1.25 and 5.19.)

The *oboe* is a double-reed instrument. The reeds are made of cane. The player, inserting them into his mouth, makes them vibrate against each other by blowing. (See Examples 2.8 and 3.18.)

The *English horn* (not used in the Mahler score) is in effect an alto oboe, pitched a fifth below the oboe.

The *bassoon,* pitched approximately two octaves below the oboe, is also a double-reed instrument. (See Examples 1.9 and 2.8.) The Mahler score shows bassoon parts written in the tenor clef (see the Ancillary Reading, Chapter 3).

Trombone

Tuba

Brasses

The brass instruments in the Mahler symphony are seven (French) *horns*, five *trumpets*, four *trombones* and *tuba* (set unusually in the score). All these instruments are played by the players' lips vibrating in a mouthpiece inserted into the end of a folded metal tube of some length. All except the trombone vary their pitch by means of a combination of valves and "overblowing" (increased tension of the lips). The trombone uses a slide rather than valves. (For trumpet, see Examples 1.16 and 1.21; horn, Examples 2.8 and 4.1; all the brass together, Example 1.26.)

Percussion

The percussion instruments shown in the Mahler score are two *kettledrums* or *timpani* (here played by two musicians), *triangle*, *cymbals* and *bass drum*. These are only some of a wide variety of percussion instruments. Others are drums of various sizes and kinds, gongs, castanets, wood block, chimes, glockenspiel, tambourine, xylophone, and many more instruments.

Strings

The four principal strings are the *violin* (usually, as in the Mahler score, divided into first and second violins), *viola, cello* (full name, *violoncello*), and *double bass* (so named because it frequently "doubled" the cello an octave lower and also called the *contrabass, bass fiddle,* or simply *bass*). These instruments all have four strings and are most often played with a bow (*arco*) but are occasionally plucked (*pizzicato*). (For the violin, see Example 1.11; for viola, contrasted with the violin, Example 1.24; cello, Examples 2.26 and 3.1; cellos and basses together, Example 1.9.)

As we noted, the orchestra playing the Mahler symphony would be composed of about 100 players—the 32 winds and 5 percussionists called for in the score, plus about 66 strings divided as follows: 18 first violins, 16 second violins, 12 violas, 10 cellos, and 10 basses. In short, the strings constitute two-thirds of the orchestra, although they require only 5 of the 29 lines in this particular score.

You may be thinking that we have overlooked some very important instruments. The organ, piano, harp, guitar, celesta, saxophone, and vibraphone are not traditionally included among the regular components of the symphony orchestra, yet they are being utilized by composers more and more frequently today. In addition, there are the so-called ancient instruments, those which became obsolete at some point but which, either as originals or modern reconstructions, have been revived in the twentieth century. Among these you may have heard the viols, recorder, harpsichord, clavichord, lute, cornetto, and shawm.

Finally, various smaller combinations of instruments, as they occur in *chamber music,* may be mentioned here:

Trio. Usually *string* (violin, viola, cello) or *piano* (piano, violin, cello).
String quartet. Two violins, viola, cello.
Quintet. String (two violins, two violas, cello; or two violins, viola, and two cellos), *piano* (piano and string quartet), or *woodwind* (flute, oboe, clarinet, bassoon, and horn).

Dynamics and Expression[7]

Dynamics

Dynamics refers to the relative loudness or softness (intensity) of musical tones. Markings derived from Italian are used to indicate dynamics. The basic signs are:

p   *piano,* soft
f   *forte,* loud

Modifications of these serve as very rough dynamic indications for the performer:

   pp   *pianissimo,* very soft
   ppp   even softer
  pppp   still softer
    ff   *fortissimo,* very loud
   fff   even louder
  ffff   still louder
   mp   *mezzo piano,* "half soft" (less soft than *piano*)
   mf   *mezzo forte,* not so loud as *forte*

  <   *crescendo,* gradual increase in loudness

  >   *decrescendo, diminuendo,* gradual decrease in loudness

---

[7] In medieval and Renaissance music there are no indications of dynamics and expression, but from the seventeenth to the nineteenth centuries they proliferate. It is in the "romantic" music of the nineteenth century and especially in contemporary music that we find the most detailed markings by composers.

Expression

Italian terms serve as indications to the performer of expressive shadings and character. Some of the more frequently encountered terms are listed below:

animato	animated
appassionato	passionate
cantabile	in a singing style
con brio	with spirit
con fuoco	with fire
con moto	with movement (moving along)
dolce	sweet (soft)
espressivo	expressive
grazioso	graceful
legato	bound together, smoothly connected
maestoso	majestic
marcato	marked, emphatic
pesante	heavy
sforzando (sf)	forcing, that is, a single note strongly accented
sostenuto	sustained
staccato	detached, short
tenuto	held (the full value of the note)

Obviously these indications of dynamics and expression are vague and subjective enough to allow for interpretation by the performer. For example, the term *appassionato* (to be played in a "passionate" manner) may have meant something specific to the composer, but it will mean different things to different performers. In a sense, the whole area of the interpretation and performance of music arises out of this terminological imprecision. And it is this imprecision, among other factors, which has led some composers recently to take their music into their own hands (and out of those of the performer) by electronically synthesizing their work.

Stroboscopically lighted exposure of a single stroke by a squash player

CHAPTER 2

Time and movement: rhythm

Marcel Duchamp, *Nude Descending a Staircase, No. 2*

Demonstration 2-1

FUNDAMENTALS OF RHYTHM   (Sides 2–3)

While our focus in Chapter 1 was primarily on sound and texture, it was necessary throughout the chapter to include time and movement in our discussion. This is not surprising since sound, in music or in the world around us, cannot exist without its extension in time. Discussing texture, for example, we noted that an active texture is created when the voices *move* rhythmically independently of one another. In contrast, a relatively inactive texture is created when the voices move more or less together. We also talked about the *rate of change* from one texture to another within a piece. For example, the Haydn *Symphony 99* excerpt (Example 1.29) changed rapidly from unison texture to rhythmic unison and then later to an active texture, ending with melody and accompaniment, all within a very short period of time. And in the discussion of the Bulgarian folk song (Example 1.17) we needed to separate the pitches in each voice from their durations in order to describe the changes from unison texture to rhythmic unison. That is, the women sang the same rhythm (same set of durations) throughout, but not always the same pitches.

In this chapter we ask you to focus your attention on the ways in which composers (or composer-performers) organize time. Actually the organization of time often accounts for your most immediate, almost visceral experience of excitement in music.

Beat and Nonbeat

Example	Composer, title	Date
2.1	Haydn, *Symphony 88*, minuet	1787
2.2	Ravel, *Daphnis and Chloé*	1909–1912
2.3	*Bhimpalasī* (sitar played by Ravi Shankar)	

46

We begin with three excerpts that are strikingly different in style (note the dates of composition) and in sound but now ask you to pay attention specifically to your experience of time. Try to clap or tap your foot as you listen to each excerpt. You will notice ⟨2.1⟩ that it is easy and quite natural to "keep time" as you listen to the Haydn symphony excerpt. The music creates a clear beat which is easy to follow. Each beat—each tap of your foot—marks off time into equal units. But in the Ravel excerpt it is difficult to find an underlying pulse—an underlying constant unit of time that you can tap out. Ravel, in this excerpt, does not invite such a time-keeping response. Rather, he seems to create a kind of suspended ⟨2.2⟩ or floating motion, not marked off or measured by an internal clock created by the music itself.

beat   nonbeat

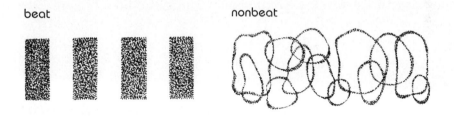

Notice, too, how differently you experience the *passing* of time in the two excerpts. Actually, both examples last slightly less than a minute as measured by ordinary clock time. But the clock's measure is an external one, different from and not relevant to your experienced time in either piece. Each piece generates its own internal temporal organization. Why, for example, does the same measured minute seem so different? You will probably experience the Haydn excerpt as being longer, or maybe shorter, than the Ravel excerpt, but most likely not the same in its total time. Whether you experience it as longer or shorter, the reason is probably much the same. In the Haydn piece many things hap- ⟨2.1⟩ pen. The rate of events is so fast that a whole section of the move-ment is played and repeated in this one minute. But the Ravel piece barely begins in the same minute of clock time; the rate of ⟨2.2⟩

events and of change is extremely slow. As in everyday life, your sense of how much time has elapsed depends on what you are doing—on how much is happening or how little. In a piece of music, the presence or absence of a marking off of time—an audible beat—also contributes to your particular experience of time. You can get a similar contrast in experience if you make the following experiment. Follow the dots below across the page, with your finger "stepping" from one dot to the next and keeping a regular pulse as you go.

. . . .
_____

Now move your finger at about the same pace continuously along the line below the dots. The total time (and the total distance) from beginning to end is more or less equal whether you "step" across the dots or move continuously along the line, but the experience is quite different. How would you describe the differences in your two trips?[1]

_____

[1] You might compare this experiment in "real" space-time with the sound-time examples in the lecture-demonstration (see p. 56), where a steady beat of a given total time (14 seconds) is played next to a continuous tone with the same total time.

Ravi Shankar playing the sitar, accompanied by a tabla player

In Example 2.3 you hear both beat and nonbeat passages. The Indian piece begins with Ravi Shankar playing the sitar accompanied by a tamboura which plays a drone in the background. Later these two instruments are joined by the tabla, a kind of drum. Listen for this change in sonority when the tabla enters and along with it a change from music without any underlying pulse to music with a very strong beat. Also notice the striking change in your experience of time and movement as this change in temporal organization occurs.

Beat Groups: Meter

Example	Composer, title	Date
2.4	*Power in the Blood* (hymn; adapted by M. Paich, sung by Mahalia Jackson)	
2.5	*Veni Creator Spiritus* (Gregorian chant)	Middle Ages
2.6	Stravinsky, *Octet for Wind Instruments,* first movement	1923–1924
2.7	Sousa, *Stars and Stripes Forever*	1896

With these examples we raise the following question: Given that a piece creates an underlying beat or pulse, can you also find and clap a slower but equally regular beat? For example, when you listen to Mahalia Jackson singing *Power in the Blood,* you can easily keep time. In fact, some of the power of the music and of the performance comes from the clearly marked beat played in the bass and drums and emphasized by the singer. But you can also find a slower beat which, in this excerpt, is doubly marked—the first syllable of "power," for instance. Notice that there is a regular relation between the slower and faster pulses. You can count two (or perhaps four) faster beats for each slower beat. (We will return to this relation between slower and faster beats in a moment.)

Listen now to the Gregorian chant *Veni Creator Spiritus.* You can probably find and clap an underlying pulse as you listen, but it is much less compelling than in the preceding example. Actually, each note (or each syllable) is of equal duration, and thus the singers create a regular but rather gentle beat. But can you clap a slower pulse without forcing it on the movement of the melody? Probably not. The beats you feel—those the monks create as they sing each note—do not naturally group together to form a slower but equally regular pulse.

The next two examples illustrate a somewhat similar contrast. The Sousa march creates a clearly audible beat, and these beats are in turn regularly grouped or marked off by a slower beat. When the two sets of beats coincide—that is, when faster and slower beats meet—they create an accent. An accented event is one that is somehow marked for attention.

In the Sousa march accented events occur just as regularly as the underlying beat itself. But in the excerpt from the *Octet* (a piece for eight instruments) Stravinsky plays with these expectations of regularity. First he lets you settle into a regular relationship between slower and faster beats. Then, having set you up, he delightfully toys with your expectations for continuation by expanding or contracting the rate of the slower pulse. He keeps you off balance by shifting the occurrence of accented events and thus shifting the grouping of the faster beats. Listen carefully to this excerpt because the shifts in accent are quite subtle.

You have heard examples with and without a clear beat (Examples 2.1–2.3) and examples with and without a regular grouping of the beats (Examples 2.4–2.7). But notice that music must first generate an underlying pulse before it can create a regular *grouping* of that underlying pulse. If there is a regularly recurring accent which groups the underlying pulse, we describe the piece as *metric*. If there is no regular grouping of the underlying pulse, we describe the piece as *ametric*. Thus, there can be beat without meter but not meter without beat. Before going on, you may want to go back and listen to the first four examples in Chapter 1, paying specific attention to the presence or absence of a beat and/or meter. This new awareness may give you some more insight into the differences in style and in character among those widely diverse examples.

Rhythm and Structure

Example	Composer, title	Date
2.8	Hindemith, *Kleine Kammermusik*, Op. 24, no. 2, fourth movement	1922

In the fourth movement of the Hindemith *Kleine Kammermusik* (*Little Chamber Music*), change in rhythmic organization coincides with change in instrumentation and texture. In fact, the movement (recorded in its entirety here) is organized around this contrast. Rhythmic unison texture along with a clear beat alternate with solo passages that do not create a clear beat. The spontaneous, improvisatory feeling of the solo passages results in part from this absence of, or freedom from, an underlying pulse. Notice, however, that each time the unison passage returns, the group plays much the same music, while each solo section is performed by a different instrument playing a new melody that seems designed for just that particular instrument. Think of the unison passages as a kind of refrain which keeps recurring, while the solo passages give each instrumentalist a chance to come forward and play his own part in his own way. Below is a diagram of the whole movement:

| refrain | flute solo | refrain | bassoon solo | refrain | clarinet solo | refrain | oboe solo | refrain | horn solo | coda |

This piece is a good one for learning more about how to follow a score, since the contrasts between the refrains (always played by four instruments in rhythmic unison) and the solo sections are quite visible. Look at the score reproduced on pages 52–53 and try to see each of the contrasting sections that are shown in the diagram.

Hindemith, *Kleine Kammermusik*

Copyright © 1922 B. Schott's Söhne, Mainz. Copyright renewed 1949. All rights for the USA controlled exclusively by European-American Music Distributors Corp. Reprinted by permission.

Notice that the score is much more detailed than the diagram. While the smallest "element" shown in the diagram is just a box which stands for a whole section of the piece, the smallest element in the score is a symbol standing for a single note. Notes follow one another on separate *staffs,* one staff (of five lines) for each of the five participating instruments. The five staffs are in turn grouped together by a *brace* at the left side of the page. As you listen, your eye must follow all five instruments along together from left to right and then shift down to the next brace of five staffs as the music continues.

Despite all this necessary detail, the contrasts between refrain and solo sections are still quite visible. The movement begins with the first refrain, which is played by all the instruments together with the exception of the flute. You can see that in this opening refrain the notes of the four lower instruments all go along together, while the flute staff is occupied only with rests. Next the flute plays alone, creating the contrast in sound and texture. The staffs of the other instruments are now occupied only with rests. Notice, too, that the vertical lines (bar lines) do not coincide with or mark off the beginnings and endings of these contrasting sections. This is an important point which we will return to in the discussion of metric in contrast to "figural" grouping. Notice that Hindemith has indicated (above the flute part) that the flutist should play freely (*frei*), which accounts for the sense of freedom from a beat. He also blurs the sense of regular pulse by telling the flutist to get faster at the end of his solo (*accel.,* for *accelerando*), thus quickening the pace of whatever internal clock the flutist was following.

When the refrain returns, Hindemith tells the performers to return to the original pace, or to play "in time" (*a tempo*), and we also once again hear a clear beat. The flute joins in for this second refrain, but the bassoon drops out in preparation for his upcoming solo. Hindemith indicates that the bassoon solo should start out slowly (*langsam*) and then, like the flute solo, speed up (*accelerando*).

Notice that if you follow the score along with your finger as you listen, you must change your rate of motion to coincide with the performers' changes in rate of motion, that is, their changes in *tempo*. So the same amount of "paper-space" may not stand for the same amount of "time-space." Finally, you will see and hear that the total time—the time proportions—of the refrains and the solo sections is not always the same. Thus, the rate at which contrast occurs also varies. For example, the third and fourth refrains are shorter, quickening the rate of change in the middle of the movement.

Now listen to the whole movement again, following the recurring refrain and the various solos as they occur in the score. The movement ends with a brief *coda* which is similar to the refrain but varied both in instrumentation and in rhythm so as to make a fitting ending.

Benny Goodman
playing the clarinet

Lecture-Demonstration (Side 3)

The next band on the record moves into a lecture-demonstration as we take a closer look at the temporal relations in both a Sousa march and a dance by Lanner. For this purpose we have used electronically generated sounds[2] which intentionally do not sound like the instruments you heard playing the march. Although artificial, this method should help you to isolate the various elements that contribute to your experience of beat and groupings of beats as well as to your experience of larger but equally regular time units.

To simplify the demonstration, the discussion is included directly on the recording (hence the term *lecture-demonstration*). Certain fundamental concepts which are illustrated on the record are defined in the text below. A graphic description of the examples is also included in the text to help you *see* the distinctions which you *hear* in the music. For further explanation of the graphic description and for a discussion of standard rhythm notation, see the Additional Materials and the Ancillary Reading sections at the end of this chapter.

Beat. The underlying pulse which marks off the passing of time into equal units. It is generated by the pattern of varied durations of a rhythmic figure together with the pitches of a melody and sometimes also by percussion instruments or bass in an accompaniment. It also functions as a unit of time for measuring these varied durations.

Meter. The organization of the beat into groups which form longer but equally regular units of time. When the groups include 2 or 4 beats (Examples 2.4 and 2.7), the meter is duple, that is, grouped in twos or a multiple of twos. When the groups include 3 beats

---

[2] The electronic sounds used in the lecture-demonstration were generated by a computer-controlled "music box" in the Artificial Intelligence Laboratory at the Massachusetts Institute of Technology.

(Example 2.1), the meter is triple. When the groups include more than 4 beats, they are usually perceived as multiples of 2 or 3 (for example, a group of 6 beats as 2×3 or 3×2, or 8 beats as 4×2 or 2×4) or as asymmetrical (and comparatively rare) groups such as 5 or 7.

Downbeat. The beats within the underlying pulse which are regularly marked for attention, that is, accented. Thus, it is the regular recurrence of downbeats which generates metric groups. The downbeat is labelled "1" to mark it as the first in each *metric* group. Note, however, that accent is not necessarily generated by *stress.* That is, the accented note need not be played louder. Its function as downbeat derives from a number of sources, including the particular pattern of varied durations as well as pitch and dynamic relations.

Upbeat. The unaccented beat preceding the downbeat, that is, the last note or notes of each metric group. The term *upbeat* reflects the active, onward movement and thus the "tension" often associated with upbeat events. The name also reflects the conductor's upward motion on upbeats in contrast to his downward motion on accented beats, or downbeats. For example, *Stars and Stripes Forever* begins with an upbeat.

Metric Grid. The regularly ordered relations among the various levels of equal time units. The metric grid, as a whole, forms a hierarchy which can be described in terms of the proportional relations among the units of time at each level of the hierarchy, for example, the relations between the beat, the lower level *division* of the beat, and the higher level *grouping* of the beats. This grid forms the underpinnings of the temporal structure; it is the organized framework in relation to which we hear the more dynamic ebb and flow of time in much of Western music.

Tempo. The rate of the underlying beat and thus (proportionally) the rate of all the other levels of the metric grid. The rate of the beat (the tempo) is often indicated in a score by reference to a device called a metronome. Through an adjustable weight on a pendulum, the metronome makes it possible to generate a variable beat and then to indicate the tempo as the precise number of beats per minute. For example, a metronome marking of ♩ = 120 means that there are 120 quarter notes per minute.

Duration. The duration of an event is measured in relation to the rate of the underlying beat which is taken to be the unit time. For example, a drum beat could be notated as ♩♩♩♩♩♩♩ with a metronome marking of ♩= 120. This would mean that the drummer should play 120 drum beats per minute or two drum beats per second. The duration of the unit time (♩) would then be one-half second.

Illustration 1. Sousa, *Stars and Stripes Forever*

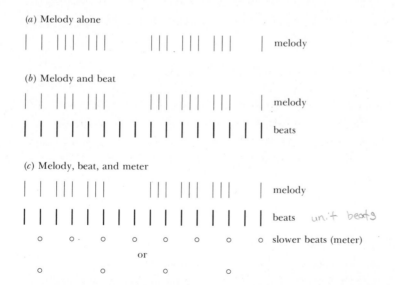

Illustration 2. Sousa, *Stars and Stripes Forever*

Organization of the rhythmic hierarchy

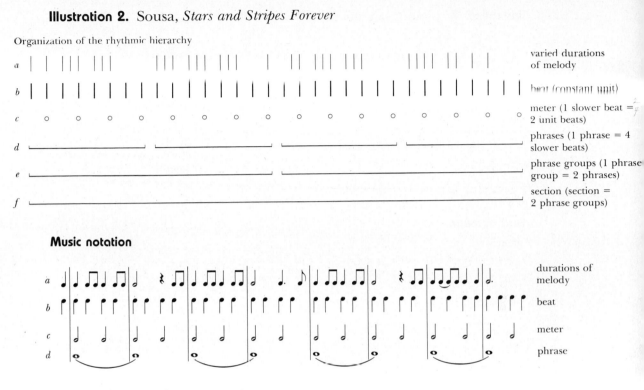

Notice when you listen to the melody (in contrast to just the rhythm played by the "drum") that the pitches are sustained, but the drum hits leave "spaces"—silence—between attacks. However, in both cases the rhythm, created by the successive attacks, is the same.

The metric grid: duple meter

Notice that at any one level the ratio is 2:1 between it and the levels above or below it—a:b = 2:1; b:c = 2:1; c:d = 2:1.

3
4

Illustration 3. Lanner, *Styrian Dances*

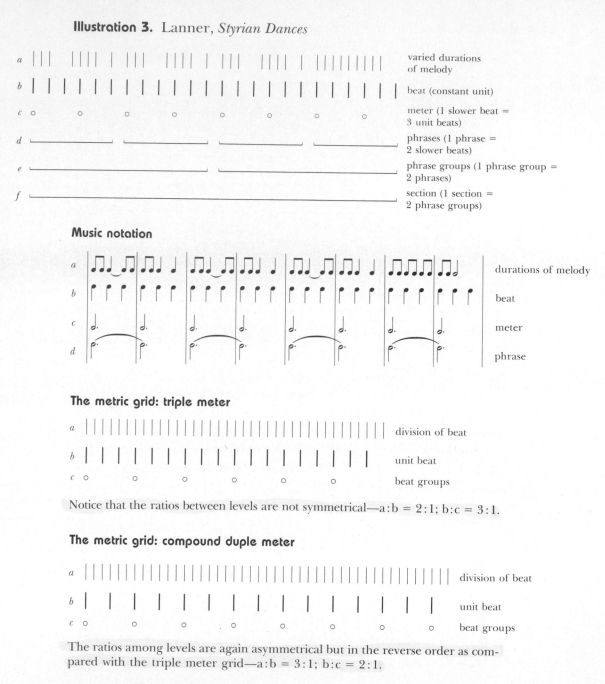

a — varied durations
of melody

b — beat (constant unit)

c — meter (1 slower beat =
3 unit beats)

d — phrases (1 phrase =
2 slower beats)

e — phrase groups (1 phrase group =
2 phrases)

f — section (1 section =
2 phrase groups)

Music notation

a — durations of melody

b — beat

c — meter

d — phrase

The metric grid: triple meter

a — division of beat

b — unit beat

c — beat groups

Notice that the ratios between levels are not symmetrical—a:b = 2:1; b:c = 3:1.

The metric grid: compound duple meter

a — division of beat

b — unit beat

c — beat groups

The ratios among levels are again asymmetrical but in the reverse order as compared with the triple meter grid—a:b = 3:1; b:c = 2:1.

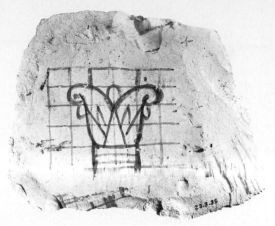

An ancient Egyptian artist's design superimposed on a grid—one a gesture ("figure"), the other a measure ("metric")

Notice that standard rhythm notation includes bar lines which indicate the higher level metric units or *measures*. The bar lines look as if they *contain* these metric groups, like boxes containing time. But they should not be interpreted as interrupting the flow of events. Unlike the notes themselves, which are symbols telling the performer to *do* something (how long to play each tone), the bar lines tell the performer *about* the music. They show the performer where events lie in relation to the metric grid. (For further information concerning meter indications, see the Ancillary Reading.)

It is particulary important to notice that bar lines do not show you the boundaries of motives or phrases. These rhythmic *figures* —the "gestures" formed by relations among events in a given melody—often overlap the measured time units indicated by the bar lines. While the listener can usually readily perceive these figural groups, they are not evident in standard rhythm notation since it is concerned entirely with measuring events in relation to some unit time.

For example, the first figural group in *Stars and Stripes* starts before the bar line and is bounded by the longer note which occurs at the *beginning* of the second measure. Thus, the figural group *ends* where the metric group *begins*. So if we count beats consecutively from the beginning to the end of this figural group, we can count 8 beats in all. But if we count beats according to the metric grid, we begin with 4 (the upbeat) and start over again with 1 at the beginning of each metric group:

| 1 | 2 | 3 | 4 | 5 | 6 | 7 | 8 | 1 | 2 | 3 | 4 | 5 | 6 | 7 | 8 | counting by figural groups |

(rhythmic notation)

beats

| 4 | 1 | 2 | 3 | 4 | 1 | 2 | 3 | 4 | 1 | 2 | 3 | 4 | 1 | 2 | 3 | counting by metric groups |

Notice that the rhythm of the second group is slightly varied. It also begins before the bar line (with an upbeat) but extends past the accented downbeat ending on the third beat of the measure.

In the Lanner dance the relation between metric groups and figural groups is somewhat different. Notice that figural groups begin and end *within bar lines*. That is, the first figural group includes the first two measures; it begins on the downbeat—on 1— and ends on the last beat of the second measure. Thus, the Sousa march can be characterized as having figures which go *to* an accent, while the Lanner dance can be characterized as having figures which begin on a downbeat, that is, proceed *from* an accent.

| 1 | 2 | 3 | 4 | 5 | 6 | 1 | 2 | 3 | 4 | 5 | 6 | 1 | 2 | 3 | 4 | 5 | 6 | 1 | 2 | 3 | 4 | 5 | 6 | counting by figural groups |

(rhythmic notation)

beats

| 1 | 2 | 3 | 1 | 2 | 3 | 1 | 2 | 3 | 1 | 2 | 3 | 1 | 2 | 3 | 1 | 2 | 3 | 1 | 2 | 3 | 1 | 2 | 3 | counting by metric groups |

It is also interesting to observe that in the Lanner dance above, the pattern of durations is the same within each figural group, with the exception of the last one. Indeed, this repetition is one factor which creates these figural groupings.

Looking back at the Hindemith piece, you will see (and hear) that sections always end at the *beginning* of metric groups; that is, each section ends on a downbeat. It is for this reason, as we noted earlier, that the boundaries of sections do not coincide with the boundaries of metric groups indicated by the bar lines.

Exercise 2-1

Meter   (Side 3)

These examples will help you practice determining the meter of a piece. Remember, however, that knowing the meter is in no sense a primary goal of listening to music. We are simply asking you to make conscious an immediate physical phenomenon, so that it may serve as a basis from which to work. If you have any difficulty in determining the meter of a piece, you may:

1. Clap the underlying beat.
2. Clap only the slower beat (sometimes, as we have seen, called the accented beat, or downbeat).
3. Clap all the beats, calling the accented beat "1." See how far you can count before you must say "1" again. If you can count to 2 or a multiple of 2, the meter is duple. If you can count to 3, the meter is triple.

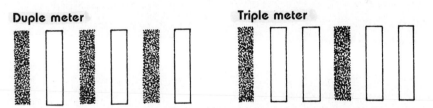

Duple meter   **Triple meter**

Listen to the examples, decide whether they are in duple or in triple meter, and mark the appropriate column. The answers are given on pages 64–65.

Example	Duple	Triple
2.9		✓
2.10	✓	
2.11	✓	
2.12		✓
2.13	✓	
2.14	✓	
2.15	✓	

CORRECT ANSWERS ·

Example	Composer, title, date	Duple	Triple
2.9	J. Strauss, *Emperor Waltz*, 1888		X
2.10	Tchaikovsky, *Marche slave*, 1876	X	

Waltzes (Example 2.9) are by definition in triple meter; as the old song goes, "Two hearts [beat together] in three-quarter time." The Tchaikovsky march is clearly in duple meter. But notice that while the trumpets always mark the strong beats (1 and 3 in the 4-beat group), the rest of the orchestra consistently plays accented notes on the "off-beats"—that is, on 2 and 4, which are the metric weak beats. The rhythmic conflict created when accents occur on events which are normally unaccented in the metric grid is called *syncopation*. Notice that these accents (played on the off-beats) are created by stress—by playing louder—in contrast to the normal metric accents which result naturally from a particular pattern of durations and pitches. Notice, too, that in the second part of the excerpt the conflicting accents stop, which leads to a lessening of tension.

Example	Composer, title, date	Duple	Triple
2.11	*Move Members Move* (spiritual; sung by Rosie Hibler and Family)	X	

The compelling character of this spiritual is created in part by the traditional clapping on off-beats; it seems almost to epitomize the notion of syncopation.

Example	Composer, title, date	Duple	Triple
2.12	S. Rollins, *Valse Hot*, 1956		X

Jazz waltzes were very rare before the mid-fifties; the music of jazz had always been in duple meter from its origins. Notice the syncopation in this "hot" waltz created primarily by off-beat drums and piano chords, but also by several striking stresses in the melody on weak beats.

Example	Composer, title, date	Duple	Triple
2.13	Sousa, *Semper Fidelis*, 1888	X	(X)

Like all marches, this one too is duple in meter (think what would happen to your two feet if you had to march to a piece in triple meter). However, in this march the two strong beats are subdivided into three rather than the usual two, as in *Stars and Stripes Forever*. When a basically duple meter is subdivided into threes, the meter is described as compound duple meter—that is, both twos and threes. Notice that there are 6 faster notes in each measure rather than the usual 8 or 4 of simple duple meter. This presents interesting possibilities for composers to play with the relations between compound duple meter and triple meter which also includes 6 faster beats in a measure. (See the diagram of the metric grid for compound duple meter and triple meter on p. 60.)

Example	Composer, title, date	Duple	Triple
2.14	*America the Beautiful* (played by the Al Cohn Quartet), 1976	X	

Here is a "jazzed-up" version of a very familiar melody. Bass, drums, and piano provide an accompaniment with the rhythmic character of the Brazilian bossa nova; in conflict with the basic beat in the drums and bass, the piano plays chords that often do not coincide with the strong beats and are thus syncopated. In the foreground, the tenor saxophone plays a relatively straightforward version of *America the Beautiful* in the first chorus, and then improvises for a second chorus.

Example	Composer, title, date	Duple	Triple
2.15	Rossini, *William Tell*, overture 1829	X	

Demonstration 2-2

RHYTHMIC COMPLEXITY   (Sides 3–4)

The preceding examples and lecture-demonstration illustrated some of the basic underlying means through which time is organized in music. These include the metric grid, which is organized into beats, the grouping of these beats to form meter, the various divisions of the beat, and the relations among these levels of the metric hierarchy. In turn, music is organized by its figures—especially in terms of the position of accents within figures, for example, beginning-accented or end-accented figures. Now that you are familiar with these "givens," which are shared by much of the music in Western culture, we will go on to see how composers have played with these givens to create interest, variety, and in many instances a special kind of almost visceral excitement.

The examples that follow are grouped according to their date of composition. While we have alluded casually to musical *style* and seen how it is associated with the particular historical period in which a composer lived, we have been more concerned up till now with juxtaposing examples because they are similar in their compositional *means* (texture, instrumentation, beat, nonbeat, and so forth), though they may be rather different in style and date of composition. In this final section examples in each group roughly share their dates of composition and thus their musical style. In addition, they all illustrate some kind of interesting rhythmic complexity. Some of these means of creating rhythmic interest will be

rhythmic complexity

found in all periods (and thus will be found in all of the following groups of examples), and yet the particular effect may be quite different within differing styles of composition. In listening to these examples, then, we are asking you to pay attention to particular means for creating rhythmic complexity. At the same time, we ask you to notice characteristics shared by music written during a given historical period, as well as the differences which result from changes in style across historical periods.

Renaissance and Baroque

Example	Composer, title	Date
2.16	C. Gervaise, *Bransle de Poitou*	c. 1531
2.17	Jacchini, *Sonata with Two Trumpets,* third movement	1690
2.18	Telemann, *Trio Sonata in D Minor,* second movement	1740
2.19	Bach, *Cantata 31*	c. 1715

Recorder players
with singer
(Italian print, 1535)

Drummer
(German print, 1562)

The first of these examples is a French dance composed during the Renaissance; the rest belong to the Baroque Period.[3] On first hearing you will probably notice that at the ends of phrases the drummer seems to be "out of step" with the recorders, who are playing the melody. Again in the middle of the dance the recorders seem to be "listening to a different drummer" as they take off on their own. Listen to the dance again and try clapping with the drum. Can you keep the beat without being pulled away by the melody?

The rhythmic conflict is quite clear here exactly because the drum is, in fact, always marking the same regular triple-meter beat while at times the recorders play between these beats. This is another example of syncopation. But unlike Examples 2.10–2.12, where the stresses were *on* the beats, the stresses in the Gervaise dance are often *between* the beats. Notice that in the middle part of

---

[3] For approximate dates of each historical period, see Chapter 8.

the dance the conflict becomes so extensive that we seem to lose a sense of meter altogether.[4]

In the *Sonata with Two Trumpets* by Jacchini we have another example of syncopation, but this time the stressed accents occur on a beat, though on a normally unaccented beat, as in the Tchaikovsky *Marche slave* and the spiritual *Move Members Move*. That is, there is a stress on the second beat of the triple meter which conflicts with the underlying accent on the first beat of the triple meter. Thus there is a kind of tension between the regularly recurring accent set up by the rhythm and pitch patterns and the stressed second beat, which so to speak attacks this given metric accent. The word *syncopation* is given to all situations in which one hears simultaneously the framework of a well-formed metric grid and events which go against the norms of that framework.

If you focus your listening on the accompaniment (organ, basses, and tympani), you will hear that they sometimes play only on the downbeats

but sometimes go on to play two notes in a row, giving an extra stress to the second

It is this displacement of the normal accent that we call syncopation.

In Example 2.18, a trio for flute, oboe, and basso continuo (that is, the background accompaniment played by the harpsichord and cello together), the accompanying instruments generally play a regular duple meter while the solo flute and oboe often play between the beats. However, this piece also differs from

---

[4] In this middle section the melody actually goes into compound duple meter played against the drum's consistent triple-meter beat.

the preceding examples in that the flute and/or oboe sometimes seem to *anticipate* the beat rather than just follow it.

In the excerpt from the Bach *Cantata* we hear rhythmic *contrast* rather than rhythmic *conflict*. The excerpt begins with all the instruments playing in unison and also playing notes of relatively long duration. Then at the end of the unison passage the melody gets faster—there are more notes per beat. This leads to a section in which this more active rhythmic movement continues, but the

begins in unison followed by a more active texture

texture also becomes more active. We hear many parts playing rhythmically independently of one another. So the excerpt includes an increase in both rhythmic activity and textural activity without any change in the rate of the underlying pulse or in the underlying meter.

Classical

Example	Composer, title	Date
2.20	Mozart, *String Quartet in G Major*, K. 387, fourth movement	1782
2.21	Beethoven, *Variations on "God Save the King"*	1803
2.22	Beethoven, *Sonata for Cello and Piano*, Op. 69, scherzo	1808
2.23	Haydn, *String Quartet*, Op. 76, no. 5, minuet	1797

These four examples are from the so-called Classical Period, and they include works by the three greatest composers of that era

—Haydn, Mozart, and Beethoven. Example 2.20, from one of Mozart's string quartets (two violins, viola, and cello), again includes contrast in rhythmic and textural activity. Like the Bach example, this one begins with notes of longer duration and changes in the second section to much faster rhythmic motion. Also like the Bach, there is no change in the rate of the underlying pulse (that is, no change in *tempo*) or in the prevailing meter (duple here, triple in the Bach). However in this excerpt slower, or *less,* rhythmic activity goes together with *greater* textural activity, while *greater* rhythmic activity (more notes per beat) goes together with *less* textural activity. In the first section, then, you hear imitation—the instruments enter one by one, each playing the same slow five-note motive. And once in, each instrument goes on to play its own individual and rhythmically independent line. Notice too that the rhythmic independence of the lines is created in large part as a result of syncopation. That is, the instruments that play against the slow-moving melody are also playing against the underlying pulse, in between the beats. In the second section syncopation disappears, and textural activity lessens. We hear one clear melody with an accompaniment, but the running melody is made up of many very fast notes. Thus when the rhythm grows more active, the texture becomes less active.

A theme followed by a set of variations on it was a favorite way of organizing music in the Classical Period. You heard another example of a theme and variations in Chapter 1—the theme and some of the variations from the fourth movement of Beethoven's *Symphony 9* (Example 1.9). Composers sometimes also borrowed themes from elsewhere, and here we have Beethoven composing variations on the British national anthem, *God Save the King* (which we in turn borrowed and know as *America*). Listening to Beethoven's setting of the familiar tune followed by one of the variations, it should be quite clear that Beethoven had a good time varying the straightforward theme by introducing syncopation. Of course, that was not all he did; in fact, you may have a little trouble at first finding the familiar tune in the variation. It may help if you sing the tune along with the variation. You will see that it fits perfectly, except you will be *on* the beat while the melody line of the variation is often between the beats. In addition, the downbeats are sometimes not sounded in the melody, leaving a silence just where we expect to hear an extra emphasis. In this way Beethoven shifts the accent to the second beat of the triple meter, most noticeably at the end of each section of the piece. Compare the effect of this shift of accent to the weak second beat with the same sort of syncopation in the Jacchini *Sonata* (Example 2.17). This is a good example of the way a composer can toy with givens—in this case the givens of the theme itself as well as the givens established by the underlying metric grid.

In Example 2.22 we again hear Beethoven making use of syncopation but this time in a rather different way and with different effect. On first hearing you may find it hard to tell which is the beat and which is the off-beat. For example, when the cello joins in, is it or the piano playing on the beat? In fact, the cello *anticipates* the beat at the beginnings of phrases and then plays on the beat and with the piano accompaniment at the ends of phrases. Notice particularly that at the end of the cello's first phrase, and again with its repetition, both cello and piano arrive together on the downbeat, but they seem to plummet into that abrupt stop as if arriving too soon. In the second part of the excerpt, the cello's syn-

String quartet (left to right: cello, viola, first and second violins)

copated notes seem to drive the piece forward to the climax, which then suddenly subsides as the syncopation ceases, giving way to a much more lyrical passage.

Finally, in the Haydn string quartet we have a beautiful example of shift in meter. In this minuet (the third movement of four in the quartet), Haydn first creates a clear triple meter. But after the repetition of this first section, there is an abrupt shift to duple meter. Haydn creates this shift in meter by simply shortening or fragmenting the figure with which the first section ends. The ending figure ♩♩ | ♫ ♩ is abbreviated to become ♫ ♩ ♩. He gives this fragmented figure to the violin, which plays a whole string of them (♫ ♩ ♫ ♩ ♫ ♩ ♫ ♩). And since the abbreviated figure is now only two beats long (instead of three), the repetitions cause the beats to group in twos instead of the initial threes. Haydn then fragments the figure still further by chopping off the last note, leaving a series of notes of equal duration (♫ ♫ ♫ ♫). For a moment the meter becomes ambiguous; we hear simply an ungrouped series of beats. With the return of the opening material, the meter is once again triple; the tension and resulting intensity subside almost as if nothing at all had happened. The fragmenting process occurs once again, this time with the cello playing the abbreviated two-beat figure. The minuet ends with a new transformation of the motive. We hear repeated statements of the original figure in its clear triple-meter form (♩ | ♫ ♩), which brings the movement to a solid and stable close. Notice that the second part of the minuet is also repeated.

Example 2.23. Haydn, *String Quartet,* Op. 76, no. 5, minuet

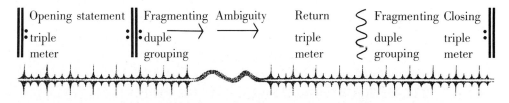

Opening statement	Fragmenting	Ambiguity	Return	Fragmenting	Closing
triple	duple	→	triple	duple	triple
meter	grouping	→	meter	grouping	meter

Romantic

Example	Composer, title	Date
2.24	Schubert, *String Quintet in C,* Op. 163, scherzo	1828
2.25	Chopin, *Mazurka,* Op. 17, no. 4	1832–33
2.26	Brahms, *Trio for Piano, Cello, and Clarinet,* Op. 114	1891

2.24

In the first of these Romantic Period examples, an excerpt from the *String Quintet in C* by Schubert (Schubert adds another cello to the string quartet), you will easily recognize the change from straightforward rhythmic stability at the beginning of the excerpt to conflict and tension in the middle to a return to rhythmic stability at the end. As in several of the earlier examples (the Telemann trio and the Beethoven cello and piano sonata) conflict is created here by an accent which precedes, or *anticipates,* the normally accented downbeat (thus syncopation). But in this excerpt the syncopation grows out of a transformation of an earlier rhythmic figure. The movement itself begins with a quick upbeat which adds power to the longer, stressed downbeat that follows. At the beginning of the excerpt you hear hints of that opening figure in the passage just preceding the syncopation. Then, at the climax (created in part by the excitement of rhythmic conflict), Schubert reminds us of the upbeat in the upper strings, but this time he withholds the downbeat! Only the cellos play the downbeat, as if teasing the upper strings to try and join them. Finally, all five strings do come together to play the original upbeat-downbeat figure with which the movement begins. It is a marvelous example of building anticipation and drive in preparation for return and stability—a subject to which we shall return in Chapters 4 and 6.

2.25

In the Chopin *Mazurka* (Example 2.25) we hear a kind of rhythmic complexity that is particularly associated with the Romantic Period of music. Not surprisingly, it is highly dependent on a "living" interaction between composer and performer. Indeed, during the nineteenth century the individuality of the instrumental performer—as virtuoso, as "star," as unique personality—comes much more to the fore. We find composers like Chopin (as well as Liszt, Paganini, and others) writing works which are in part a showcase for the performer's technical and expressive skills. One aspect of this presence of the performer as an individual is his or her use of *rubato*. The term comes from the Italian word for "robbed." It refers to the performer's freedom to slow down or speed up the tempo—to extend or shorten the time of an event or group of events. Thus it is like "robbing" time from one event or from a moment in the flow of the piece (speeding up slightly) and "paying it back" a little later (slowing down proportionally). This should not be understood, of course, as a process of actually measuring, but rather as a kind of subtle give-and-take or flexibility with which the performer treats the underlying pulse. While the purpose is one of achieving greater expressiveness, it requires a deep interaction between the structural relations of the piece itself and the performer's understanding of these structural relations, especially in their potential for expressiveness. Figural grouping plays an important role, for it is particularly in terms of figures—that is, phrases, motivic groups, gestures of the music—that the performer makes decisions (certainly not always conscious or explicit) concerning the use of rubato. In fact, a performer who might be described as using rubato tastefully is one who robs and pays back in response to such figural structure, while the performer who uses rubato in bad taste is often one who robs and pays back without sufficient attention to these structural relations or in violation of them. Besides the use of rubato to project figural groupings, performers also use it to emphasize or even prolong a climactic moment (slowing down), to reinforce a passage which is restless or driving forward (speeding up), and so forth.

Listen again to the Chopin *Mazurka* and notice particularly how the pianist "bends" the underlying beat which is always present in his left hand—that is, in the bass. Chopin encourages the pianist to let the right hand move more freely by sometimes composing a melodic line which is unmeasured with respect to the beat. For example, he writes the following:

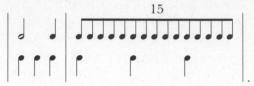

This means, essentially, "fit those 15 notes into the time of the three underlying beats in a free and expressive way." So, while it would not be quite appropriate to speak of rhythmic conflict here between the melody and the accompaniment, it does seem appropriate to note the rhythmic complexity and the expressiveness which results from the relations between the notated underlying pulse and the performer's liberties with that pulse, as well as the relations between the fairly regular bass and the relatively freer melody.

Finally, while the use of rubato is perhaps more pronounced in the performances of romantic music, it is not limited to this music. In fact, all performers include some give-and-take with the notated time in projecting structural relations and for purposes of expressiveness. This is very clear if you compare the computer "performance" with the live performance of the Lanner dance in the lecture-demonstration. Indeed, it is precisely the lack of give-and-take—the exact and rigid marking of the beat and measuring of each event—which often makes computer music sound so inhuman and mechanical.

But bear in mind that the liberties performers (including conductors) take with the rhythm of a piece as notated by the composer are very small and tasteful in the ways described above. Such liberties should not be confused with "arrangements" of a tune, as is common with popular music, and certainly not with improvisation, such as we will discuss in the next group of examples. The performance of a composed and written-out work must be faithful to the printed score. The composer notates all the pitches and their durations as well as the instrumentation (in an orchestral score) just as he or she wants them, and they are played essentially as the composer wrote them. The question of "interpretation" is precisely one of coming to understand—to "hear" the work as much as possible in terms of the composer's musical intentions—and then to find the appropriate means for projecting this understanding in performance. In a very profound sense the performer, as he or she studies a score, is also practicing the "art of listening."

2.26

The first movement of the Brahms *Trio for Piano, Cello, and Clarinet* (Example 2.26) includes in it nearly all the varieties of rhythmic complexity we have illustrated thus far—shifts in meter, syncopation (accent shifted to weak beats or between beats), changes in the division of the beats, changes in the degree of rhythmic and textural activity, as well as rubato playing by the performers. And yet the effect is not one of continuous conflict and tension as we might expect, but rather one of metric ambiguity or perhaps metric fluidity. Most of all Brahms creates a different relationship between metric and figural groupings. He asks you to focus more on the gesture—on the figural groups formed by motives and phrases which are in a dynamic, changing, almost fluid relationship to the underlying metric grid. The listener rarely loses a sense of beat but at times loses the sense of regularly recurring accents altogether, though still following the flow of the gesture from one goal or boundary to the next. Brahms writes motives that create their own inner accents which may or may not coincide with those of the initially established duple meter: downbeats are often silent or held over from the preceding upbeat; the four-beat measure is divided into three beats, obscuring the normal pulse; motives played by two instruments overlap in their grouping, placing their accents ambiguously in relation to the metric grid; a motive begins with an accent, apparently a downbeat, which turns out to have been a metric weak beat and not the metric accent at all. The result of all this is a temporal organization which is highly pliable and still tightly structured. Brahms causes time to seemingly expand and contract, ebb and flow, as it constantly frees itself from and then reaffirms an underlying pulse and meter.

With the next group of examples we move into our own century. Paradoxically, the works written most recently may sound the most strange. This is partly, as you will hear, because of the new ways some twentieth-century composers have found to organize time as well as pitch (we will return to the issue of pitch in Chapters 3 and 5). And yet we also find contemporary composers using some of the same means for creating rhythmic complexity as earlier composers but now within a musical style that gives them a rather different effect.

Twentieth Century

Example	Composer, title	Date
2.27	Stravinsky, *Petrouchka,* scene 3, waltz	1911
2.28	Bartok, *Sonata for Two Pianos and Percussion,* first movement	1937
2.29	Webern, *Five Pieces for Orchestra,* Op. 10, no. 2	1913
2.30	S. Joplin, *Maple Leaf Rag* (played by S. Joplin)	1916
2.31	S. Joplin, *Maple Leaf Rag* (played by Jelly Roll Morton)	1938

2.27

In the excerpt from the ballet *Petrouchka* we have an instance of metric *superimposition* and another example of a composer using a borrowed tune. Stravinsky took one of Lanner's triple-meter *Styrian Dances* (discussed in the lecture-demonstration) and set it against a compound duple-meter accompaniment. The excerpt begins with the bassoon playing a "melody" with notes of equal duration, but its pitch relations cause it to group into two groups of three notes each:

Lanner's melody comes in later (played by trumpet and flute)
—the same melody which Lanner himself accompanied with a
simple oom-pah-pah bass. But Stravinsky creates a playful rhythmic conflict by superimposing this triple-meter melody on his
compound duple-meter accompaniment:

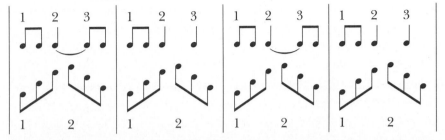

The excerpt from the Bartok *Sonata for Two Pianos and Percussion* (Example 2.28), gives us an example of a real change in *tempo*.
Unlike the Mozart quartet or the Bach cantata excerpts, where
there was an increase in rhythmic motion but no change in the
rate of the underlying pulse, in this example the actual rate of the
beat increases. This is called an *accelerando.* You saw the word and
heard its effect on a small scale in the Hindemith *Kleine Kammermusik* movement. Notice the difference between getting faster
within the framework of an unchanging metric grid (as in Examples 2.19 and 2.20) and getting faster when the framework itself
gives way. In the earlier examples we heard more notes per beat,

Percussion section of an orchestra
Timpani   Cymbals Snare drum   Xylophone

but the beat remained as fixed reference. In this example, on the other hand, there is a continuous acceleration—the actual pulse slowly speeds up rather than changing from, say, two notes per beat (eighth notes) to four notes per beat (sixteenth notes).

Example 2.29 is a complete little piece which is one of five that Webern wrote to be played as a group. Here the underlying metric grid is no longer present. In its place the structure of figural groups formed by motives and their resulting gestures becomes the basis for organizing time. With the loss of even a sense of underlying pulse, and with it, of course, the loss of meter, you may indeed feel as if the music has lost all rhythmic coherence. In fact, the piece is highly organized rhythmically, but Webern's means of organization and thus his means of generating coherence—even comprehensibility—derives from a different notion of structuring time. He asks you to attend to the unique structure formed by the movement from one figural boundary to another and by the repetition of rhythmic patterns within figures, rather than searching for the accustomed metric grid. Can you find rhythmic structure without the security of reference to a grid? It is a challenge which has been described as follows:

> Through the power of an ever new, internal logic, each work will rouse the listener from his state of passivity and make him share in its impulse, so that there will no longer be a difference of kind, but only of degree, between inventing music and listening to it.[5]

Perhaps the challenge of discovering the "ever new, internal logic" demanded by this music is also appropriate to more familiar music, in listening to which we tend too easily to fall into a "state of passivity" in simply following the norms of a regular beat and meter without listening actively enough to the unique rhythmic complexities found even in the more traditional music of earlier times.

We end this section on rhythmic complexity and the chapter on rhythm with two interestingly different performances of the

---

[5] C. Lévi-Strauss, *The Raw and the Cooked* (New York: Harper & Row, 1969), p. 26.

"same" piece. Scott Joplin plays his own rag in a straightforward way, unembellished with rhythmic complexity. Jelly Roll Morton, some 20 years later, turns Joplin's piece into a sparkling, elaborate, and virtuoso performance, in part by playing with the rhythm of the original melody so it conflicts through syncopation with the solid beat and meter which is nevertheless always clearly present. You might compare these two performances with Beethoven's variations on *God Save the King*. In Beethoven's work we hear one composer in one piece toying with a set of givens. In the two performances of the *Maple Leaf Rag*, we hear one performer "commenting" on the composition and performance of another.

But there is an important difference here. The transformations which Beethoven creates are composed and written out, and they are played essentially the same today as they were in Beethoven's own time. Jelly Roll Morton's transformations are, at least in part, the result of stylistic change; that is, they are the result of history. Within the jazz culture one person's tune (the given) becomes the very material of change. The same tune is reborn through another individual's art of improvisation. One composer's tune is another performer's point of departure. And within Morton's own performance, just as in Al Cohn's *America the Beautiful*, we also hear several variations on this performer's own version of the given tune. Comparing the Beethoven work with the performances of Joplin and Morton, we have a rich example of the possibilities of structuring and restructuring time (as well as pitch): Transformation takes place within the "history" of a single composed piece (Beethoven), through the years of history (Joplin to Morton), and within the live "history" of a single, unique, improvised performance (Morton).

Having traveled through 400 years of music history, what can we say about the changes in musical style? In order to answer this question meaningfully, we would need to consider all the dimensions of musical composition—instrumentation and texture, rhythm, pitch relations, harmony, aspects of structure and form, and the interactions among all these dimensions. It is exactly for this reason that we have left issues of stylistic analysis until the end of the book. In Chapter 9 we focus explicitly on style and stylistic change, but there we consider only a brief part of this 400-year history, namely, the period from 1860 to 1913, which includes the works of Brahms on the one end and Stravinsky on the other.

And yet, long before you will be able to say explicitly how the style of one composer differs from another (say, Bach and Brahms), you will be able to recognize and place a composition with respect to its historical period. So as you go on to study the various dimensions of musical structure, you might ask yourself what is it in the music itself that makes Bach and Telemann, for example, sound more alike than Bach and Brahms? Like other aspects of music, we would like you first to *perceive* similarities and differences; later you will be able to account for them. In the meantime, practice your ability to listen stylistically along with learning to differentiate and coordinate within and among the various dimensions of music. As you develop these listening skills, you may like to return to this short trip through music history and consider these stylistic questions again.

ADDITIONAL MATERIALS

I

While we have carefully chosen examples in each chapter to illustrate a particular aspect of music, it will often be useful to revisit earlier examples in the light of issues taken up in later portions of the book. For example, now that you have some experience with the fundamentals of rhythmic organization, you can listen again to the following examples from Chapter 1, paying attention now to their rhythmic complexity.

Stravinsky, *Le Sacre du printemps,* "Dance of the Adolescents" (Example 1.1)

As in much of Stravinsky's music, rhythm and rhythmic complexity play a central role. In this excerpt you hear a marked and steady beat throughout, but accents occur quite irregularly and thus unexpectedly. Of course, accents would not be unexpected if Stravinsky did not first set up some initial expectations—that is, some initial regularity. The excerpt begins in a clear duple meter, but with the entrance of the repeated chords we hear accents (created by stress) which confound the initial duple meter. Stravinsky notates the piece in duple meter throughout, so in these terms we might describe these accents as syncopation—they occur on weak beats or off-beats in the notated duple metric grid. However, the perceived effect seems more like shifting meter or even ambiguity of meter; we lose all sense of regularly recurring accents at times. But it is this contrast between moments of regularity of meter and moments which are ametric or ambiguous in meter, but heard in relation to the strong reiteration of an underlying pulse, which helps give the piece its wild, even savage power.

Bach, *Concerto in D Minor for Harpsichord and Orchestra* (Example 1.2)

This example also includes syncopation but in such a different stylistic environment that it seems almost inappropriate to use the same word for describing both the Bach and Stravinsky excerpts. Notice that in the harpsichord concerto we never lose a sense of the duple meter. However, you may be fooled at the outset concerning just where the downbeat comes. The movement begins with the figure ♫ ♩, which seems to place the accent on the longer quarter note following the two shorter notes. In fact, the piece begins on the downbeat, which becomes quickly clear as the piece moves on. Syncopation occurs as the excerpt continues; the downbeat accent is anticipated (in a fashion similar to the excerpt from the Telemann *Trio* in Example 2.18) and then tied over the bar line, repressing the expected accent on the downbeat.

elusive → to avoid being captured by; evade; to escape the understanding of

Moussorgsky, *Pictures at an Exhibition,* "Promenade" (Example 1.16)

In this example you hear again a clear and marked beat, but the meter seems to be elusive. Unlike the Stravinsky example, however, where our sense of meter is thrown off by unexpected accents, in the "Promenade" each beat is of equal weight with little sense of higher-level grouping of these beats. Try counting as you listen; it seems quite possible to count in twos, in threes, or in fours. But notice that the result is not one of unrest or conflict; quite the contrary, we simply move along, step by step, with the even beat. With no strong expectations for the regular occurrence of accents, we are not bothered by their absence. The steady, ungrouped beat contributes to the "promenade" aspect of the piece. (You might compare this with the somewhat similar Gregorian chant in Example 2.5.)

Beethoven, *Symphony 9,* Op. 125, fourth movement (Example 1.9)

Here we have an example of syncopation used to help articulate the structure of a melody. Notice that the theme includes an opening section, a contrasting middle section, and then a return (see Chapter 3 for a further analysis of the melody). The return is signaled, or set off, by syncopation. That is, the first note of the return comes "too soon"; it occurs on the fourth beat of the measure instead of on the expected downbeat which follows. This displaced accent is the result not only of stress but also of the melodic leap which stands out in this otherwise stepwise melody.

II

We suggest now a more active participation in the musical process which should help you to listen more responsively. For example, several students might get together to form a "rhythm band," either with toy or actual percussion instruments or simply with clapping or rapping. One player can establish the beat, another the meter by "playing" only the downbeats; then one or two others can beat various patterns, introducing syncopation or even changes of meter. Three possible rhythmic combinations are given as practice problems.

Practice problem 1

Practice problem 2

Practice problem 3

ANCILLARY READING

Rhythm Notation

Rhythm notation is based on a set of symbols that stand for the duration of an event as measured against a given unit time or metric. The ability to read standard rhythm notation assumes the ability to hear a set of durations (in a melody, for example) in relation to this unvarying beat. The beat functions, then, as a constant unit of time against which the varied durations of a melody can be measured.

The Basic Symbols

The symbols used in standard notation relate to one another by multiples of two, or, to put it conversely, by division into halves.

Notes   Rests (meaning silence, which is also measured)

o = whole note   ━

♩ = half note   ▬

♩ = quarter note   𝄽

♪ = eighth note   𝄾

♬ = sixteenth note   𝄿

To express these relationships in notational equations we have:

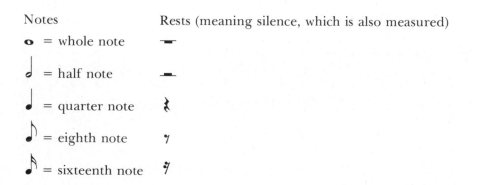

The notation may be confusing at first, because the whole note, from which the other symbols derive their names and values, is rarely used as the symbol for the unit time. The most common notation for the underlying beat is probably the quarter note. Thus if you are keeping time to a piece (as in the exercise on meter), the beat that you are clapping is most often (but certainly not always)

written as a quarter note, with the particular durations of a melody written as multiples or divisions of that basic quarter-note beat.

Meter

The higher-level grouping of beats is indicated, perhaps confusingly, by bar lines. The bar line, then, shows the reader a larger underlying metric or unit time—what we have called the "slower pulse." In terms of standard notation, then, the metric grid for duple meter (in fours) would look like this (see also p. 59):

The metric grid for triple meter would look like this (see also p. 60):

The *time signature* placed at the beginning of the piece indicates (1) the meter (the number of beats in a measure) and (2) the notational symbol which will represent the unit time or the beat. Thus in the time signature $\frac{4}{4}$, the upper number means that the beats are grouped in fours. This grouping is reflected in the division of the written music into measures, each including the equivalent of four beats, or four beats in total duration. The lower number means that the basic beat or unit time will be represented by a quarter note (♩). For example:

[musical notation in 4/4 time]

Or in ¾ time:

[musical notation in 3/4 time]

Or in ⁶⁄₈:

[musical notation in 6/8 time]

The most common time signatures are ²⁄₄, ³⁄₄, ⁴⁄₄ (or **c**), where the unit time is notated as ♩; ³⁄₈, ⁶⁄₈, ⁹⁄₈, ¹²⁄₈, where the unit time is noted as ♪; and ²⁄₂, ³⁄₂ where the unit is notated as ♩.

Other Conventions

A dot after a note is used to extend its duration by half again its notated value. Thus ♩. means ♩ + ♪, while ♪ means ♪ + ♪. The same values can be notated using a *tie:* ♩♪. The tie means "these notes are tied together; do not make another attack on the second one; the duration of the event is the sum of both." For example:

♩. = ♩♪, or ♪ = ♪♪. An indication of a triplet (♩♩♩) is a direction to the performer to play three notes in the time usually taken by two notes of the same value. Thus ♩♩♩ = ♩♩ = ♩, that is, three notes are to be played in the time taken by one quarter note. In addition, the basic 2:1 ratio among notational symbols can be circumvented as follows:

[musical notation showing groupings of 5 and 7 notes] , etc.

Tempo Designation

As we have commented repeatedly, the notation system rests on measuring time in relation to some given unit; but the symbols themselves tell you nothing about the *rate* of this unit time, that is, the tempo. The metronome provides the only precise method for representing tempo by fixing the rate for the unit time in relation to the fixed measure of the clock. Thus, if the time signature is $\frac{3}{4}$, and the metronome marking is $\downarrow = 60$, then the quarter note will be equal to one second, and there will be the equivalent of three seconds in each measure. While performers use the metronome marking to establish a basic tempo, no performer plays or measures time in this precise way throughout a whole piece; his or her performance is always responsive to the context, which results in a certain give-and-take with respect to the precisely measured beat (see the discussion of *rubato* on p. 75).

Pieces are often preceded by more general indications of tempo, and here Italian terms predominate.

adagio	slow
largo	very slow ("broad")
andante	moderately slow ("walking")
moderato	moderate
allegretto	moderately fast
allegro	fast ("cheerful")
vivace	fast ("lively")
presto	very fast
prestissimo	as fast as possible

Learning to Notate Rhythms

In the discussion of beat and meter, and especially in the discussion of the Sousa march and the Lanner dance (p. 62), we made a distinction between *metric groups* and *figural groups*. We pointed out that only metric groups are captured by standard rhythm notation; that is, rhythm notation is intended to tell the performer how to measure the time of each event. However, figural groups, which are often readily perceived by the listener, are not shown by the symbols of rhythm notation; indeed, these symbols often *look* as if they go against the grouping of events into gestures, motives, or figures.

In order to help you see the difference between these two aspects of rhythmic structure, and at the same time see how they can be coordinated with one another, we have suggested a kind of spatial notation. Our experience suggests that this spatial notation can work as an intermediary between your immediate sense experience of rhythm and the measured descriptions of rhythm found in standard notation. The following exercises will take you through the process of moving from clapping to spatial notation to standard rhythm notation.

Clap the rhythm of *Happy Birthday*. Now, with pencil in hand, "play" this rhythm on a piece of paper by tapping out the melody, making a dot for each event, as you move a piece of paper along from left to right at a regular pace. You should leave a trace that looks something like this:

. . . .

Notice that the *space* between dots (claps) corresponds to the *time* between claps; that is, larger spaces will correspond to longer times. Notice too that the trace falls into two identical figures separated by a longer space-of-time. You can see quite clearly, then, the figural grouping of the tune.

Next, turn the dots into lines, keeping the spatial relations the same:

||| | | | ||| | | |

Now clap just the underlying, regular pulse as you sing the tune. Or, if you find this difficult, get a friend to clap the rhythm of the tune while you clap the beat, and then change parts. As you play together, pay attention to how and where the beat coincides with the events of the piece—that is, try to find the beat in the piece. Now try to draw this regular beat, the underlying unit time, so that is "fits" with the tune just as your duet did:

||| | | | ||| | | |

| | | | | | | | | | | | |

The upper row of lines shows you the rhythm of the melody. The lower row of lines (all equidistant from one another) shows you the metric grid and where it coincides with events in the melody. You have here a sort of spelled out version of standard notation showing both the rhythm of the tune and the constant unit time (the beat) with which you can measure the varied durations of the tune. Now you can transform the spatial notation into standard notation. Simply follow these rules:

1. If a tune event equals the unit time, leave it alone.
2. If the tune includes more than one event per unit time (beat), join these lines together just *up to* the next beat mark.
3. If there is more than one beat for a single tune event, use a symbol for that event equal to the number of beats that go by. Now put "heads" on all the lines.

If you follow these instructions, the two-layered spatial notation will be transformed into standard notation as follows:

Notice that in the process the first three taps which previously seemed to form a little figural group are now broken up visually into 2 + 1. This is a good example of the differences between metric and figural groupings. The first two notes together equal one beat, which is exactly what the "beam" joining them indicates. Thus beams are used to indicate a group of notes that together equal one unit time, or beat. The figural group, however, includes the longer quarter note; in fact, the longer duration (♩) following the two faster notes (♫) *functions* as the goal of this small figure, though neither this function nor the group itself is represented by the graphics. In much the same way the longer half note (♩) functions to delimit or mark the boundary of the two larger figures.

To put in the bar lines, follow these instructions:

1. Clap the rhythm of the tune again.
2. Sing the tune (or get someone else to sing it) while you clap a slower, but equally regular, pulse.
3. Add a third row of lines showing where this slower pulse coincides with the tune and the beat:

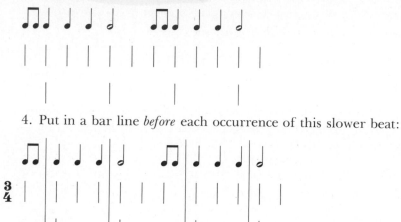

4. Put in a bar line *before* each occurrence of this slower beat:

Notice that the bar lines again interrupt, or break up, the figural groups. The bar lines show you where the downbeat occurs, and because the figural groups go *to* the accented downbeats (the figures begin with an upbeat) they are each time interrupted by a bar line.

Sometimes composers (or, later, editors) add marks which indicate figural groups or phrasing, as follows:

However, the problem of finding the figural groups is often left up to the performer. Indeed, many performers would agree that "interpretation" depends in large part on how the performer translates the notated durations into musical gestures, giving the piece both a sense of beat and meter and a sense of motion to goals. Such understandings are reflected in the performer's decisions concerning fingering, bowing (on stringed instruments), breathing (on wind instruments and in singing), dynamics, and the subtle give-and-take of the underlying pulse.

Following the same steps, now try notating *America*.

1. "Playing" the rhythm on the paper:

. . . .

2. Spatial notation:

| | | | || | | | | || | | | |

3. Two-level notation—piece and beat:

| | | | || | | | | || | | | |

| | | | | | | | | | | | | | | | |

4. Three-level notation—piece, beat, and meter:

| | | | || | | | | || | | | |

| | | | | | | | | | | | | | | | | |

| | | | | |

Before making the transformation to standard notation, notice that the events on the syllables "tis" and "lib" each include one beat plus half of the next beat, or one-and-one-half beats in all. Looking back at page 88 you will see that this can be notated either with a tie (♩ ♪) or by adding a dot to the quarter note (♩.).

5. Now you are ready to put heads on the notes and put in the bar lines:

| | | | || | | | | || | | | |

$\frac{3}{4}$ ♩ ♩ ♩ | ♩ ♫ ♩ | ♩ ♩ ♩ | ♩ ♫ ♩ | ♩ ♩ ♩ | ♩.

| | | | | | | | | | | | | | | | |

| | | | | |

Now that you have learned something about notating rhythms that you can *clap*, go back and see if you can *read* the notation in the "rhythm band" examples on p. 85.

Hokusai, *Fisherman with Cormorants* (Woodcut, 1823–1829)

CHAPTER 3

Pitch
and movement:
melody

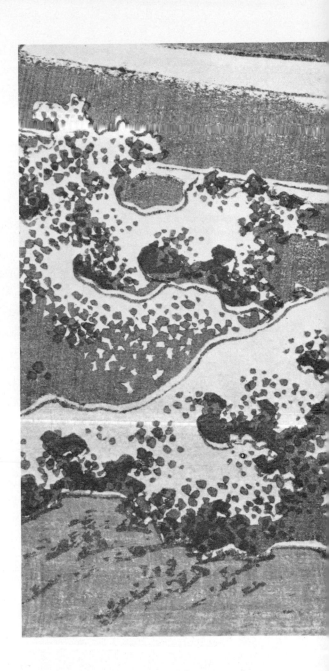

This chapter is hardly your first introduction to pitch and melody. In Chapter 1, for example, we spoke of high and low "sounds"; these can be described more precisely as being made up of high or low "pitches." Again, in the discussion of texture we spoke, for instance, of "many actively moving lines" (see page 24). "Line" is, of course, a metaphor for a succession of tones. We could say more literally (and more awkwardly) that you heard several different instruments each playing a different succession of pitches and a different rhythm. In considering rhythm in Chapter 2, you were also necessarily concerned with pitch. In fact, it is usually a succession of tones which articulates or defines time and generates your experience of a particular rhythmic structure.

We would like you to focus now on the specific relations of pitch and time as they interact to form melody. Along with rhythm, melody seems to be the most immediately tangible aspect of music—that which is often remembered, later to be hummed or whistled. But as you have seen, melody is seldom the sole component in a piece of music. Indeed, there are many compositions in which you hardly find a melody at all; you are drawn instead to action in other dimensions of the music, such as texture and rhythm. One could even dispute what is or is not "a melody". For example, some of the excerpts in Chapter 1—Varèse's *Density 21.5* and the African *Singing Game*—may not correspond to your idea of a melody. But this idea of melody—a kind of intuitive model of what a tune is—varies among cultures and even within cultures such as ours with its diversity of musical styles.

Demonstration 3-1

MELODIC COHERENCE   (Side 4)

All the melodies of Examples 3.1 to 3.6 belong to our own Western culture, and yet probably only two or three match what we think of as the prototypical tune. What contributes to the differences, and how can we account for them? Notice that the exam-

Example	Composer, title	Date
3.1	Vivaldi, *Concerto Grosso,* Op. 3, no. 6, second movement	c. 1712
3.2	Liszt, *Faust Symphony,* first movement	1854
3.3	Berg, *Wozzeck,* "Lullaby"	1925
3.4	*Did You Ever See a Lassie?*	
3.5	Mozart, *Sonata for Piano in A,* K. 331, first movement	1778
3.6	Gershwin, *I Got Rhythm* (sung by Ethel Waters)	1930

ples span more than 200 years in their dates of composition, that one is a folk song and anonymous (Example 3.4), and that another (Example 3.6), while composed, comes out of the popular culture rather than the concert-hall culture. Notice, too, that some are vocal melodies and some instrumental, and that even the instrumental melodies differ in their instrumental medium—solo piano, violin and orchestra, full orchestra. Finally, the vocal melodies are associated with a text and are about something specific, as indeed is the excerpt from the Liszt *Faust Symphony,* which is intended to convey a mood inspired by Faust's encounter with the devil. Thus the date of composition and the musical style current to the time, along with the particular subculture from which the piece comes and to which it is addressed influence the kinds of melodies we can expect. Then, too, the medium suggests particular melodic possibilities as well as constraints, as do the composer's expressive intentions.

Let us look more closely at the specific musical differences among the melodies and consider how each in its own way develops a particular sense of what a melody is or can be. Then we can go on to compare these characteristics with the perhaps banal, but for just that reason prototypical, tune *Lassie.*

We can ask, for example, what makes for coherence in the Vivaldi and Liszt excerpts. The Vivaldi is a concerto for solo violin accompanied by the orchestra. The violinist occupies the foreground role, and our listening attention is clearly focused on him.

the melody seems almost serpentine

But the melody seems almost serpentine. While it includes brief pauses which allow the listener to "frame" its movement through time, these pauses are not *predictable* in their moments of occurrence. We hear first two segments, and then time seems to be stretched. We go on and on with the unwinding melody as it slowly descends, finally coming to a close just where it began. How different from our typical folk song, in which each musical phrase or gesture is *predictable* in its time span! But if you listen again to the Vivaldi melody, you may hear that the lengthy descent is marked by repetitions of a single, brief musical figure, each repetition starting lower than the preceding one, and with the final one breaking the pattern. This process of repeating a figure starting on successively higher or lower pitches is called a *sequence,* and it accounts for one of the primary means of coherence in such continuously unwinding melodies.

3.2   Now, listening to the Liszt melody, you will notice again this sense of going on and on, again in descending steps marked by the

the melody seems to creep down, but within each small gesture it goes up

repetition of a three-note figure or *motive.* (See p. 105 for more on motives.) The melody seems to creep down, but within each small gesture it goes up. Notice, too, that while the "pitch-shape" remains the same within each gesture, the rhythm varies, helping to create a further sense of slippery elusiveness—variety within unity. As for *meter,* it is hard to find a regularly recurring accent. The *rhythmic structure* of the melody surely differs from the regular metric structure associated with our intuitive model of a sensible tune. The organization of time seems more dependent on the recurring sequential motive. Finally, notice how the melody, having descended in slow steps, then suddenly expands its range, or its scope in pitch space. The melody, still based on the same three-note motive, covers two octaves in the same time that it covered but half an octave previously, giving the illusion of getting faster as it covers more space in less time. This extension of range and the necessary use of different instruments to span it, together with the stretching and compressing of time, distinguishes the Liszt melody from both the Vivaldi and the folk tune. And, of course, the particular *choice of pitches* is also important, and we will have more to say about that in Chapter 5, on harmony.

The "Lullaby" from Berg's opera *Wozzeck,* although written 3.3 71 years after the *Faust Symphony,* has important similarities to it. As in the Liszt, the Berg melody together with the orchestral accompaniment help to convey the *quality* of the dramatic situation.

A. Berg,
from autograph
score of *Wozzeck*

As the song begins we see Marie, the heroine, standing before her window rocking her baby. Below her, soldiers are marching in the street. One of them (the drum major) is her lover, but not the father of her baby.

As in the Liszt piece, the melody moves through a very large pitch space, or range, which puts demands on the singer's voice but also helps to enrich its expressive quality. Also as in the Liszt, the melody begins rather free rhythmically, but unlike the Liszt, it later becomes quite clearly metric. These contrasts in rhythmic structure help to convey Marie's contrasting moods as expressed in the text. For example, the "Lullaby" begins with what seems an extended sigh—"Eia popeia" (Hush-a-bye)—which is followed by a motive that is almost martial in its rhythm. As in the Liszt, this motive is repeated *sequentially* and later more elaborately varied. As the song goes on, these two contrasting moods alternate, one associated with a slower, freer, almost speaking melody line, the other faster and more rhythmically marked. Listen to the song, following the text below, where the two contrasting sections are marked *A* and *B*, respectively.

A
Eia popeia   Hush-a-bye

B
Mädel, was fangst Du jetzt an?   Lass, what will you do now?
Hast ein klein Kind und kein Mann! You have a child and no husband!
Ei, was frag' ich darnach,   O, what do I care,
Sing' ich die ganze Nacht: I'll sing the whole night through:

A'
Eia popeia, mein süsser Bu',   Hush-a-bye, my sweet son,
Gibt mir kein Mensch nix dazu!   Give me no other man but you!

B'
Hansel, spann Deine sechs Schimmel an,   Hansel, harness your six white horses,
Gib sie zu fressen auf's neu   Give them something new to eat
Kein Haser fresse sie,   Not oats will they eat,
Kein Wasser saufe sie,   Not water will they drink,

A"
Lauter kühle Wein muss es sein!   Lots of cool wine it must be!
Lauter kühle Wein muss es sein![1]   Lots of cool wine it must be!

---

[1] Alban Berg, *Wozzeck.* Copyright © 1923 by Universal Edition, Wien. Copyright renewed 1951. All rights for the USA controlled by European-American Music Distributors Corp. Reprinted by permission.

So, some of the aspects which determine the particular character and coherence of a melody, and which also account for differences among melodies, are its *range* and how it moves through this range, its *rhythmic structure*, its *means* of *articulation* (how it groups into segments or gestures), the relations among these groups, the kinds of *repetition*, its choice of *pitches* and their relations, and its *purpose* or expressive intent. Let us turn now to a more traditional melody, *Lassie,* and examine these same aspects and relations to see the characteristics of melodies with which we are most familiar.

A Traditional Tune: Lassie

Consider the following questions:

1. What are the basic groupings within the melody; how many groups or phrases do you hear?
2. How would you describe the relationship among them?
3. Are any of the phrases repeated in whole or in part?
4. How are the goals of the phrases related? Which phrases end with a sense of completeness; which ones leave you with a sense of more to come? Why?

The first big point of arrival (*caesura*) occurs on the word *that:*

> Did you ever see a lassie
> > go this way and that way,
> Did you ever see a lassie
> > go this way and *that*?

The second big point of arrival comes at the very end of the song. If you count measures or beats you will find that these two points of arrival mark off segments which are equal in length. Looking more closely, we see that each of these two large segments is further divided into two equal parts:

a *[handwritten]*

a′ *[handwritten]*

contrasting
function *[handwritten]*

consequent *[handwritten]*

b *[handwritten]*

a′ *[handwritten]*

I
> 1. Did you ever see a lassie, 1st motive *[handwritten]*
>   a lassie, a lassie, second motive *[handwritten]*
> 2. Did you ever see a lassie, 1st motive *[handwritten]*
>   go this way and *that*? second motive *[handwritten]*

II
> 3. Go this way and that way
>   and this way and that way, ⎫ second motive of *[handwritten]*
>   ⎭ a stated twice *[handwritten]*
> 4. Did you ever see a lassie,
>   go this way and *that*?

Each of these four smaller segments constitutes what we call a *phrase*. Each pair of complementary phrases respectively (1-2 and 3-4) makes up what we call a musical *period,* or sentence. What is the melodic relationship among the phrases? The first two phrases are identical except for their endings. The first phrase does not end with a sense of resolution; the second phrase does. Why? It may seem surprising to realize that both phrases, in fact, end with the same *pitch*. Why, then, do their endings sound so different? Here rhythm plays a crucial role. The difference results from the metric positions of the pitches. The first phrase ends on an unaccented beat, or *weak* beat. The two-syllable word "las-sie" carries the tune on past the accented beat to the second beat—a weak beat in the triple-meter piece. The second phrase, in contrast, ends on a *strong* beat; the single-syllable word "that" occurs on an accented beat, giving the same pitch a sense of finality. Notice too that the second phrase ends with a rest—a silence—on the second beat. This silence, which still takes time, helps to separate this phrase more clearly from the one that follows.

A phrase ending is called a *cadence* (from Italian, *cadere,* to fall). The first phrase ends inconclusively on a weak beat (a beat other than *one*); the second phrase ends more conclusively on a strong beat, and the two phrases thus complement one another.[2] This is called an antecedent-consequent phrase relationship.

Notice, though, that the conclusive *ending* of a phrase can coincide with the *beginning* of a measure. In fact, it is precisely

---

[2] These two kinds of cadences are frequently referred to as "feminine" and "masculine," respectively, but we would like to see more accurate terms.

when a phrase goes over the bar line to end on the accented first beat that it sounds rhythmically most conclusive. This is a good example of how the graphics of music notation need to be read with care: The boundaries of metric units should not be confused with the boundaries of phrases! In fact, all the phrases in this piece *begin* with an upbeat, which also carries them over the bar line. With this description in mind (and ear), it will now make sense to call the first phrase *a* and the second phrase *a'*, showing that the second is a variant of the first.

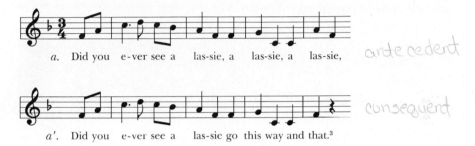

a. Did you e-ver see a las-sie, a las-sie, a las-sie,

a'. Did you e-ver see a las-sie go this way and that.³

But rhythm isn't everything. If we change only the *pitch* of the last note, keeping the rhythm exactly the same, the effect is strikingly different, and the phrase ends inconclusively:

or

(Even without playing or singing the above examples, you can get the effect by, for example, singing the same pitch on "that" as you sing on "this" in the first case, or singing the same pitch on "that" as you sing on "and" in the second.)

---

³ The learned ability to read music is certainly not a prerequisite for developing one's perception and appreciation of music. We include printed music only as one more aid or guide—in the case of a melody like *Lassie*, which everyone knows, you can simply follow the direction of the movement of the pitches, that is, the contour of the melody.

Notice that it is not a matter of the substituted pitch being higher or lower than the original ending pitch. Rather it is that the phrase must stop specifically on a particular pitch if the phrase is to sound conclusively ended. This pitch is called the *tonic.* The definition of tonic is a functional one and highly dependent on the context. That is, *tonic* can be defined as that pitch which, in a given context of pitches, sounds most stable. Thus, as a result of the particular selection of pitches included in the tune so far, together with the particular order in which they occur, this one pitch gains special significance as an "ender." Think of it for now as that pitch toward which all the other pitches in the piece gravitate. But remember that this central pitch (F in this situation) can be played in any octave, and it still maintains its *functional* significance as being most stable. Or, putting it another way, any particular F is a member of the *pitch-class* F, whose members are all the other pitches named F. If we ended this second phrase in *Lassie* on an F an octave higher or lower, it would certainly make a difference to the tune—it would not sound right. And yet on the more general level of functional stability, any F, in this context of pitches, would maintain its identity as tonic. (We will return to this subject later in the chapter.)

Many aspects of a tone contribute to its particular effect: Its position in the *metric grid,* its *pitch class,* and the function which that pitch class has gained contextually, as well as the particular *instance* of that pitch class—a higher or lower F, for instance. While all of these aspects of an event are merged or fused together in our actual experience of an event, the capacity to perceptually differentiate them can often heighten our appreciation of the subtle ways in which composers play with their various combinations.

Looking at even smaller dimensions of this simple tune, consider the following: We can further segment the first phrase into

(1) "Did you ever see a lassie":

and (2) "A lassie, a lassie":

Each of these subphrases uses different melodic-rhythmic material, or different *motives.* A motive is a small melodic-rhythmic pattern—a few notes which have some distinctive shape that is somehow bounded or self-contained to form a recognizable figure. All melodies are made up of motives. After the single tone, a motive is the smallest link in the melodic chain, and perhaps the smallest *structural* unit which the listener focuses on as a significant element in the tune.

Even in such a simple tune as *Lassie,* the relationship among motives exemplifies the basic esthetic principle of *unity and variety,* to which we have already referred. For example, through the repetition of motives, unity is achieved. Variety comes about through the use of *contrasting* motives, as well as through the modification, manipulation, or new juxtapositions of previously stated motives. The sequential repetitions heard in the Vivaldi concerto, the Liszt excerpt, and even the Berg "Lullaby" are examples of this kind of variety within unity.

In *Lassie* we have at first an example of contrasting motives. The initial motive ("Did you ever see a lassie") has a pitch shape or contour that could be described as ⌒＼ . And notice that it makes use of different note values (♪, ♩., ♩). The second motive ("Go this way and that way") contrasts with this initial one in its pitch shape (⌒⌒) as well as in its rhythmic pattern—it makes use of only quarter notes. Moving up one level in the structural hierarchy from the smaller motive to the larger phrase, we see that the second phrase (*a'*)—the *consequent* phrase—is exactly the same as the first phrase—the *antecedent* phrase—except for the last two notes—again an instance of variety within unity.

Going further into the tune, you may be surprised to realize that the third phrase in the melody—"Go this way and that way, and this way and that way"—is simply the second motive of *a* stated twice. That is, the pitches and durations for "go this way and that way" are identical to those for "a lassie, a lassie." Why do

b.   Go this way and that way, and this way and that way,

they sound so different? Here is an example of the influence of context or situation. Consider the differences in the situations in which we encounter this motive. At first we hear the motive ("A lassie, a lassie") functioning as the *ending* of a phrase. This later statement ("Go this way and that way") functions as the *beginning* of a phrase and also the beginning of a new part of the piece—that is, it comes after a big point of arrival and after a "gap" in the regular flow of events (the rest). Further, this motive is followed by itself—the same motive serves to begin and end this third phrase. The principle of unity and variety is again realized. We hear the same motive (unity) but with new effect as a result of its being embedded in a new context and with a different function (variety). One even might question what we mean by "the same". You can compare this effect of the situational embedding of a motive with the examples of *textural* embedding discussed in Chapter 1.

This third phrase, then, is different from the first two but related to them in important ways. We call it *b* to point to its contrasting function within the structure of the tune as a whole. Finally, there is a *return* to phrase *a′*, the consequent:

a′. Did you e-ver see a las-sie go this way and that?

We thus have *a, a′, b, a′*, and each of these letters stands for a phrase which is exactly four measures long. (See the brief discussion of phrase rhythm in the lecture-demonstration of Chapter 2 in connection with *Stars and Stripes Forever* and the Lanner waltz.)

This equality in phrase length we call *balanced* phrase structure by analogy, perhaps unfortunately, with weight—two phrases equal in duration are compared with two objects equal in weight. The whole tune is, in fact, balanced: The first period ($a + a'$) is equal in length to the second period ($b + a'$), and the melody can be diagrammed as follows:

Motive:	1	2	1	3	2	2	1	3
Phrase:	antecedent		consequent		contrast		return	
Period:	a	+	a'		b	+	a'	

A Mozart Melody

Let us now consider a carefully composed melody which is in many ways similar to Lassie in its general structure and yet seems much more complex and sophisticated—Example 3.5, from the Mozart *Sonata for Piano in A*. The excerpt is the theme for a series of variations. In writing a series of variations, the composer usually keeps important aspects of the *whole theme* intact during the course of each variation. For example, the whole melody may be repeated, only being varied by the sounds or textures in which it is embedded (as in the excerpt from the Beethoven symphony in Example 1.9). Thus each variation becomes a separate little whole and the entire movement a set of small pieces, each maintaining the proportions and general structure of the original theme. But as you heard in *Lassie* and in some of the other melodies, variation can also be used on a level of greater detail to transform or develop just a brief motive—through sequential repetition, new juxtapositions, and situational embeddings. Indeed, it is just the kind and degree of motivic development that perhaps more than anything else distinguishes the Mozart melody from the more ordinary, even banal, folk tune.

The overall structure of the melody, like *Lassie,* can be diagrammed as follows:

antecedent		consequent	contrast		return	extension
a	+	a'	b	+	a'	(a + b)

As in *Lassie, a* and *a'* are balanced phrases and they complement one another. Together they constitute a musical sentence (or period) which presents the basic motivic material. The term *antecedent-consequent phrase relationship* refers to this sense of complementarity—two phrases which begin much the same but in which the first ends less conclusively than the second. The relationship is somewhat analogous to a rhymed couplet in poetry:

> In poets as true genius is but rare,
> True taste as seldom is the critic's share.
>
> *A. Pope*

That is, there is a comma, or incomplete cadence, at the end of the first line (phrase), and a period, or full cadence, at the end of the second line (phrase). Together they make up a sentence, or what is called in music a period. The first two phrases of *Lassie* were described in much the same way.

The *b* section is a contrasting segment in which the initial motivic material is elaborated or developed in a more far-reaching way. It leads back to a restatement of the consequent phrase, *a'*, followed by an extension.

Let us consider more closely now the means Mozart uses to develop his initial motivic material—to explore and reveal the implications of the opening motive. Listen to just the first phrase, *a*. The germinal motive, from which the whole melody quite literally grows, is presented in the first five notes of this phrase: ♩. ♫ ♩ ♪. Clap the rhythm of this motive to become more immediately familiar with it.

Example 3.5. Mozart, *Sonata for Piano in A*

Notice that Mozart continues the phrase by simply repeating this motive sequentially, much as in the beginning of the Berg "Lullaby." Indeed, the rhythmic pattern of the two motives is quite similar. But next Mozart fragments this motive; he picks up just the last two repeated notes: ♩ ♪. Interestingly, the repetitions of this fragment, one after the other moving up the scale, cause the tiny motive to regroup, even though the pitch relations and the durations remain essentially the same. You hear the grouping indicated by the lower brackets:

Moreover, the third statement of this fragment is embellished so that the last two statements seem to merge. These repetitions of the fragmented motive bring the phrase to an inconclusive close; the phrase ends on a weak beat and on a pitch which is not the tonic.

The consequent phrase, *a'*, is itself a variation of the antecedent phrase. It begins just as *a* did, but then ascends more quickly and descends to end conclusively on a *strong beat,* with a note of *long duration* and on the *tonic*. Once again the sense of arrival at a conclusive goal is the result of a number of converging factors.

As we go on to the *b* section of the melody, variation of the motivic material becomes faster and more elaborate. We call this section *b* not because it introduces different material, but because the original material is more extensively transformed, creating more contrast and also a sense of instability or tension. For example, while the *a* section stays entirely within the pitch area defined by the first five pitches of the A Major scale,[4] the *b* section immediately moves off into the upper part of that scale, where we again hear the opening motive.

Ascending to its highest point, once more the rhythm of the germinal motive is repeated, but now with a different pitch shape (measure 10). Now the rhythmic movement becomes more continuous (♪♪♪ ♪♪♪ ♪♪♪), but a single pitch (e), the middle pitch of the range, stands out in the midst of this continuous motion (measure 11):

The germinal motive, almost lost in this wealth of variation, still remains present, however, as the primary unifying factor.

The return (*a'*) seems to be a literal repetition of the conse-

---

[4] For a discussion of scales, see pp. 116–118.

quent phrase up to the moment of expected ending where Mozart leads us on once more, spilling over the moment of anticipated resolution. There follows the brief extension, where the melody again rises to its highest point (covering nearly the whole range of the melody thus far) and, finally, dropping a whole octave, comes to rest on the tonic.

Looking back on this process of melodic invention, it seems now that the melody can hardly be described as "the same" in overall structure as *Lassie.* Once again we need to emphasize that any general description (such as $a + a'$, $b + a'$) must take into account the particularities with which that general structure is realized. And yet it is just such common procedures which underlie our intuitive sense of the prototypical melody. Some of the characteristics which we found common to both *Lassie* and the Mozart melody account for our intuitive model of what a tune is: clearly metric, balanced and unambiguous phrase structure, the sense of a tonic or central pitch to which we can relate the others, and often an overall structure described as statement-digression-return. But it is important to remember that the familiar may sometimes make it too easy to miss what is unique and special in a melody, just as the unfamiliar may lead us to dismiss a melody simply because its means of organization are different from those which we have come to take for granted—our tacit model of a sensible melody.

Motivic Development

In talking about all these melodies, we have found it useful (even necessary) to point to specific *motives*—particular melodic shapes. By pointing to motives, we were able to describe to you, the listener, the *means* by which each melody evolved and gained its unique coherence. You could hear the motive as a vehicle which carried the melody, in a particular way, through time and through its pitch-space.

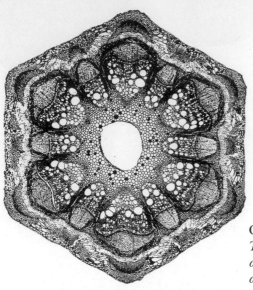

Cross section of twig
Through subtle manipulations of
a basic shape composers build unity
and also new structural functions

The motive often functions as a kind of *germinal idea* from which a whole melody can evolve. We have seen how composers, through subtle manipulations of its various features, can use a basic shape to build unity and at the same time create new melodic ideas and new structural functions. For example, the composer may subtly transform pitch-time relations, fragment the melody, or re-group its initial motivic "chunks" to create a new musical effect. Arnold Schoenberg says of this fundamental compositional process:

> Even the writing of simple phrases involves the invention and use of motives, though perhaps unconsciously. . . . The motive generally appears in a characteristic and impressive manner at the beginning of a piece. . . . Inasmuch as almost every figure within a piece reveals some relationship to it, the basic motive is often considered the "germ" of the idea. . . . However, everything depends upon its use . . . everything depends on its treatment and development.[5]

We have seen examples of this process, but to make Schoenberg's point clear, consider for a moment a very simple phrase—the first one in *Mary Had a Little Lamb*. Notice that the last two

---

[5] Arnold Schoenberg, *Fundamentals of Musical Composition*, St. Martin's Press, p. 9.

"chunks" of the phrase (T_1 and T_2) are fragments of the longer first chunk. In this sense they are both variations of the longer first chunk—a development of it.

MARY HAD A LITTLE LAMB

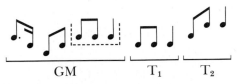

But notice that the degree of variation, or the degree of transformation, increases even within this short phrase: T_1 is a transformation of GM (the germinal motive) not only because T_1 is a fragment but also because it makes use of a *new set of pitches.* However, T_1 and the "tail" of GM are the same in their *set of durations* and in their *pitch-shape*—in each a single pitch is repeated. But with T_2 only the set of durations remains the same; both the set of pitches and the pitch-shape are varied. Indeed, the sense of tiny climax at the end of the phrase results in part from this increase in the degree of transformation. Also, T_2 moves out of the previous, very limited *range* of the tune, reaching the high point of this miniscule world. And this too can be thought of as a structural transformation. We will return to this issue of transformation, or development, in Chapters 4 and 6.

Demonstration 3-2

INTERVALS, SCALES, TONIC; RANGE AND REGISTER   (Side 4)

Throughout our discussion of melody, especially in trying to account for the contrasts among cadences—conclusive and inconclusive, complete and incomplete—as well as when pointing to the listener's expectation of a certain melodic outcome, we have spoken of the "tonic" or "central pitch," and of scales or parts of scales, and so forth. In this section we will focus specifically on these issues, setting forth in a more systematic way some of the fundamental organizing principles of pitch relations.

Probably the most obvious aspect of pitch—the one we notice and make use of even in everyday life—is simply that of *high* and *low.* We even describe the sounds of the city or of nature as "high" or "low." Actually, these everyday sounds are often made up of a pitch *continuum,* like a siren or a motor revving up. By contrast, most of the music you know is made up of discrete, or separate, pitches—a particular selection from the possible pitch continuum. The result of this process of selection is a series, or ladder (Italian *scala*), of discrete pitches. Moving upward from any one pitch, and playing all the tones in order, we find that after 12 different pitches (the *chromatic scale*) have been played, the pitches are repeated in a higher register. We call this repetition of the pitches in different registers the phenomenon of the *octave.* In the discussion of unison playing in Chapter 1, we pointed out that instruments or voices can play or sing in unison but in different octaves, as in Example 1.2, in which a group of instruments play the same melody together, the violins playing an octave higher than the violas, which play an octave higher than the cello and basses.

Putting it another way, this particular selection of 12 pitches from the pitch continuum divides the octave into 12 equidistant tones. These tones constitute all the different pitches generally found in Western music; they are separated from one another by the interval of a *half step,* or *semitone.* An *interval* is the distance between any two tones; the half step is the smallest interval. (See the Ancillary Reading, page 144, for further discussion of intervals.) The next largest interval is the whole step. The octave can also be divided into six equidistant pitches separated by whole steps. (This is the *whole-tone scale*—note the striking difference in effect between this scale and the chromatic scale.)

In addition to equidistant pitches, the octave can also be divided into seven different pitches separated by various whole and half steps. The particular ordering of whole and half steps creates

Waterdrops
*Discrete
pitches*

*A pitch
continuum*

a number of different *modes.* Two of these, the major and minor modes, are the principal modes used by composers in Western music from the seventeenth to the twentieth century. Indeed, some composers still think in terms of them.[6]

It should be emphasized that a scale or mode is not in itself a melody, but rather an abstraction derived from the pitch material of actual melodies. Thus, instead of presenting the major scale as an entity, we will demonstrate how it can be derived from the melody *America:*[7]

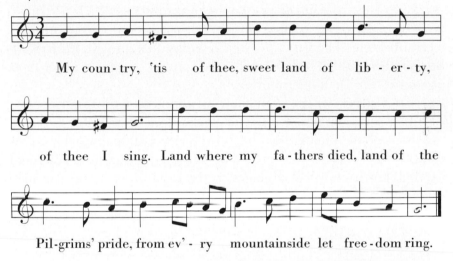

My coun-try, 'tis   of thee, sweet land   of   lib - er - ty,

of thee   I   sing. Land where my   fa - thers died, land of   the

Pil-grims' pride, from ev' - ry   mountainside let   free - dom ring.

Now if we reorder the pitches which occur in this melody, moving from the lowest to the highest, the result is as shown here:

This, then, is the complete pitch material of the melody. Now sing the tune and determine which pitch sounds the most stable,

---

[6] Before the seventeenth century other modes were described by theorists and given names derived from ancient Greek music—for example, Dorian, Phrygian, and Lydian (see p. 143).

[7] The rhythm of this melody was illustrated in the Additional Materials at the end of Chapter 2; for information on pitch notation, see page 140 of the Ancillary Reading.

the most at rest. Then sing or play the pitches as arranged from lowest to highest again, determining the most stable.

In both cases you probably found that the note G, the tone with which the melody both begins and ends, sounds most final.[8] Indeed, the sense of completeness, of finality, at the end of *America* is generated to a large extent by the function which the note G has acquired through its contact with the specific collection of pitches and their particular arrangement in this melody. Remember that the stability or instability—that is, the function—of a particular pitch derives from its relation to the other pitches which surround it. Within a different collection of pitches this same G might sound very unstable. The function, or "meaning," of a pitch, then, is always *relative* in that it depends on the context of pitches in which it is found (see Demonstration 5-2).

In a given context of pitches, the one that sounds most stable assumes a special position as the central tone in relation to which we hear all the others; the others seem to gravitate toward it.[9] This central tone is called the *tonic*. The generating of a tonic, or tonal center, has been a crucial factor in the organization and comprehensibility of music since about 1650, if not longer.

Let us now reorder the pitch material of *America,* beginning with the tonic G:

(Notice that we have used the rule of "octave equivalence" to fill out the scale—that is, the low F-sharp has been moved up an octave and the low G has been repeated an octave higher.) We have now derived a particular scale—the G Major scale. Using it as a model, we can discover exactly what combination of whole and half

---

[8] Of course, not all melodies begin or even end with this stable tone; for example, try *Happy Birthday.*

[9] Music theorists have discussed at length the question of whether this phenomenon is inherent in the natural properties of sound or whether it is the result of musical conditioning.

(Courtesy of Steinway & Sons)

steps generates the major mode and can then build a major scale
starting on any pitch. The simplest way to see the whole step-half
step arrangement is by looking at the piano keyboard (although the
best way would be to *hear* the difference between whole and half
steps). Looking at the diagram of the piano keyboard, you can observe the following: Between any two adjacent keys (even white
keys) the distance is a half step. Thus, G to A is a whole step, because there is a pitch (black key) between; but B to C is a half step,
because there is no pitch (no black key) between. So the G Major
scale has the following arrangement of whole and half steps:

DEGREE:	1	2	3	4	5	6	7	8
PITCH:	G	A	B	C	D	E	F♯	G
INTERVAL:		1	1	½	1	1	1	½

An important characteristic of this model is its division into two
symmetrical parts—Degrees 1–4 and Degrees 5–8—the two parts
being separated by a whole step. (The term, *degree,* refers to the
numbers assigned to elements of the scale. Starting on the tonic
as 1, elements are numbered from low to high, consecutively. But
notice that while numbers proceed consecutively suggesting an
equal relationship between elements, the consecutive pitches are
not related by equal intervals.)

Using this model we then can build a major scale starting on, for example F:

Looking back at *Lassie,* you can perform the same exercise. That is, order the pitches in the tune, as written, from low to high:

Rearranging these pitches, starting from the one that sounds most stable (F) and using the rule of octave equivalence, we have all the pitches of the F Major scale except for E. It is important to

note that if we had chosen to write out *Lassie* starting one whole step higher (G), keeping all the pitch *relations* (that is, all the intervals) the same, we would have all the pitches of the G Major scale except for F-sharp, and G would become the tonic pitch. Thus, any traditional melody can be played or sung starting on any pitch, but depending on which pitch you choose, a different set of pitches and a different tonic will be generated. This process of moving a tune from one set of pitches to another or from one key (tonal center) to another is called *transposition.* For example, here we transposed *Lassie* from the initial key of F to the key of G:[10]

---
[10] For more on transposition, see p. 198.

Try building scales starting on other pitches, using the model and the piano keyboard.

A model for the minor scale (below) is useful only for the first five degrees, since the upper part may take several different forms (see the Ancillary Reading, p. 111.)

Notice that the distinguishing difference in the minor mode is the half step between the second and third degrees (instead of the whole step at the same point in the major mode). In the case of G minor, then, we have B-flat at this point rather than B-natural. (Try playing *America* on p. 115 substituting B-flat for B-natural wherever it occurs.)

If you now once again play or sing *America* as it is written, you will hear that the melody is organized in two parts, the first ending with "of thee I sing." This first part is organized around the tonic —it begins there; moves below, above, and through it; and finally returns to it. The second part of the melody moves to the fifth degree of the scale and minimizes the first degree until it returns to it at the end. This organization of the melody, as in the Mozart theme, reflects somewhat the organization of the scale into two halves and points up the significance of the fifth degree (the starting point of the second half) as the second "pillar" of the tonal structure. The fifth degree is called (misleadingly) the *dominant*. We shall explore its significance further in Chapter 5.

To summarize, then, we have moved from the most general aspect of pitch (high and low) to a selection from this continuum (the 12 pitches forming the pitch material of most Western music) to a still more specific selection (the seven different pitches of the major and minor modes, which can be built from specific sets of whole and half steps). The most significant aspect of this selection is its creation of a hierarchy of stability-instability among the resulting pitches.

Having considered to some extent the pitch relationships in *America,* let us consider now how the melody moves through time. From what rhythmic patterns is the melody made, and how do these patterns contribute to its unity and variety? Tap the rhythm of the melody. As mentioned in Chapter 2, there is a rhythmic pattern (*motive*) repeated, with slight variations, a number of times: ♩ ♩ ♩ | ♩. ♪♩ |. This underlying figure helps to unify the melody. In the third statement of the motive ("of thee I sing"), the last two notes are dropped and the fourth note is extended: ♩ ♩ ♩ | ♩. |. The rhythmic activity of the phrase, not its length, is lessened as it comes to rest on the longer note. This dotted half note is also the tonic and marks off a section of the song both rhythmically and tonally. The second and concluding section contains four statements of the rhythmic pattern. The first two statements present the pattern in its original form. These are followed by two statements which give variety to the song by manipulating the basic pattern and which, at the same time, reach a climax both in pitch and in rhythmic activity. The first: ♩ ♫ ♫ | ♩. ♪♩ | is followed by: ♫ ♩ ♩ | ♩. |.

Range

In discussing the Liszt and Berg melodies (Examples 3.2 and 3.3) we noted that both had a large *range.* That is, the pitch distance from the lowest to the highest point of the melodies was relatively large. This was one of the aspects of the two melodies that seemed to distinguish them from more traditional tunes. In that discussion we also observed that the large range of the Berg "Lullaby" helped to enrich its expressive quality.

Generally, vocal melodies have a smaller range than instrumental melodies; the human voice has a smaller range than most instruments, and furthermore, folk songs or popular songs are written to be sung by numbers of people with untrained voices. The range of a melody and the way the melody moves within this range are important factors in creating its particular effect.

America, for example, is very easy to sing, and this is because it moves in small steps and avoids leaps or large intervals. (We say it is a *conjunct* melody.) The most noticeable leap occurs at a crucial point, that is, between the two halves of the melody (from "sing" to "land").

Example	Composer, title	Date
3.7	Tamil folk song (Indian)	
3.8	R. Strauss, *Ein Heldenleben* (*A Hero's Life*)	1898
3.9	Stravinsky, *Octet for Wind Instruments,* second movement	1923–1924

Examples 3.7 to 3.9 illustrate the importance of the range of a melody and the way it moves through that range in creating its particular effect.

Horn section
of an orchestra

3.7

For example, the Indian melody (Example 3.7), a Tamil folk song, has a very small range; that is, it moves within a very limited pitch-space[11] from its highest to its lowest points. The consecutive tones are very close to one another in this conjunct melody, and there are no leaps. Not being part of the Western tradition, it uses "odd-sounding" tones, that is, pitches other than the 12 of the chromatic scale. (If you try to play this example on the piano you will observe that the tones don't exactly match—you would have to play "between the cracks," that is, between the keys.) Try to sing it in the Indian fashion!

3.8

3.9

In striking contrast to the Tamil folk song, the aggressive Strauss melody, difficult if not impossible to sing, moves predominantly by leaps (*disjunct*) through a very wide range. Yet another instrumental melody, from the Stravinsky *Octet,* maintains a very small range, as in the Tamil folk song. But at the end the top boundary seems to give way as the range expands upward. Interestingly, the Stravinsky melody up to this point of expansion has exactly the same range as the Tamil song, but it somehow sounds less restricted. Perhaps the range sounds greater in part because the melody is played on the clarinet and "doubled" two octaves higher by the flute—another way of talking about playing in unison. Rhythmic factors (tempo, for instance) and the particular order in which the pitches occur also contribute to this difference in effect. If you listen very closely to the two examples, you will notice that each pitch in the Tamil song is as close as possible to the one preceding and following it, while in the Stravinsky piece there are tiny skips which, within this very small pitch world, create a significant difference in effect.

Example	Composer, title	Date
3.10	Mozart, *The Magic Flute,* aria	1791
3.11	Schoenberg, *Herzegewächse (Foliage of the Heart)*	1911

---

[11] Of course, talking about pitch-space is again a metaphor, since pitch doesn't occupy space at all. For a description of the physical properties of pitch (frequency) see the section on acoustics in the Ancillary Reading of Chapter 1.

The next two excerpts, like the Berg, are vocal melodies which span a large range. While they were composed in different centuries and represent quite different ways of relating pitch and time, they still bear a striking similarity. If you try to imagine singing either one of them yourself, for instance, you will immediately realize the incredible demands each composer makes on the singer's pitch and breath control. Not only is the range relatively large in the Queen of the Night's aria by Mozart, but much of it lies near the very top of the singer's upper register. In addition, the soprano must control the large leaps with which she moves through this range. Then, too, she must often sing *staccato* (leaving a little space between each attack) as she performs this jagged melody; this is particularly noticeable on the repeated pitches which precede each leap in the latter portion of the aria.

Schoenberg has a different idea about arranging pitches—a different notion of "comprehensibility"—but he also asks his performer to control an enormously large range. (She spans three octaves!) Moving in large leaps at the beginning, she quickly (in a slow tempo) moves from low to high. Settling in this high register momentarily, she then expands the range still further upward, gradually moving once more down again as the tension of "highness" gives way. In this piece the soprano sings *legato* (joining pitches to one another in a single breath), in contrast to the *staccato* of the Mozart aria.

Once again, the dramatic intent of the composer is important here. Mozart is trying to express in music the "blind passion of the direful Queen," and he does so by asking her to sing at the extremes of her range and to leap about dramatically within it. You might compare this Mozart melody with the theme from his *Sonata for Piano in A* (Example 3.5). Interestingly, the instrumental melody is much more constrained in its range and in its movements through that range than is the vocal melody you have just heard. The comparison should make quite clear the importance of the composer's intentions in writing a melody—just where and how he or she wants to use it. Can you imagine a set of variations based on the Queen of the Night's aria?

Demonstration 3-3

SECTIONAL AND CONTINUOUS MELODIES (Sides 4–5)

Referring back to the Vivaldi and Liszt excerpts, we noted that each differed from our prototypical tune in that it seemed "serpentine"—to go on and on as if continuously unwinding. While there were brief pauses in the melodies which allowed the listener to "frame" its movement through time, these pauses were not predictable in their moments of occurrence. We can now contrast these characteristics with the clear and balanced phrase structure of *Lassie,* with its predictable moments of arrival—an aspect of melody which seemed central to our model of a sensible tune. Melodies of the first sort we describe as being more *continuous;* melodies of the second sort we call *sectional.*

Having analyzed carefully two sectional melodies (*Lassie* and the Mozart sonata theme), listen now to another example of a continuous melody (heard earlier as Example 1.13).

Example	Composer, title	Date
3.12	Bach, *Partita 2 for Unaccompanied Violin,* gigue	c. 1720

Notice that the questions we posed on p. 101 as an introduction to our study of *Lassie* are almost irrelevant to this continuous piece. Where does the melody breathe? Where are the caesuras that mark off phrases? Where are the boundaries of groups, and how can you relate these goals to one another? After the opening complementary motives, the melody seems to unwind in a seemingly never-ending series of runs. It simply does not lend itself to the kind of schematic description (*a a' b a*) which seemed quite appropriate for *Lassie* or the Mozart piano sonata theme. What, then, constitutes its means of coherence—particularly its ways of organizing time? As in the Vivaldi and Liszt pieces, the melody is highly dependent on the use of sequences. Listening closely, you will hear chains made up of a repeated motive, the whole chain forming a sequential module—a larger structural element in the flow of the

Nautilus shell
Sequentially repeated motive

melody. The length of the larger module together with the length of the motivic units within that module create the structural rhythm of the piece. That is, time is marked off by the length of each unit of a sequential chain and, on a larger scale, by the total time of each linked module. One never knows just when a sequential chain will break, moving into a more freely structured passage, or when the more free moments will subside into the more regular pulse created by sequential repetition. It is this ebb and flow of clearly marked repetition—its interruptions and the resumption of a different sequentially repeated motive—that helps to create the underlying coherence of the melody.

In listening to the melodies that follow, we will need to ask the following: Are all melodies either sectional or continuous—one or the other? Perhaps it is best to think in terms of a continuum, with "continuous" at one end and "sectional" at the other. Most melodies will actually fall somewhere along that line—usually closer to one end or the other. *Lassie* and the Mozart piano sonata theme are of course way at the sectional end, and the Bach gigue at the continuous end. It will be helpful to think of this continuum in approaching the melodies which follow.

Example	Composer, title	Date
3.13	Gershwin, *I Got Rhythm* (performed by Ruby Braff-George Barnes Quartet)	1971
3.14	Gillespie and Parker, *Shaw 'Nuff* (performed by J. Gillespie and C. Parker)	1945

3.13

The song *I Got Rhythm* (Example 3.6), composed by George Gershwin for the Broadway musical *Girl Crazy,* was a great success and is still with us in various manifestations. The title is immediately reflected in the syncopated motive which recurs throughout the song: | ♪ ♩ ♩ | ♩ ♩ ♪ |. Characteristically in popular music, the rhythm is interpreted somewhat freely by the singer; that is, the rhythmic figure is not performed exactly the same way each time. The rhythm is stated three times, then extended the third time to end the phase. The repertory of pitches derives from what is known as a *pentatonic* scale (that is, of only five tones, related to each other as are the black keys on the piano); the melody moves up and down this scale, coming to rest on the tonic in the eighth bar.

As to overall structure, what do we find but *a a b a'*, the same as *Lassie* and the Mozart piano sonata melody. It further resembles the Mozart in that there is a little "tag" at the end of the song, adding two more bars to the standard 32-bar popular song structure. In what ways is the *b* section different from the *a*? The *b* section, known as the "bridge" (or, less frequently, "channel"), while retaining the rhythmic figure | ♪ ♩ ♩ | ♩ ♩ ♪ |, moves away from "home" by beginning higher in the scale, as well as through the use of different chords (see Chapter 5) underneath the melody.

Example 3.13 is an instrumental version of *I Got Rhythm.* In the almost 50 years since its composition, the Gershwin tune has served as the basis for countless jazz renditions, in which either the original melody is retained or the harmonic substructure alone provides the framework for new melodies above. In this instrumental version, the original tune and its *a a b a'* structure are readily apparent, even without the words. In this excerpt there are two "choruses," that is, two statements of the entire 34-bar melody. The first time through it is presented slowly by the cornet, with slight embellishment of the melody. The *b* section, or bridge, is played by the guitar. Cornet and guitar are accompanied by bass and rhythm guitar. At the end of the first statement, there is a "break" (unaccompanied solo) by the guitar which leads into a faster and freer version of the melody.

Gerry Mulligan
playing the baritone sax

3.14   The melody in Example 3.14 is presented in unison by trumpet and saxophone. It moves about very rapidly and is very difficult to sing—even to play. The unison statement is followed by alto sax and trumpet solos. Concentrating at first on the unison, are you aware of the phrases, even though it seems relatively continuous? Closer listening will reveal the same *a a b a'* structure, with each of the segments being eight measures long; but there is no strong point of arrival, for the tonic is not reached until the very end of the unison. While not readily apparent, this "bebop" melody is actually based on what jazz musicians call "Rhythm changes,"—the chord progression (harmonic substructure) of Gershwin's *I Got Rhythm*. The opening written-out unison and the two following improvised choruses by Parker and Gillespie all have the same substructure, without the tag, however. Listen closely and try to follow it; you can even sing the *I Got Rhythm* melody along with the unison and the two solos.

Example	Composer, title	Date
3.15	*Cowboy's Lament* (American folk song, sung by Burl Ives)	
3.16	*Bonnie Wee Lass* (Scottish folk song, sung by Burl Ives)	

Balanced phrase structure is readily apparent in these two folk songs. In *Cowboy's Lament* there are four lines of text in each stanza (or verse) and, correspondingly, four four-bar phrases, only the last of which ends on the tonic:

I ⎡ As Í walked oút in the stréets of Larédo,
⎣ As Í walked oút in Larédo one dáy,

II ⎡ I spíed a young cówboy all wrápped in white línen,
⎣ Wrápped in white línen as cóld as the cláy.

(Notice that lines 1 and 3 end on a weak beat, 2 and 4 end on a strong beat.)

Bonnie Wee Lass has an equally clear pattern until the ending of the fourth line, which you expect to be the final phrase. What happens at that point?

I ⎡ A bónnie wee lássie whose náme it was Néll,
⎣ Líved in a hoúse where her grándmother dwéll,

II ⎡ The hóuse it was smáll and the wíndows no léss,
⎢ Háving four pánes one néeded a gláss . . .
⎢ That níce little wíndow, that cúte little wíndow,
⎣ Swéet little wíndow where grándmother dwéll.

The fourth phrase slides right through the moment of expected rest, momentarily upsetting the regularity of the structural rhythm. Having heard two complementary phrases ("A bonnie wee lassie whose name it was Nell,/Lived in a house where her grandmother dwell,"), we are led to expect another pair of complementary phrases. Instead, the melody continues on through the expected stopping place into the next two lines of text. These last two phrases, then, are an *extension.* The song finally comes to a close at the end of the *sixth* phrase in just the way we had expected it to at the end of the fourth phrase. While all the phrases are, in fact, equal in length (four bars) and thus balanced, the regularity of phrase rhythm is upset—first by the run-on through the ex-

pected downbeat and then by stretching or extending the anticipated 2 + 2 phrase symmetry to make 2 + 4.

This may seem like a very complicated description of a perfectly obvious tune, but it is perhaps just in such small deviations
from the norm that music gains its expressiveness. Notice, however, that without the culturally acquired, and thus seemingly intuitive, sense of "norm," the whole effect would be lost.

Mozart also plays around with phrase rhythm in the duet
from *Don Giovanni* in which the aristocrat Don Giovanni (Don
Juan) plays around with the peasant girl Zerlina.

Example	Composer, title	Date
3.17	Mozart, *Don Giovanni*, duet	1787
3.18	Moussorgsky, *Khovantchina*, prelude	1873–1881

We hear first two short melodic motives sung by Don Giovanni. Together they constitute the *antecedent phrase* which ends—
inconclusively—on the *dominant.* Don Giovanni's next two melodic
motives constitute the *consequent phrase,* which ends—now conclusively—on the *tonic.* When Zerlina takes up the melody, we expect
a continuation of this balanced phrase structure, since she begins

Example 3.17. Mozart, *Don Giovanni*

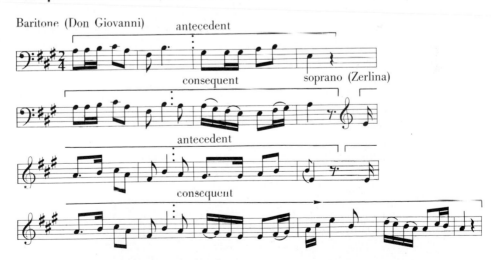

with an almost literal repetition of Don Giovanni's antecedent phrase. The consequent phrase proceeds much as before, but then the last short melodic motive is unexpectedly extended, which beautifully upsets the previously established symmetry. The

the last short melodic unit is unexpectedly extended

regularity of the structural rhythm, which the listener has come to take for granted and almost to depend on, is disrupted as Zerlina's melody continues on past the moment of expected rest—almost as if Zerlina wants to make the moment last a little longer.

Example 3.18 by Moussorgsky differs from the Mozart melody in that a normative phrase length is never established—the listener cannot predict when a goal will occur—when the melodic motion will come to rest. The effect of this melody, particularly in its sense of freedom, is quite different from the preceding examples, in which a regular structural rhythm is first established and then varied.

The mobility of phrase rhythm in the Moussorgsky prelude goes together with a lack of definition in the metric structure. In spite of the clear division of the beat into twos, there is no clear sense of a regularly recurring higher-level accent. In addition,

Oboes

there is an elusiveness about the melody line itself. Specifically, the melody is ambiguous in generating a tonic—almost as if there were a floating pitch center. As a result, the listener cannot tell whether the melody has reached a full stop—a point of rest—or will continue on.

Listen, for example, to the first two phrases in the opening statement. While the first phrase is, in number of beats, actually longer than the second, the asymmetry is not particularly evident or even important—especially when compared to the noticeable asymmetry of phrase rhythm at the end of the Mozart duet.

With the next pair of phrases another aspect of the melody emerges. While the first of these phrases is actually a variation of the initial phrase, you cannot quite be sure whether or not it is a literal repetition. In fact, this phrase is a compressed version: Three measures of the original are compressed into two here. While the pitches, except for the first, are identical, the durations of the notes are quickened to shorten the total time span of the phrase.

In the second phrase of this pair, however, the variation is clear. Moussorgsky initially varies the pitch shape somewhat but arrives in the same time span at the pitch which we expect to provide a breathing space. But the break never materializes. Instead, the melody goes on to elaborate and expand both the range and the motivic material—as if time were stretched.

While the last six examples differed in degree and kind of symmetry or balance, they are all fundamentally similar in that phrases and motives are clearly articulated. Their melodic motion can be characterized as a succession of bounded, melodic gestures which sometimes vary in their moments of arrival, but the listener can still follow the movement from one goal to the next, comparing the goals as the melody goes along. All these melodies, then, lie toward the sectional end of the continuum, with the Moussorgsky excerpt tending toward the continuous end as the listener gives in to the freedom with which gestures begin and end.

Example	Composer, title	Date
3.19	*Offertory* (Gregorian chant from the Christmastide Midnight Mass)	Middle Ages

3.19

Where does Example 3.19 lie on the continuum of sectional-continuous melodic organization? In this Gregorian chant you certainly hear melodic motion delimited by caesuras—the melody stops and the singers breathe. You can easily follow the motion from one "breath" to the next, although, as in Example 3.18, the lengths of these units are not predictable.

Page from a medieval
music manuscript

What, then, is the difference between the melodies in Examples 3.18 and 3.19? While the Moussorgsky melody did not generate a strong sense of meter, the chant is even less defined in its higher-level grouping of beats. Like the *Khovantchina* prelude, too, the chant does not create a sense of compelling motion directed toward points of rest. What is its tonic?

But the significant difference between the two melodies lies in the role played by motivic repetition and transformation. In fact, in the chant motivic patterns are neither repeated nor even structurally varied. The chant melody seems tied to—motivated by—the text and contained by the upper and lower pitch limits of each phrase. The result is a melody which, despite its "breathing spaces," seems more continuous than sectional.

Example	Composer, title	Date
3.20	Bach, *St. Matthew Passion*, aria	1729
3.21	Wagner, *Tristan and Isolde*, "Love-Death"	1857–1859

3.20

Examples 3.20 and 3.21 are even more continuous, or cumulative, in their effect than the Gregorian chant. In the Bach aria, for example, the tenor seems hardly to have an opportunity to breathe. After the instrumental introduction, with one brief vocal interpolation, the melody moves continuously forward, growing out of itself. There is no periodic phrase structure established by a

the melody moves continuously forward, growing out of itself

series of related, regularly recurring goals. The effect is one of organic growth—a constant process of becoming.

Example 3.21, from Wagner's *Tristan and Isolde*, illustrates what the composer termed "endless melody," which, in a sense, has features of both cumulative and periodic melodic processes. The melody is shared jointly by soprano and orchestra. The soprano breathes, but the orchestra continues. Through sequential

3.21

development and extreme harmonic instability (where do you settle on a tonic?), the motion is continuous in a series of increasingly intense climaxes.

Now that you have listened carefully to a wide variety of melodies and gained some understanding of the more formal properties and relations that characterize them, it will be helpful to listen again to Examples 3.1–3.6. In the light of your experience with the material in the remaining parts of the chapter, how would you now answer our initial question: What contributes to the differences among these first six melodies, and how can you account for these differences? In turn, what can you say now about the characteristics of the prototypical tune—our cultural model of a tune that makes sense?

Several aspects seem to be basic to such an intuitive model: meter, sectional organization with balanced phrase structure, and a clear sense of tonal center. Yet, as you have seen and heard in the analysis of *Lassie* and the theme from the Mozart piano sonata movement, as well as in the discussion of continuous melodies, other factors can also play an important role in creating a sense of organized movement and musical coherence. Factors such as repetition of a rhythmic pattern, sequential repetition of a melodic fragment, and manipulation, even transformation, of a germinal musical idea all contribute to creating a meaningful whole.

As you become more sensitive to these aspects of even the most familiar tunes, you may also discover these same aspects in melodies that previously seemed strange, even incoherent. Thus, a more fully developed perception and understanding of what you know and can do already, is the touchstone to learning how to appreciate music that may at first seem incomprehensible. But the virtuosity of composers (and performers) in finding new modes of expression and particular ways of building coherence demands a certain virtuosity from the listener—an expanded awareness or expanded consciousness that frees him or her to listen to a piece on its own terms. Your study up to this point, and as it continues, should help you to achieve this new and greater awareness.

ADDITIONAL MATERIALS

I

Practice Problems 1 through 4 give you only the pitches of five familiar tunes; neither their varied durations nor meter (that is, bar lines) are indicated. Play the notes on the piano or some other instrument. For each example, identify the melody and write it out with the correct rhythm and meter.

Model

Solution (*Twinkle, Twinkle Little Star*)

1

2*

* Copyright © 1935 by Summy-Birchard Company, Evanston, Illinois. Copyright renewed 1962. All rights reserved.

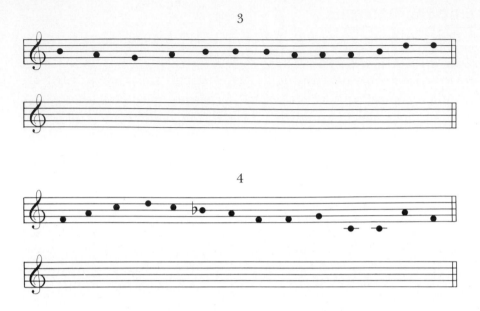

In Practice Problems 5 and 6 you are given rhythmic configurations. Provide each rhythmic configuration with appropriate pitches.

6

In Practice Problems 7 and 8 you are given pitches (this time not taken from familiar tunes) without durations. Provide each pitch shape with an appropriate rhythmic shape.

Model

Solution

In Practice Problems 9–13 you are given a set of pitches which were generated randomly by a computer. Using Examples 9 and 10 as your model, modify the remaining sets to form a "sensible tune" by deleting and/or adding pitches and by varying the durations. As you work, try to observe the bases for your decisions; from them you may be able to derive your model of a "sensible tune."

9

10

11

II

Study in detail some well-known tunes, trying to discover the fundamentals of their organization. Look, for example, for motives and their manipulation, melodic shape, and phrases and the relationships among them (length, kind of cadence, and so on). Try the following three tunes.

> *Silent Night*
> *Twinkle, Twinkle Little Star*
> *Early One Morning*

III

Listen carefully to and study (as with the familiar tunes above) some more complex melodies.

> Mozart, *Eine Kleine Nachtmusik*, K. 525, minuet, 1787 (Example 4.10)
> Schubert, songs from *Die Schöne Müllerin* (*The Beautiful Maid of the Mill*), 1823: "Der Jäger," ("The Hunter"), "Des Müllers Blumen" ("The Miller's Flowers"), "Ungeduld" ("Impatience"), and "Morgengruss" ("Morning Greeting"). Note, among other things, the readily apparent rhythmic patterns of the first three songs, compared with the almost speechlike quality and the much more subtle patterns of "Morgengruss."

IV

Contrast, as examples of sectional and continuous melodic organization, the opening melodies that you hear in the following pieces:

> Haydn, *Symphony 99,* third movement, 1793 (Example 1.29)
> Handel, *Concerto Grosso,* Op. 6, no. 2, finale, c. 1734 (Example 1.31)
> Mozart, *Symphony 39,* K. 543, fourth movement, 1788
> Bach, *Brandenburg Concerto 5,* first movement, c. 1721

V

Listen to the composer's manipulation of motives, on a larger scale, in the course of an entire movement such as those listed below.

> Beethoven, *Symphony 5,* Op. 67, first movement, 1808 (One hears almost constant development of the opening four-note motive throughout the entire movement. It appears in a seemingly infinite variety of guises.)
> Beethoven, *Quartet,* Op. 131, first movement, 1826
> Schoenberg, *Pierrot Lunaire,* "Mondestrunken," 1912
> Bach, *Well-Tempered Clavier,* Book I, C-minor fugue, 1722
> Stravinsky, *Three Pieces for Clarinet Solo,* 1920

ANCILLARY READING

Pitch Notation

As an oddity of the history of music, only seven letters came to represent the twelve tones employed in Western music. The letters A through G, with the aid of *accidentals* [*sharps* (♯) and *flats* (♭)], provide names for these twelve tones. In addition to being named by letter (which does not indicate the octave), pitches are notated on a

five-line *staff* (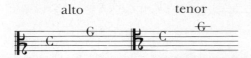). A *clef* (Latin *clavis,* "key") provides the key
to the staff, as follows:

    𝄞 is a G, or treble, clef. It fixes the G above Middle C.

𝄡 is a C, or alto or tenor, clef. It fixes Middle C. The alto clef
is used principally by the viola; the tenor clef by the bassoon, cello,
and trombone.

𝄢 is an F, or bass, clef. It fixes the F below Middle C.

    Here are the twelve tones:

Piano Keyboard (see p. 117)

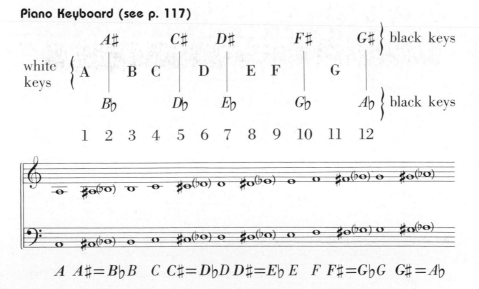

Oddly enough, A-sharp and B-flat, for example, are played by the same key; they are called *enharmonic* equivalents.[11]

Key Signatures

In tonal music (music written in a particular key) the key is indicated at the beginning of a piece by means of accidentals (flats or

Circle of fifths

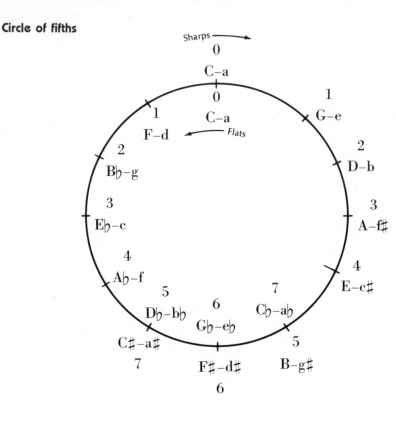

---

[11] These equivalents derive from a system of tuning called "equal temperament," which became standardized during the eighteenth century. While it is imposed on the piano by its construction, and thus on instruments playing together with it, string instruments playing together in small groups (a string quartet, for example) may make fine adjustments in pitch so that B-flat in a certain context may be slightly lower than A-sharp.

sharps) which constitute the key signature. Thus 🎼♭ means that all the B's in the piece are flatted, and the piece is in either F Major or D minor; while 🎼♯ indicates G Major or E minor. A so called "circle of fifths" illustrates the 24 major and minor keys. Starting from C Major or A minor, the keys with no sharps or flats, each sharp added to the key signature raises the key by the interval of a fifth, and each flat added lowers it by a fifth. In the circle of fifths on page 142, capital letters indicate the major keys, and small letters represent the minor keys.

Modes and Scales

The division of the octave into seven tones with varying intervals between them creates the diatonic modes shown in the following table.

Name	Starting note	Interval pattern*
Dorian	*D*	$1 \ \frac{1}{2} \ 1 \ 1 \ 1 \ \frac{1}{2} \ 1$
Phrygian	*E*	$\frac{1}{2} \ 1 \ 1 \ 1 \ \frac{1}{2} \ 1 \ 1$
Lydian	*F*	$1 \ 1 \ 1 \ \frac{1}{2} \ 1 \ 1 \ \frac{1}{2}$
Mixolydian	*G*	$1 \ 1 \ \frac{1}{2} \ 1 \ 1 \ \frac{1}{2} \ 1$
Aeolian (minor)	*A*	$1 \ \frac{1}{2} \ 1 \ 1 \ \frac{1}{2} \ 1 \ 1$
Ionian (major)	*C*	$1 \ 1 \ \frac{1}{2} \ 1 \ 1 \ 1 \ \frac{1}{2}$

* Thus playing all the white keys on the piano beginning on *D* would give you the Dorian mode, playing all the white keys beginning on *E* would give the Phrygian mode, and so forth. The interval pattern may be transposed to begin on any of the eleven other tones.

The degrees of the scale in major and minor are named:

1. Tonic
2. Supertonic
3. Mediant
4. Subdominant
5. Dominant
6. Submediant
7. Leading tone

There are three different forms of the minor scale. Note that these differences involve only the sixth and seventh degrees of the scale.

Natural Minor

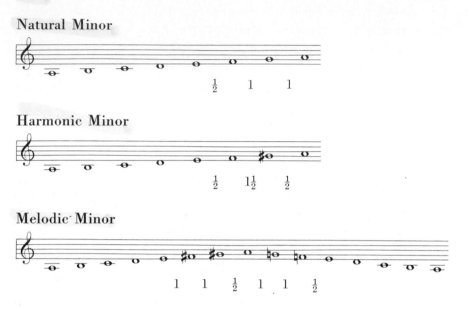

Harmonic Minor

Melodic Minor

The harmonic minor is derived from the notes found in the I, IV, and V chords in their most common form (see the Ancillary Reading for Chapter 5). The melodic minor is derived from ascending or descending melodies in the minor mode.

The term *pentatonic* is used to describe various possible divisions of the octave into *five tones* (for example, the black keys on the piano).

Intervals

The distance between any two tones is called an *interval.* In discussing scales and modes, we spoke of a half step or a whole step; these may be more properly described as a *minor second* or a *major second.* The principal intervals within the octave are indicated on page 145.

Rules for Naming Intervals

The *perfect* intervals are the *prime* (the same note; for example, two people singing in unison), *fourth* (9¼ steps), *fifth* (3½ steps), and *octave.* Lowering a perfect or a minor interval by a half step creates a *diminished* interval; lowering a major interval by a half step creates a *minor* interval. Raising a major or a perfect interval by a half step creates an *augmented* interval; raising a minor interval by a half step creates a *major* interval.

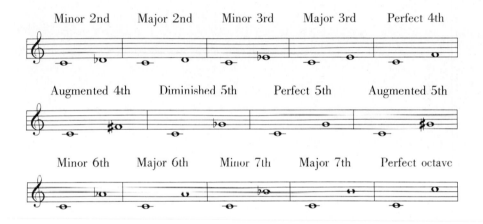

PART TWO
Process and design

Rice terraces

A particular way of building up the world . . .

CHAPTER 4

Means of organization

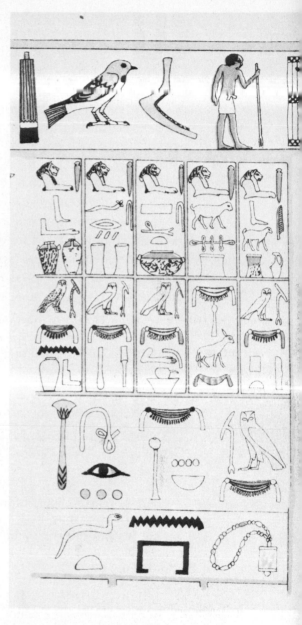

Egyptian hieroglyphics

. . . as in the creation of language.

What has happened so far in your perception of music? Try rereading the Introduction and listening again to the first seven examples in Chapter 1. Do you find that you are beginning to expand your focus? Those factors which, of necessity, have been temporarily isolated can now begin to merge. Analysis and terminology can assume their proper roles as means toward direct and immediate involvement in the total process of a work. And as you enjoy an expanded, more aware involvement, you may find justification, at least partially, for the use of language which may at times have seemed more of a hindrance than a help.

Naming an object or a relationship—such as a beat, tonic, triple meter—often appears to interfere with your response to the feelings, character, and mood which music generates. It is interesting to read what Kurt Goldstein, a biological psychologist, has said concerning the connection between language (naming) and feeling:

> [Language] is not merely a superficial means of communication, not a simple naming of objects through words; it represents a particular way of building up the world—namely, by means of abstractions. . . . In none of his cultural creations does man reveal himself as fully as in the creation of language, itself.[1]

But a problem arises because:

> If we try to become aware of them [feelings] we have to transform them into objects, and then their original character of attitudes, feelings, etc., is lost, and they are distorted into "things" . . . Thus, a phenomenon which is not experienced in a conscious form [feelings, attitudes, etc.] can never subsequently become directly conscious; and, conversely, a conscious phenomenon can never work directly upon attitudes or feelings. Only by way of the whole, by a detour, so to speak, can either influence, arouse, or disturb the other.[2]

These general comments may help you to understand this moment in a process which can sometimes appear to be a conglomeration of analytical bits and pieces rather than a total experi-

[1] Kurt Goldstein, *Human Nature* (New York: Schocken Books, 1963), p. 83.
[2] Ibid., pp. 152, 154.

ence. We have tried to emphasize, however, that an atomistic approach to the musical experience is, except as a temporary expedient, inadequate. Remember how the concerns of the previous chapters could not be kept separate? Just as our discussion of sound led to rhythmic organization, which merged into melodic organization, so our discussion of melodic organization turned to rhythmic considerations.

From now on we will pursue a broader approach. First, in Exercise 4-1, we ask you to discover specific means through which composers create a sense of unity and variety in building whole structures. Then we move to a consideration of two fundamentally different approaches to creating these structures (Demonstration 4-1). Next we introduce the subject of harmony, which "more than any other musical element, brings to music the possibility of extension, or larger design."[3] And finally, incorporating all that has gone before, we move to a consideration of these "larger designs," concentrating on their varying effects.

Exercise 4-1

Return   (Side 5)

Exercise 4-1 asks you to discriminate between those pieces which include a return to the opening musical material and those which do not. To hear the difference between these structural procedures, you will have to focus on musical events on a larger scale (in less detail, but for longer time spans than in the preceding chapters), and you will need to remember these events throughout the excerpt.

Note that Examples 4.2, 4.4, and 4.8 are each complete pieces; in these examples you will hear how contrasting procedures can influence the effect of a whole design.

---

[3] Roger Sessions, "The Composer and His Message," in *The Intent of the Artist*, ed. Augusto Centeno (Princeton: Princeton University Press, 1941), p. 111.

Remembering a musical event (or any event, for that matter) becomes easier if you can "identify" with its expressive character— becoming actively involved in it, instead of trying to remember its smaller details, such as a melodic or rhythmic configuration. A precise awareness of such specifics is extremely important when you are delving into a work, but here you can pause in your examination of details to consider larger design in one of its most general aspects. Listen to the difference between pieces in which you have the experience of returning after some kind of digression, and those in which your experience is one of continuing onward. (Note that in a number of the examples in Exercise 4-1 the composer has helped you to "fix" the initial events by repeating the opening section.)

As you listen, think not only about this fundamental difference in organization, but also, in those examples which include a return, about the differences in the way this return occurs. Is the return "announced"—are you told musically that it is approaching? Or does it simply happen without any preparation? Notice, too, that in a number of instances the return is somewhat varied, although it still clearly projects the feeling of coming back after a contrasting middle section.

We have chosen to introduce an exercise rather than a demonstration at this point to encourage you to begin your own discovery of larger design. In a general sense, this exercise also functions as an introduction to the subject of *harmony*, which plays a crucial role in determining structure. You will hear how a digression—a contrasting middle section—can lead you away from home (to a new key[4] and its tonic), while a return to a previously heard theme usually coincides with a return to the home key and its tonic. Harmony is playing a role in your perception of structure on some level perhaps unknown even to yourself.

Even with a simple melody like *Cowboy's Lament,* harmonic im-

---

[4] While the meaning of *tonic* or *tonal center* was discussed in Chapter 3, the possibility of *changing* the tonal center (and thus the key) was only hinted at in that discussion. How this change is made and its various effects will be discussed further in Chapter 5.

plications play a significant role in your sense of intelligibility; for instance, your sense of incompleteness at the end of the first three phrases, contrasted with the conclusiveness of the fourth phrase. Harmony functions in a similar way in these longer examples. You might think of it as a set of ground rules which you have learned quite naturally, much as when you were a child you naturally learned the rules of grammar which made spoken language intelligible to you.

Remember, however, that harmonic frameworks differ from one culture to another and even within cultures from one historical period to another. But we will meet these issues directly in the next chapter. For now do the exercise, keeping in mind that your sense of coherence, including contrast and return, is being generated in part by your built-in awareness of harmonic relations.

Please do not consider this exercise as a test. After you have completed the examples, look at the answers below. You will also find additional comments on some of the examples. Try listening to the examples again while reading these comments instead of simply checking to see if your answers are right or wrong. First listen carefully to Examples 4.1 and 4.2 (for which answers are given); these can serve as models in doing the rest of the exercise.

Example	No return *Continuous*	Return *Sectional*
4.1		X
4.2	X	
4.3		X
4.4	X	
4.5		X
4.6	X	
4.7		X
4.8	X	
4.9	X	

CORRECT ANSWERS AND COMMENTS

Example	Composer, title, date	No return	Return
4.1	Mozart, *Concerto for Horn and Orchestra,* no. 2, K. 417, third movement, 1783		X
4.2	Bach, *Well-Tempered Clavier,* Book I, Prelude no. 2 in C minor, 1722	X	

The first two examples demonstrate how fundamentally different structures can create strikingly different effects. In Example 4.1, the feeling of coming back is clearly prepared for by the pause of the horn together with the rest of the orchestra as well as by harmonic means. (Can you tell what happens to the harmony? Listen, for example, to the bass alone just before the return.)

Contrast the feeling of the return in Example 4.1 with the tension created by the continuously unfolding motion (followed by changes of tempo) in Example 4.2.

		No return	Return
4.3	Bach, *Concerto in E Major for Violin and Orchestra,* third movement, c. 1720		X

The contrasts between the full orchestra (called the *tutti,* meaning "all") and the solo violin with accompaniment define the sections in Example 4.3. After the solo there is a return to the *tutti* playing the opening theme. Here are two works by the same composer (Examples 4.2 and 4.3) which exemplify the different structural procedures under discussion.

		No return	Return
4.4	Chopin, *Prelude,* Op. 28, no. 18, 1838	X	

Compare the sense of ongoing movement in the Chopin prelude with that in the Bach prelude. How do they differ?

		No return	Return
4.5	Haydn, *Symphony 96,* fourth movement, 1791		X

Here Haydn has a good time playing around with your anticipation of a return before he actually presents it.

		No return	Return
4.6	Vivaldi, *Concerto Grosso,* Op. 3, no. 7, first movement, c. 1712	X	

This excerpt from the Vivaldi *Concerto Grosso* includes repetition but not return. The work proceeds sequentially. It progresses by what we might call "rhythmic stepping stones" formed by the repetition of a motive at successively higher or lower pitch levels within the same strand of the texture. In this excerpt there are two sequential passages, each with its own motive.

		No return	Return
4.7	Stravinsky, *Petrouchka,* 1911		X

Did you hear the harmonic joke in this excerpt from the ballet *Petrouchka?* Just before the contrasting section begins, Stravinsky brings things to a stop, but not to an end. The harmony at this point is directed toward a tonic which, in fact, does not materialize. The melody of the next section begins in a different key from the one intuitively anticipated by the listener. Only later, with the varied return, does Stravinsky come back harmonically to where he left off at the end of the first section. (We will return to these questions of harmony in Chapter 5.)

		No return	Return
4.8	Webern, *Five Pieces for Orchestra,* Op. 10, no. 2, 1913	X	
4.9	Bizet, *Symphony in C,* third movement, 1855	X	

The continuous motivic development (in a very brief time span) in the Webern piece may make it difficult for you to orient yourself to the piece after only one or two hearings. Why does such continuous development make return inappropriate?

Notice that in Example 4.9 you are led to expect a return. As in many of the examples in which there were returns, Bizet repeats the opening part before going on to the contrasting section. In addition, he presents a long preparation which seems to anticipate return. Instead of returning, however, the composer goes on to introduce new material.

Demonstration 4-1

SECTIONAL AND CONTINUOUS ORGANIZATION (Sides 5–6)

Demonstration 4-1 introduces you to the study of large-scale structure in music. While some aspects of structure have been discussed previously,[5] we have not yet focused on overall musical design. You will hear in this demonstration mostly short pieces or complete movements which illustrate two fundamentally different approaches to larger musical design: (1) pieces which one hears immediately as divided into parts, whether or not they include return (*sectional*), and (2) pieces which one cannot easily divide into parts (*continuous*).

[5] See Chapter 1, sonority and texture as organizing factors; Chapter 2, rhythm (beat, meter, phrase) as an organizing factor; Chapter 3, motivic development, and here in Chapter 4, return.

Egyptian vase
Sectional organization

American Indian pot
Continuous organization

This fundamental distinction was discussed in Chapter 3 where continuous melodies were contrasted to those "with clear and balanced phrase structure and predictable moments of arrival." But now when we refer to dividing a piece into "parts," we mean not smaller units (such as phrases defined by caesuras) but rather those larger structural units that stand out as the significant sections of a piece—those units which lend themselves to schematic representation and can, for example, be meaningfully designated A, B, C, and so forth.

Of course, these larger sections are, in turn, composed of smaller units (phrases), and the relations among these phrases generate the particular character of the section. In a whole piece you can hear a kind of hierarchy of structural relations: phrases combine to make up sections, sections combine to make up still larger parts, and these larger parts combine to make up the whole.

The Distinction Illustrated

Example	Composer, title	Date
4.10	Mozart, *Eine kleine Nachtmusik* (*A Little Night Music*) K. 525, minuet	1787
4.11	Chopin, *Prelude*, Op. 28, no. 18	1838

Examples 4.10 and 4.11 should make the fundamental distinction between sectional and continuous organization clear. Example 4.10, by Mozart, is a late-eighteenth-century stylized dance movement, the third movement of a four-movement instrumental work. It is clearly divided into three large parts, the first and last being identical (except for the absence of repeats in the last part). Its overall structure may be diagramed as follows:

$$\text{A} \qquad\qquad \text{B} \qquad\qquad \text{A}'$$

$$\|{:}a{:}\|{:}b + a'{:}\| \qquad \|{:}c{:}\|{:}d + c'{:}\| \qquad a\ \ b + a'$$

Note that each of the three sections is "closed out," or relatively complete in itself; in addition, within each of the larger sections, A, B, and A', one hears a somewhat similar inner structure: $\|: a :\|\|: b + a' :\|$. Notice, that unlike the clear delineation between B and A', *b* and *a'* flow into one another; thus they are designated *b + a'* rather than *b a'*.

minuet

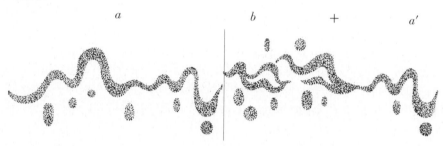

In addition, note that section *b* is made up of the same motivic material as *a* (and *d* bears a similar relationship to *c*). In fact, its function is to create something new out of the old by developing the motives already present in section *a*. By contrast, B presents entirely new material not drawn from A in any obvious way at all. The comparison demonstrates nicely the hierarchical relations mentioned above: sections *a* and *b* are separated from one another and are clearly different, but both the separation and the degree of difference are significantly less than that between A and B in the larger design of the piece. A and B are therefore not only *longer* than *a* and *b*; they also present a higher degree of contrast and distinctness.

With these basic distinctions in mind, what other differences do you hear between the ABA' structure and the *a b + a'* structure, and what specific differences do you hear among the smaller parts—*a, b,* and *a'*?

In contrast to the Mozart minuet, the Chopin prelude (Example 4.11) cannot be divided into parts—it moves continuously

cannot be divided into parts

forward in spite of the caesuras, or "breathing" pauses. It would not be possible to make a schematic representation of the structure of this piece, such as ABA, for example. We will return to Examples 4.10 and 4.11 in Chapters 6 and 7, respectively.

Sectional Pieces

Example	Composer, title	Date
4.12	Schubert, *Ländler,* Op. 171, no. 4	1823
4.13	Mozart, *Variations on "Ah, vous dirai-je, maman,"* K. 265	1778
4.14	M. Reynolds, *Little Boxes* (sung by Pete Seeger)	1962

The next three examples, like Example 4.10, are sectional, yet each is organized differently. The Schubert dance (Example 4.12) is in two clear sections: A B. Each part is repeated, ‖: A :‖: B :‖, but there is no return (see the Additional Materials for further discussion of this dance).

The theme of Example 4.13 will certainly be familiar to you, though under a different name. Included here are the theme and two of the twelve variations that Mozart wrote on this theme. In Mozart's time it was common for composer-pianists to improvise in public on well-known melodies. Mozart's composed piece gives us some idea of what such a performance might have been like.

a theme and variations

The theme may be diagramed as follows: $\|{:}a{:}\|{:}b + a'{:}\|$. Each of the two variations included in Example 4.13 follows this same large design. In addition, each variation also follows the underlying structure of the theme. For example, in the theme and in each variation you will hear:

> The same phrase structure and the same relations between phrases (like antecedent-consequent)
> The same basic pitch-shape for each phrase (although this skeletal shape is "dressed" differently each time)
> The same set of harmonic relations (like full and half cadences, which occur in each variation just as they did in the theme)

Try to follow the structure of the theme as it is realized anew in each variation. At the same time you will discover that each variation has its own character. What means does Mozart use to give each of these larger sections its individuality? Finally, even though not all the variations are included in this excerpt, you can sense the additive quality of the piece. Each large section (variation) is added on to the previous one, and all of them together make up a particular kind of whole.

Another kind of additive piece is the simple verse form of the ballad. In the song *Little Boxes* (Example 4.14), as in most ballads, it is the words that hold your interest, and it is only the words that change. You take for granted the exact repetition of the music (melody and harmony) that marks off each section of the song. In contrast, each of the variations of Mozart (Example 4.13) repeats the general structure of the theme, but each time the structure appears in a new guise—sometimes more in a disguise.

The differences between the song and the variations have much to do with the social function of the two pieces. One listens to the words of the ballad to agree (or disagree?) with its message. The music is only a medium—a vehicle that exists perhaps to strengthen the verbal message or, occasionally, as with *Little Boxes,* even to create a musical picture of it. With the Mozart variations, however, one listens to the medium itself—the medium *is* the message!

Continuous Pieces

Example	Composer, title	Date
4.15	Palestrina, *Missa Aeterna Christi munera,* Sanctus	c. 1590
4.16	Bach, *Two-Part Invention in F Major,* no. 8	c. 1720

Examples 4.15 and 4.16 are organized so as to create a continuous structure, but one listens to each of them rather differently. The Renaissance piece by Palestrina (Example 4.15), a movement from a setting of the text of the Catholic Mass, is active in texture; the parts enter in imitation and are rhythmically independent. The piece creates an effect of unceasing movement characterized by melodic homogeneity. There is, however, a contrast in tone color as well as an increase in textural density as the parts pile up on top of one another.

The piece is continuous, with few obvious breaks in the musical flow. But if you listen closely, you will hear four "sections" marked off by carefully concealed points of arrival. In this polyphonic piece the text is a significant structural determinant, for a new series of imitative entries occurs with each line of text:

Sanctus, Sanctus, Sanctus,
Dominus Deus Sabaoth,
Pleni sunt caeli et terra gloria
    tua,
Hosanna in excelsis!

Holy, Holy, Holy,
Lord God of Hosts,
Heaven and earth are full of thy
    glory,
Hosanna in the highest!

What musical elements create the "section" boundaries? How are these points concealed?

The Bach invention (Example 4.16) is also active in texture, but this time, since there are only two "voices," the texture is thinner throughout. As in the Palestrina, the piece begins with imitation. However, the Bach piece has a clear point of arrival one-third of the way through (see also the Additional Materials at the end of this chapter).

An eighteenth-century harpsichord with two keyboards.

(The Metropolitan Museum of Art, New York; The Mr. and Mrs. Isaac D. Fletcher Collection: bequest of Isaac D. Fletcher, 1917)

Rondos

Example	Composer, title	Date
4.17	Rameau, *Suite in E*, gigue no. 2	1724
4.18	Haydn, *Trio in G*, "Rondo all' Ongarese"	1791
4.19	S. Reese, *Which Side Are You On?* (sung by Pete Seeger)	1932

Examples 4.17–4.19 are again sectional. Unlike Examples 4.15–4.16 they can be meaningfully diagramed—a diagram will represent the progress of the piece and the perceived relationships among the parts. Rameau's piece (Example 4.17) can be thought of as having a refrain (A), the entire gigue proceeding as follows: $\|: A :\|$ BACADA. (How do the various sections differ? Are they each in themselves relatively sectional or continuous?)

The Haydn trio[6] (Example 4.18) proceeds similarly, although it is much more extended in each of its parts, and consequently much longer. It may be diagramed as ABA′CA″ Coda. Unlike Rameau, however, Haydn further subdivides each section into two or more smaller parts. A, for example, may be diagramed as $a + a' \|: b + a' :\|$. The type of structural procedure illustrated by Examples 4.17 and 4.18 is called a *rondo*.

You are probably more familiar with the rondo procedure as it appears in a ballad, such as Example 4.19 with its refrain (A) sung to the words "Which side are you on?" But as in the previous ballad, *Little Boxes,* it is the words more than the music that make for change in the contrasting sections of the song. Considering *only* the words, we might diagram this ballad the same way we diagramed the Rameau gigue: ABACADA. The impact of the returns to A, sung by the whole audience after each word-contrasting section, demonstrates the powerful political and social function return can have in songs such as this one, written during a bitter coal strike in Kentucky. Furthermore, the effect of return in this verbal context points up the function of returns in a non-verbal context, where the contrast is purely musical—as in the rondos of Rameau and Haydn.

[6] The title "Rondo all' Ongarese" means "Rondo in the Hungarian Style," a reference to Hungarian gypsy violin music.

a rondo

A	B	A	C	A

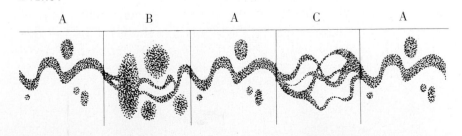

Frank Lloyd Wright,
"Fallingwater" House, 1936
Sectional or continuous?

Continuous or Sectional?

Example	Composer, title	Date
4.20	Schubert, *Impromptu*, Op. 90, no. 2	1827
4.21	Schoenberg, *Six Little Piano Pieces*, Op. 19, no. 4	1911
4.22	J. Lewis, *Django* (played by the Modern Jazz Quartet)	1960
4.23	Stravinsky, *Le Sacre du printemps*, introduction	1913

In categorizing a piece as sectional or continuous, it might be best (as with melodies) to think in terms of a continuum with "sectional" and "continuous" at opposite ends; most pieces will lie somewhere on that continuum, closer to one end or the other. The Schubert *Impromptu* (Example 4.20) may at first appear to be continuous because the melody is a series of rapidly flowing notes that seem never to stop—there is no caesura in this upper part of the texture. But would the piece be accurately described as continuous? No, but why not? The answer lies in the very clear balanced phrase structure generated by the chords in the left-hand accompaniment.

In comparison, the Chopin prelude heard earlier (Example

4.11) seems, on the most immediate level, very discontinuous, proceeding in fits and starts. Yet the overall impression, created primarily by the restless unstable harmony, is that the music never really stops at the breaks—that it synaptically flows onward until the final cadence.

You can also compare the Chopin prelude with the stylistically different Schoenberg piece (Example 4.21). Both have a continuously onward impulse despite clear caesuras. Both have a rhythmic and melodic freedom which gives them an improvisatory air; yet both grow unceasingly out of the initial motivic material, which undergoes almost magical transformation. Continuous pieces like these often gain their unique coherence through just such continuous development of a germinal motive.

4.22 John Lewis's piece *Django* has at least one point of similarity with the Schubert *Impromptu*, that is, a seemingly continuous surface above a less immediately apparent sectional substructure. The piece begins with the shared statement of a melody by vibraphone ("vibes"), piano, and bass—slow and without a steady beat at first, then gradually picking up the tempo. With the entrance of the drums (played with brushes), we proceed to a series of improvised "choruses" by first the vibes, then the piano. The underlying substructure (the basis for each improvised chorus) might be diagramed as follows:

a	*a*	*b*	*a'*	*c*	sections
6	6	8	4	8	number of bars (measures)

Though 32 bars in length, this is more complex and harder to hear than the traditional *a a b a* structure (cf. Chapters 3 and 5). The signpost for *b* is the repeated note in the bass (called a "pedal"); that for *c* a "bluesy" theme in the bass.

There are three choruses by the vibes followed by a brief codetta (Italian, *coda* + *etta,* "little tail") leading into two choruses by the piano. The group slows down in the *c* section of the last piano chorus, leading into the restatement of the opening theme and conclusion. (The excerpt includes only the three choruses by the vibes.) You might compare this set of variations on a "theme" with the Mozart variations discussed above (Example 4.13).

Listen now to the Bach aria heard previously as Example 3.20, and characterized as follows: "After the instrumental introduction, with one brief vocal interpolation, the melody moves continuously forward, growing out of itself. There is no periodic phrase structure established by a series of related, regularly recur-

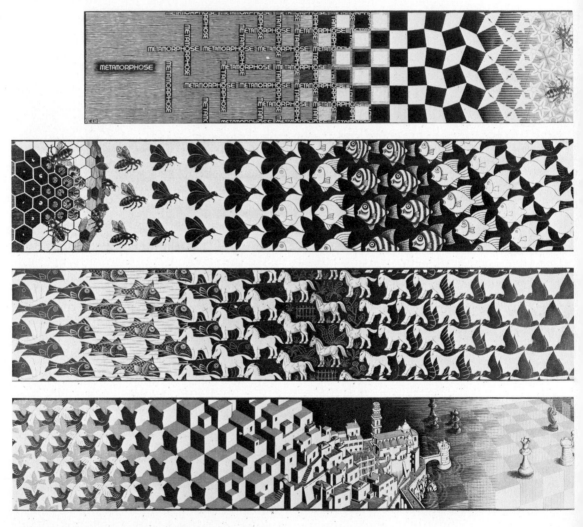

M. C. Escher, Metamorphosis. (*Escher Foundation, Collection Haags Gemeentemuseum, The Hague*)

ring goals. The effect is one of organic growth—a constant process of becoming."

While we were speaking there of only one aspect of organization *melody*, you can now hear how a continuous melody tends to generate a continuous structure, which is further reinforced by homogeneity of texture and singleness of theme.

Example 4.23, the beginning of Stravinsky's *Le Sacre du prin-*

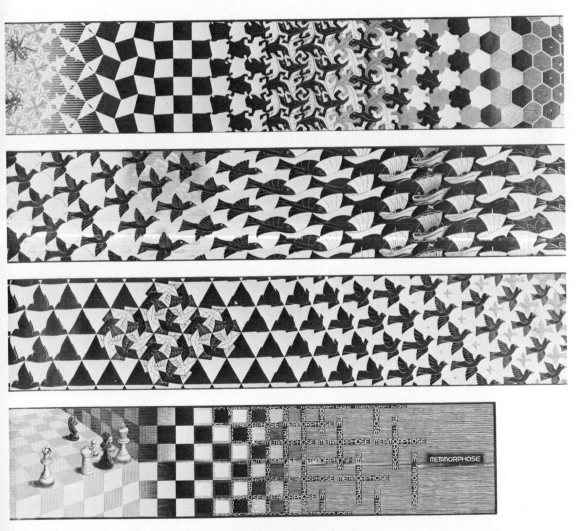

The whole evolves dramatically
and organically out of its initial fragment.

temps, has no caesuras. Paradoxically static and in motion at the same time, its feeling might be characterized as one of dynamic stasis. There is a gradual build-up to a climax: Beginning with a solo bassoon in its upper register, Stravinsky gradually adds more and more instruments (predominantly winds) until the loud muted trumpets bring us to the peak. The solo bassoon then ends the excerpt as it began. Changes in sonority and texture create a sense of kaleidoscopic motion, yet the motion is inhibited by the persistence of a few melodic and rhythmic fragments.

You might go back now and listen again to two pieces heard earlier in the chapter (Examples 4.2 and 4.8). They are both relatively continuous pieces without a return. The Bach prelude is a kind of perpetual motion piece until the freer, more improvisatory closing; there are, furthermore, no caesuras marked off by conclusive cadences.

In the Webern piece one hears, in contrast, a filigree of sounds so tightly interrelated that, as in the Schoenberg piano piece (Example 4.21), the whole evolves dramatically and organically out of its initial fragment. If you listen to this brief composition several times, you will gradually come to hear more details, more events, and more contrast. At the same time the piece may appear to get longer and even less continuous as your perception of contrast leads you to hear the momentary articulation of structural divisions. Perhaps we will find that *sectional* and *continuous,* like many other terms used to describe music, do not define discrete and unvarying characteristics of an entire work but rather *tendencies* toward which a work or moments of a work seem to lean.

ADDITIONAL MATERIALS

The examples in Demonstration 4-1 were chosen primarily as illustrations of the difference between sectional and continuous structure. We can now consider some of these examples and several additional ones more deeply in order to perceive the individual aspects of works and at the same time become aware of further general aspects of musical design. Consider the following questions carefully in relation to all the works in this section.

1. Does the piece divide into larger sections which are readily perceived?
2. Within these larger sections, is the structure basically sectional or continuous?
3. Does a schematic representation of the piece, such as ABA, come readily to mind?
4. If there are no clearly defined sections, what creates structure?
5. What defines or marks off sections?
6. What is the relationship among sections?
7. What are the sources of contrast? Of unity?

I

Listen again to the following two pieces, both of which were included in Demonstration 4-1:

Schubert, *Landler*, Op. 171, no. 4, 1823 (Example 4.12)
Bach, *Two-Part Invention in F Major*, no. 8, c. 1720 (Example 4.16)

In Demonstration 4-1 Schubert's work illustrated a sectional piece; Bach's illustrated a continuous one. The two pieces are superficially similar in that each reaches a point of arrival—a caesura—dividing it into two parts. Nevertheless, they operate on fundamentally different structural principles. Schubert's texture is *homophonic* (consisting of a melody and accompaniment), and it proceeds in clear, four-measure phrases—two phrases in Part A, two in Part B—creating two equal halves. The relationship between the first two phrases is rather different from the relationship between the second two phrases. The first two are essentially antecedent and consequent phrases. What generates the sense of tension in the third phrase, and why do we have almost a sense of return—at least return to stability—in the concluding phrase?

Bach's invention, on the other hand, is a *polyphonic* piece which begins imitatively and continues with an active texture in which the two parts, though similar melodically, retain their rhythmic independence throughout. This rhythmic independence does not allow for the kind of clear, balanced phrase structure heard in the Schubert *Ländler* (which, in fact, defined it as sectional). Why? When one part momentarily pauses, the other, pursuing its own path, continues on to *its* goal. Each part overrides the caesura of the other, creating an unceasing onward flow.

The continuous flow is finally interrupted with a caesura (not, however, exactly at the midpoint, where it came in Schubert's piece, but only one-third of the way through). Following the caesura, the opening imitation reappears, but not in the tonic key of the piece and without a strong sense of return to the opening—it is merely another phase in the continuous development of the initial figure. (Can you hear how Bach exploits motives from that figure throughout the piece?)

The last portion of the invention is exactly the same (except in a different key) as the part before the caesura, yet we do not hear this repetition as a return. Why? Primarily because the "return" does not *begin* with a clear statement of the theme. As the passage continues, however, it emerges as a restatement of the opening portion of the piece up to the caesura—but *without* the characteristic theme with which the movement began. Bach creates a return of *becoming* rather than an abrupt, announced one. It is, in short, a return consistent with the continuous nature of the piece as a whole.

II

Listen to and compare the following two pieces. You heard the Haydn minuet as Example 1.29; however, now we ask you to consider its organization on a larger scale.

Mozart, *German Dance,* K. 605, no. 1, 1791
Haydn, *Symphony 99,* minuet, 1793 (Example 1.29)

The *German Dance,* like the Mozart minuet in Example 4.10, illustrates a clear ABA′ structure. A and B in turn are divided into $\|:a:\|\|:b + a′:\|$, while A′ is the same as A without repeats. The Haydn minuet could be schematically diagramed in exactly the same way, yet it is a much larger, more imposing work. What happens within A and B to sustain the greatly expanded proportions? Notice, for example, that while the *a* section of the *German Dance* is a simple two-phrase, antecedent-consequent statement, the *a* section of the Haydn minuet is only one-third complete at the end of its opening antecedent-consequent statement. It continues on to a section which generates more tension and ends with a closing passage which is more stable. What causes these differences in effect? How does *b* differ from *a,* how is the return to *a′* effected, and what surprising events occur in this return? A careful study of the Haydn minuet should give you an appreciation of its composer's genius in generating out of very simple musical material a work filled with contrasts. It is a dance, but it also has suspense, humor, and climax—all making a tightly packed, eminently satisfying whole. (This minuet is discussed again in Chapter 6.)

III

The following are large complex pieces, a detailed discussion of which would require many pages. Listen to them on your own, for they will provide invaluable experience in coming to grips with extensive pieces. Ask the seven questions listed at the beginning of the Additional Materials as you listen to each piece.

Purcell, *Dido and Aeneas,* "Dido's Lament," 1689
Wagner, *Tristan and Isolde,* prelude, 1857–1859
Handel, *Concerto Grosso,* Op. 6, no. 2, c. 1734 (Example 1.31)
Mozart, *Sonata for Piano in F,* K. 332, first movement, 1778

Victor Vasarely, *Oeta,* 1959

CHAPTER 5
Harmony

Constantin Brancusi, *The Kiss*, 1908

The subject of harmony has come up several times in previous chapters, but we have reserved the detailed discussion of it until now. Of course, you already have gained a general sense of the role of harmony as it articulates or defines structure. For example, you heard in the Liszt and Wagner excerpts (Examples 3.2 and 3.21) and the Chopin prelude (Example 4.11) how harmony can create a restless mood and consequently a less defined structure. In the discussion of the Mozart sonata theme in Chapter 3 you heard how harmony functions to create complete and incomplete cadences, and we discussed scales and their relation to the tonal center (which necessarily involves harmonic relationships). Likewise, in Chapter 4 you noted the role of harmony in creating return. All these earlier experiences with sound, time, and pitch should help you to understand this crucial, but sometimes difficult and elusive, aspect of music.

Demonstration 5-1

HARMONIC FRAMEWORKS   (Sides 6–7)

Harmony is often defined as "the relationship among chords," a *chord* being the sounding together of two or more pitches. We will broaden the meaning to consider harmony as the *basic pitch framework* of a given piece or even of a particular kind of music. Indeed, when we speak of sound—the sound of African music or the sound of Renaissance music (as in Chapter 1)—often we are referring to the particular harmonic framework of the style. In addition, when you single out a special moment in some composition and exclaim, "Listen to that sound!" you probably have been attracted by an unusual combination of pitches—a chord—which is somehow unexpected in the context of that piece. Thus harmony has both broad and very detailed, specific implications. It is this dual aspect that often makes harmony difficult to talk about:

174

The context defines the particulars, and the particulars generate the context.

For example, the study of harmony traditionally means the study of *tonal*, or *functional*, harmony—the framework within which most Western composers have worked from about 1650 until into the twentieth century. Most of the music with which you are familiar takes this framework as an assumption, and you tacitly absorb this assumption as a basic means of comprehension. In order to help you become aware of this assumed framework, we begin with some examples in which functional harmony is *not* the underlying basis for coherence—where, in fact, it is not operative.

Possibilities Other Than Functional Harmony

Example	Composer, title	Date
5.1	*Dodoitsu* (Japanese)	18th c.
5.2	*Citombe* (East African)	
5.3	*The Moon Shines* (Bulgarian)	

Examples 5.1 and 5.2 are both from non-European cultures. Example 5.1 is a Japanese love song with accompaniment on the *shamisen;* Example 5.2, an East African dance tune played on the *mbira,* or thumb piano, and recorded in Southern Rhodesia. Example 5.3, while from European Bulgaria, does not operate within the pitch framework of functional harmony either. For the people of these areas, this music is as natural, coherent, and meaningful as tonal music is to us. Indeed, Japanese, Africans, or Bulgarians who have grown up singing, playing (often by ear), and listening to music with different assumptions from ours are likely to find our music as incomprehensible as we find theirs. Those who study music of other cultures (*ethnomusicologists*) are able to isolate and describe the various bases of pitch organization which give the music of each culture its particular coherence. In doing so, they

Japanese shamisen

reveal a framework that is both systematic and complex. What may appear chaotic to us in the music of other cultures seems so only because we are unaware of another order.

Notice that we are speaking of harmony not so much in terms of chords but in terms of a framework of pitch material and pitch relationships: the selection of pitches from the continuum (see

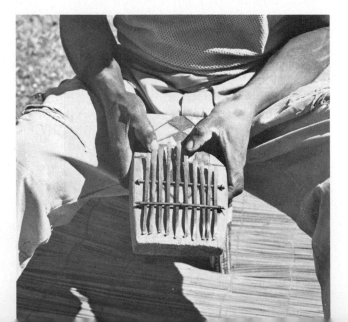

African mbira

Chapter 3) and the various ways in which these pitches character-istically are combined, either simultaneously or in succession. In this sense a melody like the Japanese song, where there are no chords even in the accompaniment, also establishes and works within a harmonic framework.

While tonality and functional harmony provide the frame-work for the music with which we are most familiar in our own Western culture, music before the mid-seventeenth century and after the early twentieth century operates within different har-monic frameworks. The next two examples illustrate music writ-ten before and after the central tradition of tonal music in our own culture—a tradition which we usually tend to take for granted.

Example	Composer, title	Date
5.4	Gesualdo, *Dolcissima mia vita*	1611
5.5	Boulez, *Le Marteau sans maître*, "Après l'artisant furieux"	1955

5.4 In the Gesualdo example, for instance, you hear chords and chord progressions which sound familiar, but there are moments of unexpected sound or an "odd" progression from one chord to the next. You sometimes expect certain chords but they don't ar-rive. This sense of expectation derives exactly from our habitual ways of listening and understanding within a tonal framework. You will also notice an uneasy, slippery quality to the pitch motion —it sometimes seems to lose its direction. In fact, it is precisely this sense of *directed* pitch motion that is most characteristic of tonal harmony. Once this framework has been learned, simply through persistent contact with the music that is most often around us, we take it as a norm—a given. But, as you can hear in this example, it is not always an appropriate set of assumptions; it has not always been the underlying principal of harmonic organization. Notice, too, that Gesualdo at times uses harmony for what is called "word painting." That is, he uses a particular chord as an expressive means to help convey the feelings intended by the words. For example, on the word *morire* (die), you hear a harmony that sounds particularly poignant. You will discover other instances of "word painting" as you listen again to the Gesualdo example and follow the text:

Dolcissima mia vita,	Sweetest love,
A che tardate la bramata aita?	Why do you hold back the desired aid?
Credete forse che'l bel foco ond'ardo	Do you think perhaps my ardor
Sia per finir perchè torcete'l guardo?	Will come to an end, because you avert your face?
Ahi, non fia mai ché brama il mio desire	Alas, this will never be, for I must
O d'amarti o morire.	Either love you or die.

Leaving this pretonal world and skipping over the seventeenth through nineteenth centuries (the age of tonality in the West), listen to the short movement from Boulez's *Le Marteau sans maître* (*The Hammer Without a Master*). Much of its strangeness in sound results from Boulez's abandonment of the previous tonal framework and his development of other ways of relating pitches to one another. On first or second hearing the piece may seem to be simply without organization—random or chaotic. In fact, it is a highly organized, tightly composed piece, and given sufficient experience you can come to perceive it as such. For the moment, however, the piece can serve to raise questions concerning not only its particular means for creating structure, order, and changing effect, but also those means for creating structure that we take for granted in more familiar music. These examples, together with the ones from other cultures, should make clear, then, that music which depends on functional harmony for its underlying coherence actually belongs to a limited culture and to a limited historical tradition.

5.5

FUNCTIONAL HARMONY

With the next examples we ask you to narrow your focus to music that *does* operate within the framework of functional harmony. We will deal first with the contrasts between harmonic stability and instability. Then later in the chapter, when you have had some experience discriminating among these general harmonic functions, we will concentrate on the detailed and specific means that generate them.

Examples 5.6–5.12 illustrate three kinds of structural functions that tonal harmony can create: statement, stasis, and waiting. They are grouped together here because each of them depends for its effect on there being a single tonal center in relation to which all the events are heard. That is, each of the excerpts remains in one key. In this broader sense they are all harmonically stable. This broader sense of harmonic stability is reflected in your perception of clear and ordered direction in the music. You have the feeling of knowing where you are and what to expect. With this sense of orientation goes an intuitive awareness of tension and repose—harmonic movement away from the tonic, associated with tension, and harmonic rest when the tonic returns. That is, you can spontaneously recognize when a passage arrives at a point of rest or when it is still moving toward such a point.

Statement Passages

Example	Composer, title	Date
5.6	*Old Blue* (sung by Burl Ives)	
5.7	Weber, *Invitation to the Dance*	1819

In Chapter 3, we described the tonic as the pitch which gives a melody a sense of arrival. The chord which is built on this tonic note—the one which harmonizes, elaborates, or reinforces it—is called the tonic *triad*. We will return to a further discussion of triads in Demonstration 5-2. In Examples 5.6 and 5.7 you will hear only two chords: the tonic chord and, in contrast to it, the dominant chord built on the fifth degree of the scale. As you listen, notice that it is the movement from one to the other—the interaction between them—which creates both movement and rest within the framework of a single tonal center. The tonic always sounds relatively stable; the dominant, by contrast, provides movement away and the expectation of return once again to the tonic and rest. Examples 5.6 and 5.7 then, are straightforward, unambiguous *statements* created by the two basic *harmonic functions,* tonic and dominant, to which the term "functional harmony" most explicitly refers. Listen for the change from one chord to the other—tonic (at rest) and dominant (in motion).

Harmonic Stasis

Example	Composer, title	Date
5.8	Wagner, *Das Rheingold,* prelude	1854
5.9	Beethoven, *Symphony 3*, Op. 55, fourth movement	1803

While Examples 5.6 and 5.7 might be described as *statements* setting forth the stable and complementary relations between tonic and dominant chords, Examples 5.8 and 5.9 can be described as *static*. Both include simply an elaboration of the tonic harmony. But the *harmonic stasis* created by the use of one central chord functions rather differently in each piece. The Wagner example is the *beginning* of a dramatic work, and it sets the scene and mood as well as the central tonality. The Beethoven excerpt is the *ending* of a whole symphony; it brings the intense, rhythmically active final movement to an extended and solid conclusion.

Waiting Passages

Example	Composer, title	Date
5.10	Bach, *Brandenburg Concerto 5,* first movement	c. 1721
5.11	Beethoven, *Sonata for Piano,* Op. 31, no. 3, second movement	1802
5.12	Schubert, *Quintet in C,* Op. 163, second movement	1828

Examples 5.10 and 5.11 also make use of only one chord, but the difference between these two examples and Examples 5.8 and 5.9 is crucial, the effect almost opposite. Both Examples 5.10 and 5.11 are built on the dominant harmony in contrast to the tonic chord of Examples 5.8 and 5.9. The result is a sense of tension, but a tension that is clearly directed. You know where you are going tonally, and you sense a continuous build-up as you move unswervingly toward the inevitable goal—the tonic. Such passages, generating *directed tension,* function within the structure of the piece as *waiting passages.*

In the Bach excerpt the dominant tone is sounded by the cellos (and bass of the harpsichord) on the first beat of every measure (the first of every eight cello tones). Above this underlying dominant, the chords change every measure. Notice the fast moving right hand harpsichord figures and, especially, the trills in the flute and violin. And experience the resolution of tension with the return of the theme and the long awaited tonic.[1] In a somewhat analogous passage, though for solo piano, Beethoven prolongs the dominant harmony with rhythmic elaboration, leading to a return of the opening theme and the tonic harmony. An interesting and quite different dominant waiting passage can be heard in the *b* section of the jazz piece *Django* (Example 4.22).

Example 5.12 provides a transition between the broadly stable

[1] This is not the tonic of the piece, but of just this part of the piece.

harmony which results when a piece remains clearly centered in one key and the next group of examples, which are fundamentally less stable because they include a shift from one tonal center to another. As in the passages of directed tension, the harmony in the Schubert quintet creates an effect of search; but here the search seems endless, and one loses all sense of time. Although the harmony at times wanders (undirected), it repeatedly approaches a tonic cadence (directed tension), only to go on without reaching resolution. Finally the process is halted, not by arrival but by the appearance of a new element which is equally unstable. We have the feeling of being lost and searching for rest within a world of unending motion.

Changing Tonal Centers

In the next group of examples the general stability created by the consistent reference to a single tonal center gives way to a broader sense of movement and instability as the music shifts out of one key and into another. Just as the movement from tonic to dominant *chords* within the boundaries of one key creates contrast between motion and rest, so on a broader scale the movement from the frame of one whole *key area* with its particular tonal center to another whole key area with its new tonal center creates a more expanded motion and subsequent rest. Indeed, we can speak of levels of harmonic movement—*within* one key, where all chords are heard in relation to a single tonic, and *among* keys, where chords are heard first in relation to one tonal center and then, by a usually significant shift, in relation to another tonal center. Within the larger framework of tonality, then, these shifts create contrast, broad harmonic movement (change of key), ambiguity, and often greater intensity. Notice, however, that as with your response to rhythmic conflict (syncopation or shift of meter), your response to these moments of change or ambiguity is predicated on your assumption of a norm—in this case a normative "key feeling." In all these examples the composers either generate a clear tonal center (a harmonic norm) and then move away from it, or else imply one or more tonal centers but avoid explicitly establishing them. Such compositional means can create their desired effect only if you can assume and accept the tonal framework within which they operate.

Example	Composer, title	Date
5.13	Mahler, *Symphony 1,* second movement	1888
5.14	Johann Strauss, *Voices of Spring*	1868
5.15	Tchaikovsky, *Symphony 4,* second movement	1877

Examples 5.13–5.15, for instance, all move from one key to another, but they do so in different ways. In Example 5.13 the change is immediate. Mahler states his motive in one key, then immediately begins again with the same motive but in a new key. There is no transition, only juxtaposition.

In contrast, Example 5.14, an excerpt from Strauss's *Voices of Spring,* has a short but decisive transition which shifts the tonal center. The first two phrases (the second is somewhat extended) are clearly in one key, ending with a cadence on the tonic. This same chord which forms a tonic ending to the first portion is then transformed, through the addition of a pitch "foreign" to the initial key, so that the tonic becomes the dominant in the new key. The extension of this transformed chord—now functioning as a dominant—becomes the harmonic basis for a brief waiting passage that leads to the new melody and to the new tonic.

Putting this process another way, we might say that when the chord that functioned as the chief tonic chord (I) in the first part of the excerpt is dethroned by a "foreign" pitch (belonging, as it does, to a different tribe of pitches), it becomes second in rank (I becomes V) in the new collection of pitches, or new key. This single chord plays the role of "pivot" between the two tonalities, serving as the central chord of the first tonality and then, when transformed, as the dominant, foreshadowing chord of the second. After a short transition, the excerpt continues with a new melody in the new key. Can you hear the moment of change in this excerpt? Go back and try to sing the tonic during the first two phrases. Then try to sing the new tonic as the excerpt goes into the new melody, which ends (here) on the new tonic chord.

Example 5.15 resembles Example 5.14 in that you hear first one melody, then a transition where the tonal center shifts, and then a waiting passage which functions as a preparation for a new melody in a new key. But in the Tchaikovsky excerpt the transition takes longer. Where Strauss used a relatively abrupt pivot chord, Tchaikovsky moves more gradually from the first tonal area toward another. This process, called a *modulation,* creates a momentary tonal no-man's-land.

Notice that the first melody is heard twice: first played by bassoon and violas, then repeated an octave higher by the strings with added figuration in the winds. This shift in register should not be confused with modulation. In modulation the crucial factor is not a change in register but rather a change in both the fundamental set of pitches being used and the pitch that sounds most stable or central.

If you listen carefully to the excerpt, you will hear the modulation occurring during a sequential passage where each statement of the melodic fragment (♫ ♫ ♩ ♩ ♩) serves to shift and confound your sense of tonal direction. The modulation settles into a waiting passage where you hear the new dominant harmony extended through repetitions of a short melodic figure that again shifts only in register. The motive is played first by the flutes in a high register; then (descending in register) by the clarinet, the horn, and, in an abbreviated version, the violas; and finally by the cellos. The transition to the new key and new melody is very smooth. Your musical vantage point is gently eased from one view of the pitch universe to another.

Paris, Etoile
*A single tonal center . . . clear and ordered direction
. . . you have the feeling of knowing where you are.*

Boston, downtown section
*Tonal ambiguity . . .
you lose your sense of
orientation and direction.*

Chromaticism

Example	Composer, title	Date
5.16	Bach, *Well-Tempered Clavier*, Book I, fugue no. 24 in B minor	1722
5.17	Beethoven, *String Quartet*, Op. 133 (*Grosse Fuge*)	1825
5.18	Liszt, *Faust Symphony*, first movement	1854
5.19	Coltrane, *Giant Steps*	1959

In Examples 5.16 through 5.19, the tonal no-man's-land which characterized the transition between the two tonally stable statements in Example 5.15 becomes much more extensive—nearly all-pervasive. You hear long passages of tonal ambiguity. You lose the sense of orientation and direction created by the relation of all the pitches and chords to a single, central one—the tonic. Such dramatic moments are generated by the composer's use of pitches that belong to more than one "family" of pitches.

You will remember from Chapter 3 that major or minor scales (sometimes called *diatonic* scales) include a particular subset of the 12 possible pitches. Each of these collections of 7 pitches constitutes what we can call a *family*, each family of pitches centering around one particular pitch. There are 12 such families, each centering around one of the 12 possible pitches. Thus the key of C Major has C as its tonal center and includes the family of pitches found in the C Major scale. The key of B Major has B as its center and includes the family of pitches found in the B Major scale. In these passages of tonal ambiguity composers include pitches from more than one family, sometimes introducing all 12 possible pitches in close succession. In this way they upset your tonal equilibrium but also create a feeling of greater expressiveness as harmonic relationships take on new meaning and are enriched by new, sometimes not yet realized, possibilities. Such passages are described as *chromatic* (from the Greek *chroma*, or color) because of their use of all or most of the 12 pitches of the chromatic scale in contrast to the 7 pitches of a diatonic scale.

Listen, for example, to the Bach excerpt (Example 5.16) which is the first part of a fugue (see Example 1.11 and Chapter 7). It begins with a single unaccompanied melody, called the fugue *subject.* Try to sing the melody. You will probably find it difficult because while it begins with the pitches of the tonic triad, the subject quickly introduces all 12 tones of the chromatic scale and also modulates from the initial B minor to the key of F sharp minor.

Example 5.16 Bach, *Well-Tempered Clavier,* Book I, fugue no. 24

A second part then enters with essentially the same melody (though starting on a different tone), then a third, and finally a fourth part at the top of the texture. The very active texture complements the harmonically unstable (though periodically resolving) harmony.

Example 5.17, by Beethoven, sounds almost chaotic on first

hearing. Harmonically, the excerpt is an example of extreme chromaticism: At some moments we hear a series of shifting tonal centers, but at others tonality seems to be nearly obliterated. Listen to the example several times. Does it become less chaotic? What constitutes its means of achieving comprehensibility?

The beginning of Liszt's *Faust Symphony* (Example 5.18) was discussed in Chapter 3 in the context of melodies different from those we are used to. There we commented on the continuousness of the opening motive, itself created by the particular relationships among the pitches of the melody. We can now make these relationships more explicit. The four statements of the rising three-note motive form a *chromatically* descending sequence which includes all 12 pitches of the chromatic scale. The three-note motive itself confounds your sense of tonal center. The three pitches are equidistant—the distance of two whole steps. Together the three pitches of the motive form an *augmented* triad (see the Ancillary Reading for this chapter)—a triad that does not exist within the family of pitches belonging to any one major scale.

Example 5.18 Liszt, *Faust Symphony,* opening theme

The transformations of this germinal motive form the fundamental material for the rest of the passage. Note the elusiveness of the beat and meter, the large range, the big melodic leaps (often contrasted with half-step motion), and the limpid sound of solo woodwinds or of strings playing in unison. The diabolical character of the piece (Faust makes a pact with the devil) can be directly related to these rhythmic, melodic, and sound relationships as well as to the continuously moving and shifting tonal framework.

John Coltrane, who wrote *Giant Steps,* plays it here on the tenor saxophone. The piece probably derives its title from the unusual chord progression with which the piece begins and which then serves as the basis for Coltrane's improvisation. It is chromatic and seems to go on without end, without a stable center, a place of rest. Yet how different it is from the previous three chromatic examples. Why? Obviously instrumentation and rhythm are crucial factors.

Structural Functions of Harmony

Example	Composer, title	Date
5.20	Chopin, *Étude*, Op. 10, no. 3	1832

5.20   In the Chopin *Étude* (one of many "studies" Chopin wrote for the piano) we hear a piece with the familiar ABA′ structure—statement, contrasting middle section, and return. But in this piece Chopin creates contrast by dramatically introducing chromatic harmony into an initially straightforward tonal setting. The

John Coltrane
playing the soprano saxophone

piece begins with two statements of the opening melody accompanied in the lower part (played by the pianist's left hand) by a somewhat syncopated repeated rhythmic figure. The second statement reaches a brief climax and then subsides into a cadence on the tonic.

The middle section begins slightly faster as the piece becomes somewhat more agitated. This increase in intensity is created also by movement away from the stable tonality. Chopin passes through several new key areas repeating the same musical material in each one. This is followed by a slow build-up to the climax of the whole *Étude*. In the process we lose all sense of clear melody as the pianist plays only chords; at the same time we lose all sense of tonal center as the harmony becomes highly chromatic. The chords are themselves ambiguous; neither major nor minor, they seem to defy direction or specific implications for resolution.[2] In addition, Chopin repeats the same ambiguous chord in continuously ascending and descending chromatic steps, up and down the piano keyboard.

The grand climax subsides as the tempo again slows down, and we hear hints of the initial melodic material. The harmonic motion once more becomes clear and directed as Chopin arrives at and extends the dominant harmony to create a waiting passage—a preparation for return. Harmonic tension is finally resolved as we return to the opening melodic material harmonized by the tonic chord calmly alternating with its dominant, each reaffirming the other. The *Étude* concludes with a quiet cadence on the tonic chord which is briefly extended as the melody also descends to the tonic note.

This *Étude* is a beautiful example of the use of harmony to create *structural* functions—statement, ambiguity and climax, wait-

---

[2] Like the successive pitches in the Liszt melody, these chords are made up of simultaneously sounding pitches separated by equal intervals. They are called *diminished seventh chords* (see Ancillary Reading), where each pitch of the chord is a minor third away from each other pitch. Interestingly, this is the chord often used in the past in movies when the situation gets frightening or dangerous— most typically when the "bad guy" enters the scene.

ing, and return. Each of these structural functions is largely dependent for its effect on the *harmonic* functions defined by the network of relations we call tonality. While its workings may seem complex when analyzed and spelled out in words, it is a kind of "grammar" that everyone in our culture seems to learn and respond to as spontaneously (and remarkably) as the grammar of our own spoken language. We will return to the structural functions of harmony in Demonstration 5-3.

Demonstration 5-2

FUNDAMENTALS OF TONAL HARMONY

Now that you have had some experience listening to relations within (and without) tonal harmony, we ask you to consider in greater detail factors that generate these tonal relationships. Unfortunately, constraints on recording space-time limit us to discussion only here. It is important therefore that you go back and listen to the examples in Demonstration 5-1 again as well as those which follow in order to bring to life the theoretical discussion in this Demonstration.

The basic building block of tonal harmony is the *triad*. A triad is a chord made up of three tones (*tri*-ad). Strictly speaking, a triad is a chord built up in a particular way from its lowest tone called the *root*. The term *root* derives from the notion of a root-tone from which the triad grows. More exactly, the root of a triad is the note which the triad elaborates, reinforces, or extends. A triad can be built on any degree of the scale, each triad elaborating that particular degree:

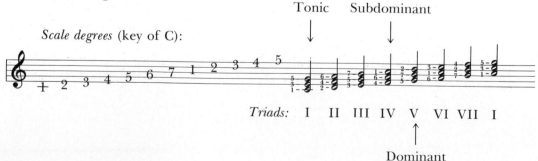

The triad is built by adding to its root the pitches which lie a third and fifth above it in the scale. For example, the tonic triad, or I, is built on the 1st degree of the scale. Its root is the tonic note and above it are added the 3rd and 5th degrees of the scale. The dominant triad, or V, is built on the 5th degree of the scale. Its root is the 5th degree and above it are added the 7th and 2nd (or 9th) degrees of the scale. (Notice that scale degrees are represented by arabic numerals while triads are represented by roman numerals.) The notated triad when in root position (that is, with the root pitch as its lowest tone) forms a pattern of notes all of which are either on lines or in spaces.

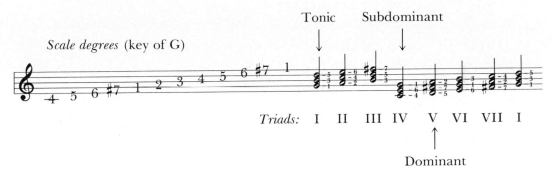

As you have heard (Examples 5.6 and 5.7), the tonic and dominant triads, along with the subdominant triad built on the 4th degree of the scale, form the pillars of tonality. Notice that the root of the V chord is an interval of a fifth *above* the I chord while the root of the IV chord is an interval of a fifth *below* the I chord (giving it the name *sub*dominant, meaning *under*-dominant.) It is the relationships among chords as they progress from one to the next that establishes our sense of tonal center. Any triad by itself is ambiguous in its tonal function or meaning. Only when we hear two or more triads can we be sure which one is the most stable—the one to which we will give the name *tonic*. It is these relationships, then, which establish a particular tonal context, the *key.*

Throughout the book we have emphasized the importance of context in giving meaning to an event. In discussing sound and texture we heard how the same melody can sound quite different

The same figure or chord will sound quite different when embedded in different environments.

when embedded in a new sound context (Examples 1.8-1.11, for instance). In discussing melody we noticed that the same motive or figure could sound quite different when it occurred at a different place in a tune and with a different function. For example, the same motive which *ends* the first phrase of *Lassie* (". . .a lassie, a lassie") sounds different when it functions as the *beginning* of the *b* section ("Go this way and that way"). In similar fashion the same chord will sound quite different when embedded in different tonal environments. The name given to a triad—tonic, dominant —names its harmonic function. However, the same triad can function as a tonic in one key and the dominant in another. For example, the C triad will be called the tonic when it functions as the most stable chord in the key of C, but it will be called the dominant when heard in the key of F, or the subdominant if it is heard in relation to G as the tonic:

Key of G: I 2 3 IV V 6 7 1   I   = Tonic

Key of G: 1 2 3 IV V 6 7 I   IV   = Subdominant

Key of F: 1 2 3 IV V 6 7 I   V   = Dominant

In listening to music we respond most readily to these tonal functions—for example, the sense of waiting and its associated tension in Examples 5.10–5.12 where we hear predominantly dominant-function chords, in contrast to Examples 5.8 and 5.9 where we hear predominantly tonic-function chords. In fact, two triads that have the same function but different pitches (two tonics) may sound more similar than two triads that have exactly the same pitches but different functions. It is precisely this chameleon-like quality of chords to take on meaning according to their harmonic environment that makes it possible for composers to shift or slide so smoothly from one key to another. For example, in the Strauss, *Voices of Spring* (Example 5.14) a single triad functions at one moment as the tonic and in the next moment as the dominant.

The word *function* is used in several different but interrelated ways in this chapter and in music theory generally. To help prevent understandable confusion about the use of this word, two distinct uses of it should be clarified. In Demonstration 5-1 we used the word *function* to refer to the *structural functions* of certain passages (statement, stasis, waiting). The structural function of a passage, then, can be described as the particular role the passage plays in a whole piece. (We will return to this sense of structural function in Chapter 6.) In this Demonstration we are speaking of the *harmonic function* of a particular chord within the framework of a given tonality. The interaction between two chords, the movement from one to the other, usually defines the function of each. For example, hearing one chord (perhaps a C chord) in juxtaposition with another chord (a G chord) allows us to label one (C) as tonic and the other (G) as dominant. It is a reciprocal relation, like friendship or an argument—you need a two-way interaction to define each member.

There is an important connection between structural functions and harmonic functions. A passage which functions as a statement within a piece will often include only tonic and dominant harmonic functions. Thus, the two uses of the word are related like means and ends: the use of only tonic and dominant harmonic functions is a means toward the end of creating a passage which has a stable structural function within the piece as a whole. This relation of means and ends will be developed at greater length in Demonstration 5-3 (see also the discussion of the Chopin étude on p. 188).

Returning now to the fundamentals of tonal harmony, notice that the interval of a fifth plays a special role within this framework. Its importance can be seen on the smallest and the largest levels of musical structure. For example, the triad, the basic element of the harmonic framework, is outlined or bounded by the interval of a fifth. Chords whose roots are related by fifths (IV-I-V) are pillars within a tonality, they establish the *key* of a piece (in many ways, the key *to* the piece). Fifths also define the harmonic "distance" *among* keys. For instance, keys related by the interval of a fifth (C-G-D, and so forth) are most closely related because their pitch collections differ only by one pitch. The so-called circle-of-fifths shows the harmonic distance among all the keys (see p. 142 for a picture of the circle of fifths). Any two keys next to one another around the circle are most closely related; they share six pitches and four triads in common.

Composers make use of closely related keys to create both unity and variety in larger pieces. For example, at the end of the *a* section of a minuet (see Chapter 6) there is often a *modulation* to the closely related key of the dominant—that is, from C to G or from A to E and so forth. The change in tonal center creates variety while still maintaining unity through the shared pitches and triads among these closely related keys. Similarly, the second group in the exposition of a sonata form movement is usually in the key of the dominant (see Chapter 6); the second entrance of the subject in a fugal exposition is also in the dominant (see Chapter 7). We can even construct the notes of a major scale by moving around the circle-of-fifths. For example, F-C-G-D-A-E-B gives us the pitch collection of the C major scale. In fact, from the point of view of harmonic relations, this is a more meaningful description of the pitch collection than simply the arrangement of these pitches from low to high as in the scale. Finally, most folk songs and much of jazz and rock use primarily I, IV, and V chords to harmonize their melodies. In Demonstration 5-4 you will hear a number of twelve-bar blues. A particular sequence of I, IV, and V chords forms the harmonic skeleton for all of them.

Having set forth some of the general aspects of the tonal framework, we list below further components and possibilities composers and performers use to flesh out or expand these basic tonal relationships.

Inversion: A rearrangement of the pitches of a triad so that the root is no longer the lowest tone:

C-triad   F-triad

Root   1st inversion   2nd inversion   Root   1st inversion   2nd inversion

Interestingly, Rameau, an eighteenth-century composer and theorist, was the first to observe systematically that even when the pitches of a given root position triad are rearranged (as in an inversion), the resulting chord can still be considered "the same" as when it is in root position. That is, it was Rameau who developed a theoretical framework in which this rearrangment of the same pitches could be considered an inversion of a single, fundamental chord. Along with this came Rameau's systematic description of triads in terms of their root functions—that is, the use of roman numerals to represent the harmonic function of a chord in terms of its root. The illustration above shows you the three possible positions or rearrangements of a triad. Notice that inversions allow composers to create contrast even *within* a single triad or harmonic function. For example, a I chord in first inversion will be somewhat less stable, less solidly I than the same chord in root position. In the Haydn minuet from the *Symphony 100,* for instance (see the score on p. 205), only root position chords are used in the opening statement section (except for one inversion in measure 7). Later, in the *b* section where Haydn begins to develop his material, we find him also using more inversions—in measure 18, for example, where we hear an inversion on a strongly accented event.

Arpeggio or broken chord: The notes of a triad played one after the other rather than played simultaneously:

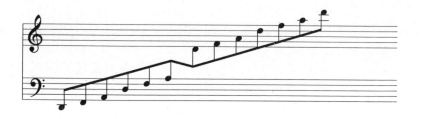

A triad can be animated or stretched out through time and pitch-space in this fashion. A good example of this stretching out of a triad is the opening of Wagner's opera, *Das Rheingold* (Example 5.8). You hear first simply a single, long sustained tone played by the string basses, and then gradually the other pitches of the triad emerge over this initial root tone. The whole passage is an extension of that root tone through its triad. In the next example (Example 5.9) you hear Beethoven stretching out the closing tonic triad over several octaves and considerable time to bring the movement to a resounding close. On a much more detailed level, broken chords are often used as the basis for common accompaniment figures. For example, in the minuet from Haydn's *Symphony 100,* again, the second violins and cellos play a broken chord figure in measures 9 and 10. In this way Haydn creates a more animated version of the opening passage found in measures 1 and 2 where the same tonic triad is played as a simple chord, a group of simultaneously sounding tones.

Full Cadence: The progression from the dominant chord to the tonic chord at the end of a phrase.

Half Cadence: The use of the dominant chord at the end of a phrase. For example, in the song "Old Blue" (Example 5.6) the first phrase ends with a half cadence (". . . and his name was Blue"). The word *Blue* is harmonized by a V chord. The second phrase ("And I betcha five dollars he's a good one, too") ends with a full cadence. The entire second phrase is harmonized by the V chord followed by the I chord on the last word, *too.* The contrast between full and half cadences is usually quite obvious since the full cadence sounds more complete and more stable than the half cadence which sounds incomplete and less stable. See also the discussion of phrase structure and cadences in Chapter 3, especially the discussion of the Mozart piano sonata theme. The exercise on full and half cadences (pp. 202–204) will give you practice in hearing the difference between the two kinds of cadences, and perhaps more importantly, give you some good, clear examples of what the terms refer to.

Consonance and Dissonance: The terms consonance and dissonance refer most specifically to the relationships between two pitches—the interval formed by the two pitches. In traditional tonal theory intervals are classified as either consonant or dissonant (although the classification has changed through the course of history, along with changing musical styles). For example, intervals of a third, fifth, sixth, and octave are usually considered consonant, while intervals of a second, fourth, and seventh are usually considered dissonant. (For further discussion of intervals see the Ancillary Reading for Chapters 3 and 5.) However, the terms also refer more generally to harmonic movement within the context of a particular piece or even a particular style. This usage of the terms is much more difficult to define. A description of its meaning (rather than a definition) must include the notion that consonances tend to be stable, even conclusive, while dissonances tend to be dynamic, in need of resolution. This more general sense of consonant and dissonant is related to another use of the terms which is widespread but often misapplied. With this usage the term consonant tends to be associated with "pleasing," while dissonant is associated with "disagreeable," "harsh," or even "incoherent." For example, to describe a whole piece as sounding dissonant or sometimes "unharmonious," is to refer, most likely, to its general harmonic framework when that framework is something other than a tonal one. You might be tempted, for instance, to call the Boulez piece (Example 5.5) dissonant. In terms of tonal harmony it does, in fact, make use of traditionally dissonant intervals and few simple triads. But, as we have pointed out, the means Boulez uses for creating contrasts in stability and instability are not based on the assumptions of tonal or functional harmony. Thus, to describe the whole piece as dissonant is to describe it in terms of a harmonic framework which does not apply. Further, the description will tend to befog the underlying bases for comprehensibility and coherence which Boulez and other twentieth-century composers have established.

Transposition: The process of rewriting a melody (or a whole passage) so as to keep the successive relationships the same but making use of a different set of absolute pitches. Or putting it another way, if we play a melody in the key of C and play the same melody in the key of B, we will keep the intervals between pitches the same and the scale degrees the same but these same numbers will now refer to different pitches. For example, *Lassie* begins with a broken tonic triad—the scale degrees, 1-3-5, followed by 6, and then a return to the starting tonic, 5-4-3-1, again basically outlining the tonic triad. No matter what pitch we begin with, as long as we agree that it is the tonic, thus calling it 1, the subsequent scale degrees will be the same. However, if we name the pitches, instead of the scale degrees, we will find that the two versions of the same tune look different. Thus a transposed melody is both the same (in interval relations) and different (in actual pitches) from its initial statement:

Lassie:	1-	3-	5-	6-	5-	4-	3-	1
C:	C-	E-	G-	A-	G-	F-	E-	C
B:	B-	D♯-	F♯-	G♯-	F♯-	E-	D♯-	B
F:	F-	A-	C-	D-	C-	B♭-	A-	F

Scale degrees: **(key of C)**

Pitch material reordered:

1 3 5 6 5 4 3 1 1 2 5 5 3 1 1 3 5 6 5 4 3 1 1 2 5 5 1   5 6 (7) 1 2 3 4 5 6 7 1

Tonic Dominant

Scale degrees: **(key of B)**

1 3 5 6 5 4 3 1 1 2 5 5 3 1 1 3 5 6 5 4 3 1 1 2 5 5 1   5 6 (7) 1 2 3 4 5 6 7 1

Tonic Dominant

If one were actually to write this melody in B major, the sharps would be assimilated into the key signature as shown here:

Exercise 5-1

Major and Minor; Full and Half Cadences (Side 7)

This exercise has a somewhat different purpose from Exercise 4-1. The earlier exercise was intended as an initial step toward your discovery of structure. This exercise, coming after you have had some experience with musical organization (return, sectional and continuous structure, and harmony) is intended simply to give you practice in hearing two rather specific aspects of harmony: (1) major and minor modes and (2) phrases which end either on the tonic (full cadence) or on the dominant (half cadence).

Major and Minor

In Chapter 3 (p. 119 and Ancillary Reading) we briefly discussed the difference between the major and minor modes. You may remember that the essential difference between the two modes lies in the third degree of the scale: While the third degree is a *major* third above the tonic (two whole steps) in the major mode, it is a *minor* third above the tonic (a whole step plus a half step) in the minor mode. Or, putting it more simply, the third degree of the scale is a half step closer to the tonic in the minor mode than it is in the major mode. The tonic *triad,* which involves this third degree, is therefore also different in major and minor. The Ancillary

Tonic Triad in C Major   Tonic Triad in C Minor

Reading sections for Chapter 3 and for this chapter show the various forms of minor scales as well as the resultant triads.

The following exercises will give you some practice in distinguishing between pieces in the major and minor modes. While pieces in major and minor do indeed sound different, no rules can be given for acquiring the ability to distinguish between them; we might compare the problem to finding rules for distinguishing between red and pink. In fact, the difference between major and minor is like a change in the color of a tonality, for it is not a change in the key, or the tonal center itself. (Often, though not always, the effect of major is happy, that of minor, sad.) Learning to distinguish between colors or between modes comes basically from experience and practice. In the case of the modes, it is useful to be able to *hear* the difference (particularly as a source of contrast within a piece). Naming that difference is simply a way of focusing your attention on it.

Listen to each example and determine whether the piece is in the major or minor mode, or whether it changes from one to the other during its course.

Example	Major	Minor	Major → minor	Minor → major
5.21		✓		
5.22	✓			
5.23		✓		
5.24			✓	
5.25				✓
5.26			✓	

CORRECT ANSWERS

Example	Composer, title, date	Major	Minor	Major → minor	Minor → major
5.21			X		
5.22	Mozart, *Sonata for Piano in A,* K. 331, first movement, 1778	X			
5.23	Mozart, *Sonata for Piano in A,* K. 331, first movement, 1778		X		
5.24	Beethoven, *Violin Concerto,* Op. 61, first movement, 1809			X	
5.25	Schumann, *Album for the Young,* "The Wild Horseman," 1848				X
5.26	Schubert, *Die Schöne Müllerin,* "Tränenregen" ("Rain of Tears"), 1823			X	

Full and Half Cadences

In this group of examples you are asked to discriminate between phrases which end on the tonic (I)—a full cadence—and phrases which end on the dominant (V)—a half cadence. The significant factor in this perception is the feeling of stability or completion in the full cadence in contrast with that of incompletion or of being left suspended in the half cadence. You should go back and refer to the discussion of *Lassie* in Chapter 3 and also the Mozart sonata theme, where this distinction was illustrated through melodic aspects alone. However, melody and harmony are inextricably interrelated in tonal music; thus the sense of incompleteness of an antecedent phrase results from the absence of the tonic in both melody and harmony at the cadence, while the consequent phrase ends solidly on the tonic.

Guitarists know about the two chords I and V, usually either in D Major (D = I, A = V) or A Major (A = I, E = V). A song like *Clementine*, for example, uses only these two chords: beginning on the tonic, reaching the dominant on "Clemen-TINE," staying
$$V$$
there until "for-GOT-ten," then to V and back to I at the end. In
$$I$$
general, it is important to remember that while a piece need not begin with the tonic harmony it almost always ends with it.

Listen to each of the examples and determine if the excerpt ends on the tonic (full cadence) or on the dominant (half cadence).

Example	Tonic (I)	Dominant (V)
5.27	✓	
5.28		✓
5.29	✓	
5.30		✓
5.31		✓
5.32	✓	

CORRECT ANSWERS

Example	Composer, title, date	Tonic (I)	Dominant (V)
5.27	Brahms, *Variations on a Theme by Haydn,* Op. 56a, 1873	X*	
5.28	Haydn, *Symphony 104,* first movement, 1795		X*
5.29	Beethoven, *Septet,* Op. 20, third movement, 1800	X	
5.30	M. Reynolds, *Little Boxes* (sung by Pete Seeger), 1962		X
5.31	Bach, *Suite in B Minor,* minuet, c. 1721		X*
5.32	Schubert, *Die Schöne Müllerin,* Der Muller und der Bach (The Miller and the Brook), 1823	X	

* Phrases do not end on the first beat of the measure.

Demonstration 5-3

HARMONY: STRUCTURAL FUNCTIONS   (Side 7)

We will now turn to a Haydn minuet in order to show how harmony serves various structural functions. The written material requires very close reading, and even more important, the analysis demands that you listen very closely to the music. You should go back and play the examples a number of times. The score is printed on the following pages, and will aid you in the discussion.

Example	Composer, Title	Date
5.33	Haydn, *Symphony 100,* third movement, minuet	1794
5.34	*a* section of minuet	
5.35	*a'* section	
5.36	*b* section	
5.37	*b* section (measures 17–35)	
5.38	*b* section with artificially imposed return	
5.39	*b* section with return as Haydn wrote it	

Example 5.33 Haydn, *Symphony 100*, Third Movement (Minuet)

The overall structure can be diagramed as follows: $a \quad a'\|{:}b + a''{:}\|$ It is essentially an expanded version of the structure heard in the Mozart *Eine kleine Nachtmusik* minuet (Example 4.10). In this Haydn minuet, however, the parts are all expanded; in addition, instead of being literally repeated, the first *a* section is repeated with varied instrumentation and dynamics.

Listen to the *a* section alone (Example 5.34). There are two balanced phrases, the first moving from the tonic to the dominant (half cadence), and the second moving from the dominant back to the tonic (full cadence). Notice that the *harmonic rhythm*—the rate at which the chords change—speeds up in the second phrase: One chord remains for two bars in the first phrase, and there are one or two chords in each bar in the second. The effect is of an acceleration toward the end of the period. In addition, the harmony in the second phrase is enriched by the use of chords other than I and V. Listen to the varied repetition of *a* (*a'*) (Example 5.35), noting particularly the differences between the two phrases. The changes of harmony and harmonic rhythm are indicated in Diagram 1.

Diagram 1

First phrase   *Second phrase*

Listen now to the *b* section of the minuet (Example 5.36). Notice that the balanced phrase structure of section *a* is no longer present in *b*, and that the *b* section is longer than *a*. We hear fragments treated sequentially, there is a more active texture (two rhythmically independent lines), and later in *b* there is a momentary shift in meter.

In *b* then, a fragment of the theme (♪ ♩ ♫ ♩ ♪) becomes a building block for sequential development; this process contrasts

---

* Means V of VI, that is, the dominant of VI; since in this example VI is E minor, this chord is B⁷.

with the regular, balanced phrases of *a*. As a result *b* is more continuous. For example, there is a continuously directed motion
without any caesura, until the twelfth measure of section *b* (bar
20), in contrast to the cadences which occur every four measures
in section *a*.

Listen to the first portion of *b* more closely (bars 17–35),
trying to discover what means Haydn uses to generate continuousness, tension, and contrast through the development of material
heard previously in *a*. There are three phases in the motion to the
cadence in the twelfth measure of *b*, and a fourth phase which extends this cadence. What are the differences in effect and in the
means used in these four phases (Example 5.37)?

The first phase has a wandering effect—we momentarily lose
our bearings, we are in flux (*b*, measures 17–20). In addition, the
texture is polyphonic (while in *a* there was a melody and subordinate accompaniment): Notice the tension between the top part,
played by the first violins (doubled by the oboe), and the lowest
part (violas and cellos, then cellos and basses). Following this, we
sense, in Phase 2, a more directed tension (*b*, measures 21–24), and
in Phase 3 the resolution of this tension in a cadence (*b*, measures
25–28). Finally, in Phase 4, we hear a kind of stasis (*b*, measures
29–35).

The harmonic means contributing to these changing effects
are the following: In Phase 1 tonality is shifting (a mixed family
of pitches); in Phase 2, the establishment of the new key, first by
an emphasis on its dominant—a waiting passage; then, in Phase
3, through a cadential passage which has as its goal the solid arrival
at the tonic, a full cadence in the new key. In Phase 4 the new tonic
is extended by its reiteration in the bass with chord changes over
it, some of them distrubing the stability of the new key. In addition, the stability of Phase 4 is weakened by an active texture and
rhythmic conflict. Notice, for example, that the opening motive of
a appears in truncated form in both the upper and lower parts of
the texture in imitation. This results in a shift to duple meter,
which conflicts with the prevailing triple meter and also sets up a

cross-accent as the two fragments oppose one another. Following Diagram 2, listen to this part of section *b* once more (Example 5.37). Comparisons among the four phases are summarized in Table 1.

Diagram 2

Phase 1	Phase 2	Phase 3	Phase 4
Shifting tonality	V becomes tonic (waiting)	V-I in new key	Extension of new tonic

Table 1

Phases:	1	2–3	4
Affect:	Instability, flux	Directed tension, then release	Stability (shaky)
Means:	Shifting tonality	Extended V of new key, then resolution to I of new key	Pedal on new tonic with chord changes above it
Structural function:	Modulation to the key of the dominant; tonic (G) → dominant (D)	Arrival at contrasting key area (D)	Confirmation of contrasting key area

Thus, this passage from *b* creates a motion from the tonic (I) in the *a* section to the dominant (V) in the *b* section on the larger level of tonal centers themselves. In the *a* section a single tonal center was established through the movement of chords within that one key: I to V and back to I. Now, on a larger scale, and over a longer period of time, a harmonic motion has been generated from a key which we called the tonic to another key which we had previously heard as a dominant. In *a* we spoke of being *on* the dominant chord (at the end of Phrase 1); in *b* this same chord has become a tonic, and we speak of being *in* the dominant key. We have modulated from G to D (cf. Example 5.15), and Phase 1 is our "tonal no-man's-land."

We have hinted, however, that in Phase 4 the new key is not quite solidly established; there is still a certain restlessness—both in rhythm and in key. (Are we *on* the dominant or *in* the dominant?) In any case the dominant (key or chord) must resolve ultimately to the original tonic. Indeed, the return could take place at this point. Listen to how the *b* section would sound if *a* did return after Phase 4 of the *b* section (Example 5.38). Then listen to what Haydn actually does (Example 5.39). What is the difference?

In our artificial return the structural rhythm is speeded up; *b* is shortened and is not allowed to unwind itself gradually. Haydn, in contrast, slips back into *a* through a highly chromatic, unstable passage which even at its end generates a rather fuzzy "waiting passage," Phase 5. Thus Haydn has composed a kind of musical joke by preparing us for a return at the end of Phase 4 of *b* and then diverting this expectation with the sliding, modulatory, delaying passage which eases back to the tonic key and to the return of the thematic statement of *a*. Our feelings about the return itself are also different in Examples 5.38 and 5.39. The abrupt juxtaposition of *b* and *a* in Example 5.38 simply puts us down into the stability of *a*'s statement; in Example 5.39 the clarity and stability of key, phrase structure, texture, and rhythm in *a″* constitute not only a return to familiar material but a return to the comfort of stability after a period of feeling "Where am I? Where am I going?" In short, Haydn provides us with a more dramatic contrast than exists if we bypass Phase 5.

Listen now to the whole minuet (Example 5.33). You will notice that *a* returns with still further changes in instrumentation and with the addition of a coda. Comparing it with the minuet from Mozart's *Eine kleine Nachtmusik* (Example 4.10), you will notice that this Haydn minuet has a considerably more dramatic effect. While the *b* section of the Mozart remained fixed harmonically and only hinted at a contrast in key area, this minuet, in its considerably lengthened *b* section, introduces modulation into a new key, establishes it (although we have some doubts in retrospect), and then wends its way back to the original key. Thus, the Haydn minuet is more dramatic; as you become aware of its details you respond to its greater variety of emotions over a longer period, but still this is variety on a small scale.

Demonstration 5-4

THE TWELVE-BAR BLUES (Side 8)

> What I think about that makes the blues really good is when a fellow writes a blues and then writes it with a feeling, with great harmony, and there are so many true words in the blues, of things that have happened to so many people, and that's why it makes the feeling in the blues.[2]
>
> J. D. SHORT

Now that you have had some experience with harmony, both on the level of the individual chord and in larger dimensions, you can listen with new insight to the following group of pieces, all of which are based on a chord progression involving basically only the I (tonic), IV (subdominant), and V (dominant) chords.

Example	Composer, title	Date
5.40	J. Yancey, *How Long Blues*	1943
5.41	J. Wood, *Mean Old Bedbug Blues* (sung by Bessie Smith)	1927
5.42	B. Holiday, *Fine and Mellow*	1939
5.43	L. Armstrong, *Muggles*	1928
5.44	C. Parker, *Relaxin' at Camarillo*	1947
5.45	King and Josea, *Be Careful With a Fool* (sung by J. Winter)	1969

---

[2] J. D. Short, as quoted in Samuel Charters, *The Poetry of the Blues* (New York: Avon Books, 1963), p. 17.

In *How Long Blues* (Example 5.40) you hear a series of variations on a theme. The pianist was improvising, and thus there was no fixed number of variations. When this recording was made in 1943, the three-minute 78 rpm record would have been the sole determinant of the number of variations. The theme on which the pianist improvised is the following basic harmonic progression:[3]

$$| \quad I \quad | \quad I^7 \quad | \quad IV \quad | \quad IV \quad | \quad I \quad | \quad V \quad | \quad I \quad | \quad I \quad |$$

---

[3] In the progression, $I^7 = V^7$ of IV, or V^7/IV. That is, adding the flatted seventh degree of the scale to the tonic chord (I) transforms the function of the chord into the dominant (V^7) of the IV chord:

See also Example 5.14 (*Voices of Spring*), where the same progression is used by Strauss to get from one key area to another and from the first to the second theme.

A "jam session" with
Al Cohn on tenor sax.

A simple bass accompaniment played by the pianist's left hand outlines the basic triads, and over this accompaniment you hear a free melodic improvisation.

The basic blues progression, however, is a twelve-bar progression, much more common than the eight bars of *How Long Blues.* The next five examples are all twelve-bar blues, spanning a period of about 50 years. You will hear vocal and instrumental blues, slow and fast blues, music of different styles and periods. At the same time you should gain a feeling for the intimate relationship between harmony and phrase structure in tonal music.

Listen to Example 5.41, which is sung by Bessie Smith, one of the great singers in the early history of jazz. If you analyze the melody, you will hear that each phrase is four measures long and that three phrases (one for each line of text) constitute a stanza or chorus. There are twelve bars in all—thus the "twelve-bar blues". Generally in vocal blues, as in these, the singer ends the phrase at the beginning of the third measure, leaving almost two full measures for the instrumentalists to fill in. The phrases relate to each other in both text and melody as *a a' b:*

a Bedbugs as big as a jackass will bite you and stand and grin, [instrumental]
    I   **I**   **I**   **I**

a' Bedbugs as big as a jackass will bite you and stand and grin; [instrumental]
   IV   **IV**   **I**   **I**

b We'll trick all those bedbugs 'fore them turn around and bite you again.[4] [instrumental]
   V   **V**   **I**   **I**

This constitutes only the first verse, or stanza; there are three stanzas, but the last is only eight bars long. Listen to the example again, this time concentrating on the harmonic underpinning, or chord progression. Notice that although the text and melody are essentially the same in the first two phrases (*a* and *a'*), the har-

---

[4] *Mean Old Bedbug Blues,* lyrics and music by Jack Wood. © Copyright 1927 by Jack Wood. © Copyright renewed by Jack Wood.

mony is different. You will feel the changes as the second phrase
(*a'*) begins. The progression of the twelve-bar blues can be represented in its essential form as follows:

	a				a'				b		
I	**I**	**I**	**I**	**IV**	**IV**	**I**	**I**	**V**	**V**	**I**	**I** $\quad$ **V**[5]
1	2	3	4	5	6	7	8	9	10	11	12

Can you hear the difference between the IV → I progression
in *a'* and the V → I progression in *b*? It is the V chord that gives
the final phrase in each stanza not only its conclusiveness but also
its fresh quality (which always coincides with the fresh words of the
b text). To hear this harmonic progression clearly, listen to the
piece several times and concentrate on the instrumental accompaniment. Finally, listen to the piece once again, focusing on what is
most important—the singer herself.

In Billie Holiday's blues (Example 5.42), recorded 12 years
later than *Mean Old Bedbug Blues*, the fundamental twelve-bar
blues pattern is the same, but there are slight differences (in addition to those resulting from the more advanced recording techniques). We hear first a four-measure introduction on tonic harmony played by the saxophones, which first repeat a one-measure
motive, then compress it, and then restore it to its original form.
Billie Holiday comes in after the muted trumpet, singing:

a My man don't love me, treats me oh so mean;   [instrumental]

  I   **IV**   **I**   **I**

a' My man he don't love me, treats me awful mean;   [instrumental]

  IV   **IV**   **I**   **I**

b He's the lowest man that I've ever seen.[6]   [instrumental]

   V   **V**   **I IV**   **I**

---

[5] The V at the end leads into the next chorus.

[6] Copyright Edward B. Marks Music Corporation. Used by permission.

Listen closely to the harmony, which is essentially as follows:

	a				*a'*				*b*		
I	**IV**	**I**	**I**⁷	**IV**	**IV**	**I**	**I**	**V**	**V**	**I IV**	**I**
1	2	3	4	5	6	7	8	9	10	11	12

How does this harmony compare with that in Bessie Smith's blues? With the exceptions of measures two and eleven, the chords are the same. Although you probably cannot identify all the chords in this piece, you should be able to hear how the basic progression and its subtle variations relate to the organization of the text into lines and stanzas. There are three stanzas in this excerpt. Listen several times, comparing Billie Holiday's blues with Bessie Smith's more prototypical version.

Now listen to Louis Armstrong's *Muggles* (Example 5.43). In this instrumental blues, the musicians take the fundamental twelve-bar blues progression as the basis for extended improvisation. There are five variations on a theme here, the theme being not a melody but the basic blues harmonic progression. In a live performance the players might have continued to improvise on the blues progression for a half hour or more.

Muggles begins with solo piano, not playing a theme but rather improvising on the tacitly understood blues progression. The pianist, Earl Hines, plays around with the chords and their rhythmic placement in an interesting way. Then a solo trombone, clarinet, and trumpet (Louis Armstrong) each, in turn, plays a chorus; Armstrong plays two and surpasses by far the trombone and clarinet. Notice how Armstrong enters in the last two bars of the clarinet solo with an excitingly syncopated ascent, as the orchestra goes into double time behind him with sustained chords. Armstrong reiterates the tonic note, jumping up and down the octave and subtly varying the syncopated patterns.

In improvisation creative musicians play around even with

the given material (the constant), so the blues progression is still more varied in this example than it was in the two previous ones. Nevertheless, the piece still retains its essential I → IV → I → V → I progression. Listen to how beautifully Louis Armstrong plays with the larger structural rhythm. Although he never loses sight of the twelve-bar phrase rhythm, always coming out right, he freely weaves his way between and around both the metric and the harmonic downbeats—the returns to the tonic in measures 3 and 7, the motion to IV in measure 5, and the return to I in measure 11. The actual harmonic progression of *Muggles* is roughly:[7]

a				*a'*				*b*			
I	II⁷ V⁷	I	I⁷	IV	IV (minor)	I	I V♭9/II	II⁷	II⁷ V⁷	I IV	I V
1	2	3	4	5	6	7	8	9	10	11	12

Those of you who have had some experience playing the twelve-bar blues might like to compare the progression in Example 5.43 with the essential blues progression given for Example 5.41. Even if you cannot hear each individual chord change, listen very carefully, and try to follow the fundamental progression in the twelve-bar structure: to IV (bar 5) in the second phrase, back to I in bar 7, to V in bars 9 and 10, and once again back to I in bars 11 and 12.

Nineteen years later (a big time span in jazz history), Charlie "Bird" Parker recorded his own "line," or "head," based on the blues progression. This highly syncopated melody, played in unison by the group after a piano introduction, recurs at the end of the piece. After this beginning there are improvised solos by alto saxophone (Parker) and tenor saxophone (two choruses each);

---

[7] Roughly because there are slight variants from chorus to chorus. For a further explanation of seventh and ninth chords, see the Ancillary Reading at the end of this chapter.

Miles Davis playing the trumpet

the excerpt ends at that point. This is the style of jazz called *bebop,* and the harmony is still more varied than in the previous examples.

Finally, listen to Example 5.45, *Be Careful With a Fool,* a recent rock blues. Notice how the accompaniment plays a slow four-beat measure, with each of the beats divided into a faster triplet rhythmic pattern:

The harmonic progression is simpler than in the last two examples, closer, in fact, to the earlier blues. And as in the earlier vocal blues, there is an instrumental fill-in between the singer's phrases. The rock style, however, though retaining the shell of the old twelve-bar blues, has a very different mood.

Listen again to all six pieces (Examples 5.40–5.45.) They should have

1. Given you some lively practice in hearing the workings of the I, IV, and V chords.
2. Focused your attention on the role of harmony as a fundamental skeletal framework.
3. Pointed up the distinction between the larger design of a work (in this case a harmonic progression and a rhythmic structure) and its details, which, even though they constantly change, are always related to that larger design.
4. Demonstrated how a framework such as the blues progression can become so internalized—such a natural way of thinking—that it liberates rather than limits the musicians' imagination.
5. Shown you a variety of jazz styles over a 50-year period.

While these aspects of musical composition may be more obvious in relation to the twelve-bar blues, they are equally relevant to many of the other pieces which we have discussed. Indeed, one of your principal goals should be to hear the relation between the larger design of a piece and its details—to discover that the larger design both contains and is realized by its details. Perhaps this kind of awareness is even one definition of perceptive listening.

Your experience with the twelve-bar blues should help you to realize that other procedures (the simple *a b + a'* phrase form, or the minuet and the sonata forms discussed in Chapter 6) can also be a natural way of thinking for composers who have truly internalized the fundamental relations of these procedures. The whole question of limits and freedom of expression, which has become such a large part of our harmonic considerations, will be one of the principal issues returned to in the concluding chapters.

Example	Composer, title	Date
5.46	Mozart, *Serenade in C Minor*, K. 388, fourth movement	1782

5.46

With these thoughts in mind, turn now to a performance of the final movement of Mozart's *Serenade in C Minor* for two oboes, two clarinets, two horns, and two bassoons. Similar to the pieces based on the twelve-bar blues, this movement is also a theme and variations. The structure of the theme is the familiar ‖: *a* :‖: *b* + *a'* :‖.

(sixteen bars in length). The design of the theme differs from that of the twelve-bar blues in that it includes a clearly defined middle section *(b)* and a return *(a')*. In addition, each of the two large sections is repeated, so that there are 32 bars from the start to the finish of each variation. The general harmonic motion is

			a								b		+		a'	
C minor:	I	V	I	V	I	V	V/V	V	V/IV	IV	IV V/V	V	I	V	VI II V	I
				G: IV	I	V	I									
	1	2	3	4	5	6	7	8	9	10	11	12	13	14	15	16

In the Mozart serenade, with the exception of the second variation, the harmonic foundation is not created by underlying sustained chords (such as those in *Muggles*), around and within which the melody instruments improvise. Here the harmony is created primarily by the individual melody lines of each instrument. Indeed, this is a significant factor in differentiating the improvised examples from this composed work.

Nevertheless, as in the blues, the I, IV, and V harmony again predominates. Notice that the first phrase establishes the tonic (just I and V), while the second phrase moves strongly to the key area of the dominant (a small-scale modulation). In the *b* section, the harmony quickly moves from an emphasis on IV (bars 9 and 10) to an emphasis on V (bars 11 and 12), which prepares the return. The *a'* section, unlike *a*, ends with a clear, full cadence on the tonic.

In this movement, the theme and each of the first four variations in the movement all follow exactly the same harmonic progression as well as the same phrase structure. (The fifth and final variations are in major.) While you may not (and need not)

follow the chord-to-chord progression, you should be able, as in the blues, to hear the general harmonic movement and its relationship to the phrase structure: the movement from I to V in *a*, the shifting harmony in *b*, and the return to stability in the final phrase, *a'*. Mozart creates marvelous contrasts in character and sound from one variation to the next by changes in instrumentation, rhythm, and texture; but he does so within the limits of his own initial design.

Once again limitations seem to liberate the imagination—as if to say, "How many ways can one find to create anew the same simple set of relationships?" The structure becomes a kind of Phoenix, reborn with each new variation.

ANCILLARY READING

The Basic Triads

The four types of triads are:

In the course of time, additional thirds were added to the basic triads, creating sevenths, ninths, elevenths, and so forth:

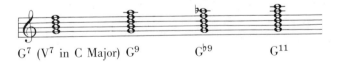

Triads can be built on each scale degree within a key. The following are the basic triads in C Major:

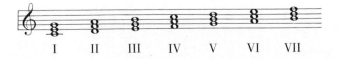

The triads on I, IV, and V are major; II, III, and VI are minor; and VII is diminished.

Below are the basic triads in C minor.[8] The triads on V and VI are major; I and IV are minor; II and VII are diminished; and III is augmented.

Inversion

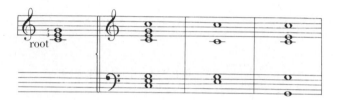

There are numerous possible arrangements of the notes of a chord. Here are four examples of a C Major triad. In the second example the root (C) is heavily "doubled." In the third, the triad is played in *first inversion,* that is, with the third of the chord rather than the root in the bass. (See Example 3.17, with its deceptive cadence to a first inversion tonic chord in Zerlina's phrase extension.) In the fourth example, the chord is in the *second inversion.* This chord is often referred to as a *six-four chord* because the upper two notes are a sixth and a fourth above the lowest, rather than a third and fifth as they are in a root-position triad.

Cadences

In the traditional study of harmony, chords are written in four

---

[8] The harmonic minor scale is derived from the practical use of these triads, particularly I, IV, V; see Chapter 3, p. 144.

parts. Various cadences are illustrated below in the traditional manner.

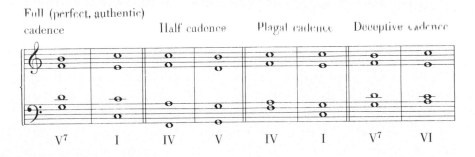

ADDITIONAL MATERIALS

As in the Additional Materials for Chapter 2, we suggest that you look back over some of the earlier examples, now from the point of view of their harmonic interest.

Mozart, *The Magic Flute,* aria (Example 3.10)
Schoenberg, *Herzegewächse* (Example 3.11)

In Chapter 3 these two examples were paired as illustrations of "vocal melodies which span a larger range" but also as representing "quite different ways of relating pitch and time." We also hinted that Schoenberg has a different idea about arranging pitches—a different notion of "comprehensibility." From your study of harmony you can now make this "different notion" more explicit. In fact, the Mozart melody, while certainly including large leaps and an enormous range, still remains solidly in one key. Actually, the soprano is often singing the pitches of the I, IV, or V chords, sometimes stretching them out over an octave or more, which accounts for the large range and the leaps. The Schoenberg song, in contrast, is not only chromatic but is so to the extent that no tonal center is established at all. The chords in the accompaniment are not triads but rather sonorities made up of intervals other than, or in addition to, thirds and fifths. Thus, the functional harmony on which we usually depend for our sense of direction and orientation is not applicable here. And still, if you try to listen to the song on *its* terms instead of listening in terms of previous stylistic expectations, you will hear a structure defined by clear phrases marked by caesuras and repeated pitch-shapes characterized by a large leap followed by a slow descent. Starting with these musical gestures, you may find this so-called "atonal" music beginning to take shape and to become comprehensible. But you can only enter into this search for coherence once you realize that the conventions of functional harmony are not going to be the key. It's a little like listening to French and hoping it will turn into English. But just as you can use the internalized knowledge of your own language to help you understand an unfamiliar one, so your deepening knowledge of aspects of familiar music that you may not have been aware of before will help you to discover the means of comprehensibility which Schoenberg's music shares with this older music.

Schoenberg, *Six Little Piano Pieces,* Op. 19, no. 4 (Example 4.21)

In Chapter 4 this brief piano piece by Schoenberg was used to illustrate the continuous development of a germinal motive. This is a good example of music that is not tonal (no tonal center and no tonic or dominant functions as such) but where the means of organization are not entirely unfamiliar. Notice, for example, that the ending of the first phrase is marked by a slowing of the tempo and by a fuller texture—the melody line is only now accompanied by chords in the bass. The chords reappear in the next phrase, and at the cadence you will hear, if you listen carefully, that the melodic motive is much the same as at the first cadence—a rising, three-note figure. Finally, the third phrase begins with exactly the same pitches as the first phrase but now transformed by a different rhythm. But perhaps more "hearable" is the strong punctuation at the end by the two chords in the bass followed by a single note in the melody which together seem to achieve resolution—arrival. In the terms set up by the piece, then, each small section has a *structural* function even though these are not dependent on the *har-*

monic functions associated with tonality. The first phrase sets forth the motivic material; the second phrase develops this material rhythmically and elaborates its sonorities; the third phrase further transforms the initial motivic material rhythmically and uses the bass chords so as to form a conclusion—an ending. Described in these terms, the structure of the piece and the means Schoenberg uses to create this structure sound quite familiar—an increase in texture and sonority at the cadences, rhythmic transformation of motives (as in the *b* Section of the Haydn *Minuet*) and the use of textural punctuation to set up an ending. But in the Schoenberg piece everything is much more compressed; you need to be very attentive to all the details or the piece is gone before you "tune in."

Wagner, *Tristan and Isolde,* "Love-Death" (Example 3.21)

This is another wonderful example of chromatic harmony, still within a basically tonal framework. Unlike the examples just discussed where chromaticism is so complete as to obliterate tonal functions, Wagner uses chromaticism so as to keep the listener in touch with key centers but often without actually stating their tonics. Thus, for example, you hear extended dominant harmonies heading toward a specific tonic resolution (a waiting passage), but the resolution never arrives. Instead, Wagner shifts away from the expected tonic to set up a different one. In this way the tonal center is continuously shifting, but nonetheless the music depends on tonal functions for its effect—precisely the effect which the example initially illustrated, that is, continuous organization. Heading toward a tonal goal but then veering off to suggest another, Wagner keeps the music moving onward, increasing in tension and excitement almost from the beginning of one act of the opera to its conclusion. (See also, Chapter 9, p. 336.)

Sourwood Mountain (Example 1.19)

Verdi, *La Traviata* (Example 1.20)

Rossini, *William Tell,* overture (Example 2.15)

M. Reynolds, *Little Boxes* (sung by Pete Seeger) (Example 4.14)

S. Reese, *Which Side Are You On?* (sung by Pete Seeger) (Example 4.19)

All of the above examples are good ones for practicing your skills in hearing I and V chords. In fact, they all use predominantly just these two chords. *Sourwood Mountain,* for instance, hardly moves from its one sound—a single chord—and this single chord is the tonic. The whole song is sung over the repeated tonic chord—another example of "harmonic stasis" but quite different from either the Wagner or Beethoven examples heard earlier (Examples 5.8 and 5.9). In the Verdi aria, the first two phrases are harmonized by only I and V. The next two phrases, a kind of middle section, move away from the tonic momentarily but set up the return with a clear V again. The last phrase is again harmonized with I and V, ending with a full cadence on the tonic. The *William Tell* overture also begins with just I and V harmonies. Then moving away briefly to a different key and to the minor mode, Rossini makes a waiting passage on the dominant that almost caricatures the notion of a waiting passage as it sets up the return. *Little Boxes* and the refrain of *Which Side Are You On?* are both harmonized by just I and V. Listen to them again and see if you can hear the chord changes.

Haydn, *Symphony 8,* first movement (Example 1.5)

Finally, it is interesting to compare Haydn's early *Symphony 8* (Example 1.5) (1761) with his later *Symphony 100* (Example 5.33) (1794). The excerpt from *Symphony 8* is the beginning of the first movement; the excerpt from *Symphony 100* is the third movement, a minuet. Notice that the *Symphony 8* movement begins with two phrases, both of which end on the tonic chord, while the *Symphony 100* movement begins with an antecedent-consequent phrase relationship—the first phrase ending on the dominant, the second on the tonic—creating a sense of closure or of complete statement. The *Symphony 8* excerpt continues with movement between dominant and tonic—a unison phrase outlines the V chord, then the little flute motive outlines the tonic and then two motives which end first on V, then on I. This is the segment printed on p. 7, and it is the first statement section of a movement in sonata form (see Chapter 6). The differences in harmonic structure between it and the minuet movement discussed in this chapter are important to the broader differences between these two ways of organizing music. Listen to the *Symphony 8* excerpt and compare its harmonic structure with that of the *Symphony 100* excerpt—both make use of only I and V in their first sections, but their relations to one another are quite different in each work. It will be interesting to return to this comparison when you study the minuet and the sonata forms in Chapter 6.

For additional jazz examples, you might listen to some of the following blues to supplement those presented on the recordings:

King Oliver, *Dippermouth Blues,* 1923 (Epic)
Louis Armstrong, *West End Blues,* 1928 (Columbia)
Lester Young, Charlie Christian, *Ad-Lib Blues,* 1940 (Jazz Archives)
Sonny Rollins, *Blue Seven,* 1956 (Prestige)
Miles Davis, *Walkin',* 1961 (Columbia)
Roy Eldridge and Earl Hines, *Blues for Old "N's",* 1965 (Xanadu)
Jim Hall, *Two's Blues* (a blues in minor), 1975 (CTI)

Finally, a fascinatingly instructive illustration of the interrelationships among harmony, structure, and jazz improvisation can be seen in the jazz version by Al Cohn of *America the Beautiful,* 1976 (Xanadu). (See Example 2.14.)

PART THREE
Structure: form and function

Piet Mondrian, *Composition in Red, Blue and Yellow*, 1937–1942

CHAPTER 6

Sectional organization

Byzantine Mosaic, Ravenna, Italy

In Chapters 6 and 7 we finally bring together the various aspects of music which have, of necessity, been discussed separately throughout the book. We are at the moment promised in the Introduction, when you should be able to perceive the effects of the various aspects of music "not as isolated factors but as parts of an inseparable whole, combining and influencing one another to generate the events, motion, and process of a unique work." In this chapter we will be observing the varying roles or functions of certain passages as these interrelate to create particular kinds of musical design or "forms."

First, we must distinguish between the immediate experience of a work and those abstract concepts called *musical forms.* Forms (such as the minuet, sonata form, and rondo) represent a generalization from many works that share, in some sense, the same structure.

On the one hand, you can directly experience a musical work as a series of events—we mean, now, events on a larger scale. You might first sense such events in terms of passages of stability, moving away, tension, culmination, and so forth; and then later in terms of structural function, such as statement of a theme, digression, development, return, or ending. This series of events, when completed, constitutes the form. And, depending on their inner relationships, you can move from the particular experience of these events to a more generalized experience, recognizing the totality as a minuet, a sonata form, a rondo, a theme and variations, or some other structure.

On the other hand, you can begin, as we do in Demonstration 6-1, with the generalization—the abstract schema of a form. In doing so, you will be anticipating the order of events. The strength of this vantage point is that you can focus on the *differences* among a group of works (that which makes each of them unique) in the light of the very general organization which they all share. In concentrating on their uniqueness, you can then listen with fascination (as we did in choosing the examples) as each piece unfolds, revealing some of the myriad possibilities that composers have found in realizing a single, basically simple structure. These differences may stem from the particular germinal materials, the personal choices of the composer at the moment, or the specific musical style. (The examples in Demonstration 6-1 span a period of 138 years.)

At first, you may feel more informed and comfortable with the second approach. But as you gain experience in listening to various forms, you may find yourself taking both approaches simultaneously—responding to the unique events of each piece as they happen but also enjoying the process as a particular experience within a more general framework.

Remember, however, that what we think of now as "classical forms" were labeled (and their "rules" codified) only after the fact —that is, after the works themselves already existed. The term *sonata form,* for example, was first used in the 1840s—well after Beethoven's death. The composers who wrote in the "classical forms" were not

> following a recognized pattern but rather were giving their music the shape which the scale of their work, in terms of the materials available to them, seemed to demand. . . . What we call musical form is the design that results from the musical impulse itself, a design of a temporal and in no way predetermined nature.[1]

You may note that in dealing with *sectional forms*—specifically, the minuet and sonata form—we concentrate on music written after the middle of the eighteenth century. Sectional forms became more prevalent after 1750 because of a number of stylistic factors, the most significant being the emergence of tonality as a fundamental syntactical force. Our purpose here is not to survey sectional forms (by looking at all types from all periods), but rather to consider carefully the general characteristics of two

---

[1] Roger Sessions, *Questions About Music* (Cambridge: Harvard University Press, 1970), p. 37.

forms and, through these more specific considerations, to extend your musical perception.

Central to the expansion and increased complexity which you will find in these works are the possibilities engendered by transformation. The ability to hear development of a germinal idea through various kinds of transformations is therefore crucial to the appreciation of these larger works. It is for this reason that we have returned repeatedly to the notion of transformation. Beginning with the transformations created by changing sound environments (Chapter 1), we then considered melodic transformation by fragmentation and sequence in the discussion of the Berg aria (Example 3.3) and the theme from the Mozart *Piano Sonata* (Example 3.5). In the section which followed, Motivic Development, we specifically anticipated the importance of transformation by looking carefully at a very simple instance of melodic transformation in "Mary Had a Little Lamb." In Chapter 5 you saw (and heard) how the function of a single chord could be transformed as a result of its harmonic context. To develop your awareness and perception of these processes of transformation is a major goal of the book. In these last chapters this growing awareness will help you to participate more fully and more appropriately in these large-scale compositions. This chapter and the next should serve, then, as a culmination of your work thus far and also help you to make sense of where you have been as well as how far you have come.

Demonstration 6-1

THE MINUET AND THE SCHERZO (Sides 8–9)

On the most general level, the pieces in Demonstration 6-1 (all of which are in triple meter) can be described as shown here:

A	B	A' return
minuet	trio	minuet (*da capo*)[2]
$\|:a:\|:b + a':\|$	$\|:c:\|:d + c':\|$	$a \quad b + a'$

In Chapter 4 you became familiar with the internal organization of each of the three large sections just diagramed: the minuet, the trio, and the return to the minuet. Here we are concerned not with a new musical design but rather with the possibilities of extending this design into a larger work and the remarkably varied ways in which this extension can be realized.

The sections are indicated on the record, although not exactly at their beginning, so that you can experience these structural events yourself. In a few examples, because of the lack of recording "time-space," the trio and minuet *da capo* have not been included.

Each composer has played with the possibilities inherent in this general schema. Notice particularly the following:

1. The nature of the return to *a'*. Is there a "waiting passage" or not? Is the return varied?
2. The development of thematic material. Where does it occur, or does it?
3. The nature of the contrast between *a* and *b*.
4. The nature of the contrast between the minuet (or A section) and the trio (or B section).
5. The addition or lack of a coda.
6. The proportions of the whole, and the parts to the whole.
7. The nature of the thematic material itself and how it influences the realization of the overall structure.

---

[2] *Da capo* (D.C., literally, "from the head") is an indication to the performers to go back to the beginning and play the first part of the piece over again. It is most often found at the end of the trio section, indicating a replaying of the minuet ("Minuet *da capo*").

As you listen to this collection of works you should discover a richer significance in the simple notion of statement-contrast-return (set forth in Chapter 4) and the influence that stylistic change can have on it.

THE MINUET

Example	Composer, title	Date
6.1	Mozart, *Eine kleine Nachtmusik*, K. 525, minuet	1787
6.2	Haydn, *Symphony 99*, minuet	1793

You are already familiar with Examples 6.1 and 6.2. The minuet from Mozart's *Eine kleine Nachtmusik* (Example 6.1) presents the minuet structure in its irreducible form. On first hearing, the *a* section sounds like one long, continuous, eight-measure phrase. Closer listening, however, will reveal its antecedent-consequent phrase structure, concealed by the increased rhythmic activity in the fourth bar. There are, in fact, two phrases here, as determined by both harmonic and melodic means: the movement to the dominant at the end of the first phrase (fourth bar) to create a half cadence, and the repetition of the first part of the melody at the beginning of the consequent phrase (bars five and six). Of additional interest in this deceptively simple piece is the effect of duple meter against the basic three in the consequent phrase.

The brief *b* section provides contrast in almost every dimension: in dynamics (softer), texture (thinner as the bass drops out), and harmony (moving away from the tonic it touches on the "relative minor"). For melodic material Mozart uses in *b* the little figure from the fourth bar of *a* (♩ | ♪♪♪♪♪ |), which served there to conceal the articulation between phrases. In what ways does the trio contrast with the minuet?

In Example 6.2, from Haydn's *Symphony 99*, the proportions

Example 6.1 Mozart, *Eine kleine Nachtmusik*

From Edition Eulenburg Publication #218. Reprinted by permission of the publisher.

Menuetto da Capo.

Wolfgang Amadeus Mozart, 1789

minuet (A)

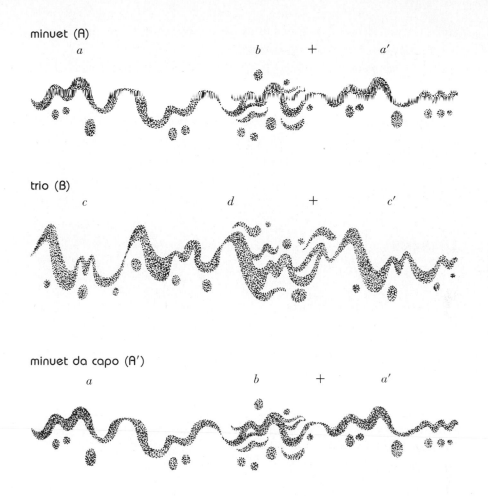

trio (B)

minuet da capo (A′)

of the movement are considerably expanded. You may remember that in studying the Haydn symphony movement in Chapter 1 (Example 1.29), we noted that *a* itself included three sections, each with a different function: a *statement,* consisting of antecedent and consequent phrases; an *extension* and *elaboration* of this material, generated by a more active texture; and a *closing* section. In *b* the contrast (indeed, the basis for calling it a new section) is created by *development* of the initial thematic material. Haydn transforms the germinal musical idea. He inverts it (the melody goes up now rather than down), fragments it, and embeds it in a more active texture and a less stable harmony.

The return is prepared for by the gradual emergence of the opening material. Imitative statements of the initial motive evolve into a complete statement of the original theme with its rhythmic unison texture. Can you next hear how the change in *a'* creates a sense of greater finality? What seemed in the *a* section an elaboration or exploration of implications becomes in *a'* their resolution.

TWO SCHERZOS

Example	Composer, title	Date
6.3	Beethoven, *Quartet,* Op. 18, no. 1, scherzo	1799
6.4	Schubert, *Quintet in C,* Op. 163, scherzo (without trio and scherzo *da capo*)	1828

The third movement of a symphony or quartet changes in Beethoven's hands from a minuet to a scherzo. While the "form" remains, the character of the scherzo takes this movement even further away from its elegant courtly origins. Notice the following in Example 6.3:

1. The extreme brevity of *a* and, to a lesser degree, of *b*
2. The greater expansion that takes place in *a'*
3. In the trio, the almost unrecognizable return in *c'*
4. The lack of repetition of *d* + *c'*, which stems from the varied nature of *c'*

How does the nature of the thematic material in the trio influence the effect of return in *c'*? At what point in the process do you finally feel the stability usually associated with return?

Example 6.4, taken from the Schubert *Quintet in C,* is the longest of all the movements heard so far. Unlike Example 6.3, this scherzo also has an expanded *a* section; in it all the sections (*a, b,* and *a'*) are nearly equal in length.

Notice that the opening material is already considerably elaborated in *a*: The harmony becomes more complex, contrasting material is introduced, and the section ends with a codetta. The *b* section introduces not only further development of the opening material of *a,* but also a new melody (though one that seems to derive from *a* material). The *b* section leads into *a'* with a prolonged waiting passage. This passage was included as Example 2.24 where it was used to illustrate syncopation.

You can hear now how the rhythmic agitation, along with the harmony and the repeated melodic figure, help to generate a waiting passage—a preparation for return that is followed by the return itself. Note how your increased ability to perceive rhythmic stability and instability furthers your ability to respond to the evolving structure of a work as well as to its overall effect. The excerpt ends with a coda following *a'*. In this performance *b + a'* is not repeated.

While the music you have heard in these first four examples spans a period of only 41 years, from 1787 to 1828, its variety in the light of our point of departure, the minuet from Mozart's *Eine kleine Nachtmusik,* is remarkable. The changes can perhaps best be summarized by noting the proportions of stable melodic statements to unstable elaborations, developments, and codas. While the Mozart minuet is composed primarily of melodies—their appearance, disappearance into brief "development," and reappearance—the later works are concerned primarily with realizing the *implications* of briefly stated thematic material through subtle transformations of it. And the thematic material is itself often dramatic and unstable. As a result, the character and purpose of the minuet is dramatically transformed from its original function as music for the royal ballroom.

Woodwind trio (left to right: bassoon, clarinet, flute)

LATER "MINUETS"

Example	Composer, title	Date
6.5	Mahler, *Symphony 1*, second movement	1888
6.6	Schoenberg, *Suite for Piano*, Op. 25, minuet	1925

The movement by Mahler from his *Symphony 1* (Example 6.5), marked simply *Kräftig bewegt*—"lively, animated," couples two seemingly disparate musical phenomena: the simple, diatonic tunes of the Austrian village band on the one hand, and a very large orchestra and much expanded (chromatic) harmonic vocabulary on the other. The result is a piece rich in contrasts of sonority and full of "sound effects." Within the structure of A, notice the following:

1. There are no literal repeats.
2. The *b* section is relatively long in relation to *a* and has greater contrast in harmony,[3] sonority, and texture. Note particularly the in-

---

[3] The beginning of the *b* section was used in Chapter 5 (Example 5.13) as an illustration of change of key by juxtaposition: "Mahler states his motive in one key, then immediately begins again with the same motive but in a new key." In context, you hear these means as contributing to the greater contrast of the *b* section.

crease in textural activity and the thickening of the texture at the climax, followed by a thinning of the texture down to only one group of instruments at the waiting passage before the return of a'.

3. a' is introduced softly and with a thin texture, followed by a full orchestration of the original theme, which is then varied to create a dramatic coda.

The trio (B) provides contrast in almost every dimension and is freely structured. The return to A includes essentially only the a' section with its coda.

In Example 6.6, from his *Suite for Piano,* Schoenberg has adapted the old minuet form to a new harmonic context—chromatic and without a tonal center. What creates stability of thematic statement and instability of development? The traditional structure within the minuet is in many senses maintained: a is repeated literally; $b + a'$, however, is not (literal repeats are rare in Schoenberg); and only portions of a return exactly in a'. The larger structure—minuet-trio-minuet *da capo*—is also maintained.

Note that the sense of dramatic possibility which we saw emerging even in the earlier minuets is developed still further in the last two examples. In particular, the returns are consistently more varied. They generate within the structure exactly the kind of drama—almost in the narrative sense—that is inherent in the attitude which sought a new kind of personal expression in the Romantic Period (see Chapter 9).

Demonstration 6-2

SONATA FORM   (Side 9)

This demonstration differs from Demonstration 6-1 in two ways:

1. While in Demonstration 6-1 we began with an abstract schema—minuet form—in Demonstration 6-2 we begin with events them-

selves. We concentrate on the varying functions which passages can assume, only later arriving at the generalization—in this case *sonata form.*

2. In Demonstration 6-1 we considered a number of examples written over a relatively long time span and reflecting great diversity in musical style. Here, in contrast, we concentrate primarily on the music of only two composers, Mozart and Beethoven. In addition, we consider only one complete movement.

The difference in approach in these two demonstrations stems largely from the nature of the sonata form itself, particularly its greater length and complexity. Therefore, instead of using a historical approach, as with the minuet, the emphasis here will be on music from the Classical Period. But for contrast, in the Additional Materials we suggest pieces from both the nineteenth and twentieth centuries.

Structural Functions: Means and Effect

Example	Composer, title	Date
6.7	Mozart, *Symphony 40,* K. 550, fourth movement	1788
6.8	Mozart, *Symphony 40,* K. 550, fourth movement	1788

Begin with Examples 6.7 and 6.8; listen to them several times. While they both work with the same material, one of the passages is more stable. Why? Which of the two might be the opening statement of the theme?

Example 6.8 is the initial *statement* of the theme; Example 6.7 is a subsequent *development* of it. The stability of the statement is generated by balanced phrase structure and by the emphasis on tonic and dominant harmony, as well as by the clear (now familiar) structure shown below.

Example 6.8 Mozart, *Symphony 40,* fourth movement (initial statement)

Later in the movement (Example 6.7), Mozart develops this theme, beginning somewhat as he did originally but quickly breaking up the germinal material—dissecting it and in effect keeping the listener guessing by avoiding clear tonality, rhythm, and phrasing. Listen to Examples 6.7 and 6.8 again—now in their proper order—as Examples 6.9 and 6.10.

Example	Composer, title	Date
6.9	Mozart, *Symphony 40,* K. 550, fourth movement, measures 1–32	1788
6.10	Mozart, *Symphony 40,* K. 550, fourth movement, measures 125–205	1788

These two excerpts bring together in one work the kinds of contrast that we have seen in excerpts from individual works and have discussed separately in previous chapters. Using the same motivic material, Mozart changes the initially stable statement into one of dramatically different effect and function.

In his reworking of the theme the harmony is ambiguous; it moves rapidly through a series of tentative key areas. The metric and phrase rhythm are also less regular and less clear, and the balanced phrase structure of the statement gives way to a phrase structure blurred by active, imitative texture. In short, all dimensions are transformed. Your sense of clear sectionality in the initial statement becomes one of continuous and agitated motion in the later development of the opening thematic material.

Evolving Musical Shapes

Excerpts 6.9 and 6.10 illustrate a basic distinction in the presentation of musical materials. We might describe them as music of *being,* that is, thematic statement (6.9), and music of *becoming,* that is, of development or transition (6.10).

Example	Composer, title	Date
6.11	Beethoven, *Quartet*, Op. 18, no. 1, first movement, measures 101–114	1799
6.12	Beethoven, *Quartet*, Op. 18, no. 1, first movement, measures 101–154	1799
6.13	Beethoven, *Quartet*, Op. 18, no. 1, first movement, measures 115–186	1799

Next listen to Example 6.11 to determine its character and its place in the movement. Actually, this excerpt closes off a large section of a work. The static harmony restrains the forceful rhythmic and melodic motives. Over an embellished tonic pedal played by the cello, the other instruments play, with rhythmic regularity, a series of V-I progressions followed by scale passages. The effect is one of further extending or elaborating the tonic harmony. This is a *closing section*.

Listen to the excerpt again with its continuation (Example 6.12). Unlike the closing section, this continuation is highly unstable and charged with excitement—modulating and avoiding clear cadences. The whole passage is characterized by a rapid rate of change and a continuous transformation of motivic material. This section is concerned with *development,* or "analysis," in the sense of breaking up and revealing the implications of previously stated material. This continuation constitutes the first half of the *development section* of the movement.

Now listen to the entire development section and its continuation (Example 6.13). Toward the end you have an exciting experience of return to familiar territory—to stable ground—in fact, to the tonic of the piece and to the very opening of the work. This return is anticipated by a lengthy *waiting passage*—an ornamented dominant *pedal*[4] with a very agitated rhythm. The waiting passage gives way to return through the striking change in rhythmic and

---

[4] Known as a *pedal* because in organ works the performer would hold his or her foot on a single bass pedal.

textural activity. With the entrance of the melody (return to opening material), the rhythmic motion slows down, the texture becomes less active, and agitation subsides into calm.

Once again these examples demonstrate the combined use of various musical dimensions—sound, rhythm, motivic manipulation, harmony—to generate the contrasting passages which define and articulate structure. Relationships which initially might have seemed dichotomous (for example, active and inactive texture, sectional and continuous melodic organization, diatonic and chromatic harmony) are now heard as the tools of musical process—the means of creating an ever-evolving, organic, multifaceted whole.

A COMPLETE MOVEMENT IN SONATA FORM

Example	Composer, title	Date
6.14	Mozart, *Quartet in G Major*, K. 387, first movement	1782

Example 6.14 presents the entire first movement of Mozart's *Quartet in G Major*, K. 387. It falls into nine sections, more or less clearly articulated by the kinds of contrasts you have heard in previous examples, but now operating within one movement. Each section has its role—its *function*—in the evolution of the total work. Listen carefully, trying to hear the structural functions of each section. Ask yourself the following questions:

1. Is there a tune or a well-defined *thematic statement,* with clear phrasing and stable harmony?
2. Or is the music unstable, fragmented, changing frequently in texture, and harmonically ambiguous or modulating—thus *transitional* or *developmental* in character?
3. Or is the harmonic movement directed toward a certain goal—a *waiting passage?*
4. Or does the music seem to be cadential in some way—a *closing section?*

Listen to the entire movement at least once before reading the analysis which follows. Try to listen on a broader scale. Step back, as it were, and use your increased awareness of musical possibilities to take in and respond to the larger gestures of the music. You should now be able to absorb the details of your molecular analysis into a more intense response to the total design.

The various sections, their respective structural functions, and the relationships among them together constitute what is generally known as *sonata form*.

Section 1 states the *opening* theme. Mozart uses material from this opening prominently throughout the entire movement. The phrasing is clear, the harmony stable within the tonic key—here, G Major.

In Section 2 the thematic material is fragmented; there is a change to a more active texture, contrast in textural density, and imitation. The passage is much more continuous and is modulatory in harmony. It finally arrives at a waiting passage in the new key, the dominant, in preparation for the statement of another theme. This is a *transition* section.

Section 3 presents a contrasting melody. What means are used to create a melody different in character from that of the opening theme?

In Section 4 you hear a series of extended cadences always returning, sometimes with delay, to the tonic of this section. This is a *closing* section.

Sections 1–4 together constitute the *exposition* of the movement.

Section 5, a *development* section, is characterized by the greatest rate of change. Motives from the themes of the exposition are manipulated and thrown off balance. We are ushered into this section by a marvelously unsettling transformation of the opening theme. As it proceeds the tone colors of the instruments are exploited, and the texture is varied in both activity and density. The harmony is at first ambiguous, then shifts from one key to another, coming to rest in a passage reminiscent of the closing section of the exposition. But the deceptiveness of this closing is revealed as we move into a waiting passage which prepares for the return of the opening theme and the return to stability.

Sections 6–9 together constitute the *recapitulation;* they parallel Sections 1–4 of the exposition. Thus in Section 6 we have the opening theme; Section 7 parallels Section 2 (the transition); Section 8 parallels Section 3, stating the second, contrasting theme. Finally, Section 9 parallels Section 4, the closing section which completes the movement.

Listen again to the entire movement. Its dramatic evolution is created by the composer's imagination and skill—his command over the musical means we have discussed throughout the book and which you now hear in guises appropriate to making this movement a whole. Listen to Mozart's use of sonority and texture,

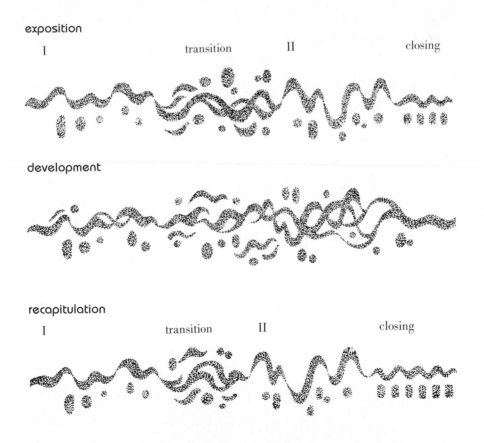

exposition

I   transition   II   closing

development

recapitulation

I   transition   II   closing

his contrasting and combining of rhythmic and melodic shapes, and the varieties of harmonic motion.

The generalized structure of the Mozart quartet movement, as well as that of any movement in sonata form, can be outlined as follows. But please remember that this is a generalization, that is, a description of a procedure which represents a number of works in general but may represent no one of them in particular.

SONATA FORM

(Introduction—found only in some allegro movements)
Slow, exploratory, and wandering in character; modulatory and often tonally ambiguous until just before the end; leads directly into the exposition.

Exposition

1. Theme Group 1. *One or more themes in the tonic key, characterized by the harmonic stability and generally regular phrasing of thematic statement.*
2. Transition. *Modulating, generally more active in texture, motives broken up and regrouped, more continuous.*
3. Theme Group 2. *One or more themes in another key (usually the dominant) which contrast in character with those of Theme Group 1.*
4. Closing Section. *Cadential in effect; closes off the exposition with emphasis on the new tonic.*

Development

5. *"Analysis" and exploration of material presented in the exposition, characterized by modulation, tonal ambiguity, melodic material fragmented and in other ways transformed, and a rapid rate of change. This section is more active in texture and more continuous; occasionally a new theme is presented.*

Recapitulation

A repetition of the sequence of events in the exposition:

6. Theme Group 1.
7. Transition.
8. Theme Group 2. *Now in the tonic of the piece.*
9. Closing Section.

(Coda)

May take the form of further development of material before ending the piece in an even more final fashion than the closing section.

Two points should be made about the above outline as a generalization:

1. *The sonata form (or any musical form) as described in a diagram is a generalization made from a large number of works, each of which is unique—as you have heard in listening to the minuets. A musical form is not a mold like those into which you pour plaster, hoping that each cast will be identical. The generalization is most useful, in fact, not in categorizing or labeling but in perceiving distinctions. Given sufficient time and experience, you can come to hear within a given framework not devices or formal sections but rather organic movement, function—you can respond to the composer's musical gestures.*

2. *The second point concerns the effect your knowledge of forms has on your expectations. For example, when you listen to the first movement of a symphony by Mozart, you can with justification anticipate a different series of events from those that will occur when you listen to the third movement: The first movement will almost certainly be in sonata form, while the third will be a minuet.*

What are the differences in your expectations for the minuet and sonata-form movements? The sonata form is larger in every sense. More happens. There are two contrasting statement areas; these necessitate a transition between them and often a closing section before the development. The development is the heart of the sonata form. Here the composer reveals to the listener the implications of what may have seemed straightforward, simple melodies in the exposition. The recapitulation, in turn, is not heard as simply a repeat of the exposition—you hear the music now in a new light, having experienced the development, where the potential of the thematic material was explored.

As a result, this first-movement form, as it is sometimes called (though not correctly, since it may occur in a second or final movement), is expansive, organic, and dramatic. So much happens in a movement in sonata form: transformations in both motivic material and in character, conflict, revelations of hidden implications, and so forth.

In the minuet your expectations are different. The experience is of two usually quite separate wholes and a third which repeats the first: minuet-trio-minuet. This is quite different from your experience of dramatic growth in the sonata form. When we consider any of the three parts of the minuet (since we do consider them separately), our sense of proportion is much smaller than it is when we listen to a movement in sonata form. There is but one theme in the *a* section; development of the material of *a*, primarily in the *b* section, is on a considerably smaller scale than what we can expect in the development section of a sonata-form movement; and return will be less dramatic because of the shorter, less revealing excursion.

Put in these terms, however, the comparison is inherently dangerous, since it pits the minuet against the sonata. Each deserves to be heard on its own terms. We must listen to the way each composer realizes or exploits the possibilities of a particular set of formal relationships. Thus, on the one hand, each piece must be heard as a unique series of events. But on the other, these events must be perceived as realizing in some way the set of formal relationships which the piece shares with other works.

THE INFLUENCE OF STYLE

Finally, we urge you to listen to the first movement of Brahms's *Symphony 3* (not included in the recordings), which was written over 100 years after the Mozart *Quartet in G Major*. Notice how the style of a composer is reflected in his particular manner of handling the various structures common to the works of many composers. For example, in Demonstration 6-1 we observed that in the chronologically later works the dramatic possibilities of the minuet form came to the fore, particularly in the movements by Schubert and Mahler.

To continue with the consideration of stylistic differences, listen to the opening of the Brahms symphony. Then compare it with the openings of the Mozart symphony and quartet movements discussed earlier. Think about the general character of each, and notice the striking differences between the opening theme of this movement and the other opening themes. Sing them. You will notice immediately the wide range, large leaps, and varied, often irregular, rhythm of the Brahms melody. It seems to evolve out of itself, each "bit" growing out of the previous one by subtle transformation. In contrast to the clearly articulated, balanced phrases of the other opening statements, this process generates one enormously long gesture. (See also Example 2.26.)

Perhaps most striking are the differences in Brahms's orchestration and harmony. The "romantic" character of Brahms's opening depends greatly on his use of a large and varied orchestra and his thick, almost muddy texture within which the tone colors of specific instruments, particularly the horns, are exploited.

Brahms's use of harmony is often coloristic, bringing the concepts of harmony and sonority very close together. For example, between the first two chords there is an interesting change in color: A major tonic triad is followed by a functionally ambiguous chord which includes the tonic note but hints at the minor mode. This chord suggests both tonic and dominant functions by its particular sonority. (These two chords and the third, together with their upper melody line, below, pervade the entire movement.)

Brahms, *Symphony 3*

As the large gesture continues, major and minor are juxtaposed, along with chords which exploit the "edges" of the tonality. Brahms creates a kind of chromatic harmony composed of chords not strictly within the key but not changing the tonality either— merely enriching and coloring it. The result is a statement of thematic material that is, in comparison with the earlier sonata-form movements, unstable, wandering, and charged.

Given this style of grand gesture, enriched harmony, exploitation of instrumental color, and affective, almost associative character, is the model of the sonata form valid for the Brahms symphony movement? On what level is the generalization possible?

Listen to the rest of the movement. Notice, for example, the second theme (played by clarinets and bassoons), with its contrasting character, prepared for by the transition and a waiting passage. Note the closing passage, which evolves out of the contrasting second theme and then, by harmonic and motivic manipulation, merges into the development. (There is no clear end to the exposition, as in the other movements discussed.)

The development section includes a remarkable transformation of the second theme. Listen to its rapid shifts in key and its more active texture. The recapitulation emerges slowly through hints at the familiar motives, followed by the two opening chords which lead, finally, into the rebirth of the opening gesture. A long coda is added which includes further development and expansion.

The crucial relationships of the sonata form are thus revealed —almost more as essence than actuality in the light of these changes in style. The structure itself seems to have been altered in some ways: proportions are changed, and the continuous aspects of the form—the areas of organic growth—pervade the entire movement. The functions of the sections are clear, but they are rarely delineated by caesuras or cadences. Even clearly articulated phrase structure is rare; melodies are characterized by large gestures coalescing out of fragments.

Indeed, it is the notion of the sonata form as *sectional* which seems to have changed most as we compare this movement with the Mozart quartet movement (Example 6.14). We are carried along by a process of transformation and change already present in the harmony of the opening chords and in the evolving nature of the first theme. This emphasis on continuous growth, together with the associative implications of Brahms's instrumentation, harmony, and melodic-rhythmic design, generates a "Romantic" work. The course of events, like a narrative, continuously changes our perception of those elements which remain constant.

Exercise 6-1

STRUCTURAL FUNCTIONS   (Side 10)

Having analyzed the different structural functions of passages within a sonata-form movement in Demonstration 6-2, you can test your ability to perceive these musical events. As in the demonstration, we focus here on excerpts from instrumental works by Haydn, Mozart, and Beethoven. These three composers are the "greats" of the Classical Period (c. 1750 to 1827; 1827 being the year of Beethoven's death). It was in the Classical Period that the sonata form became a fundamental way of thinking for composers of instrumental music.

Listen to each passage twice. Determine whether it can be characterized as one of the following, and check the corresponding column in the table below.

A. Statement

B. Transitional-development

C. Waiting passage[5]

D. Closing section

---

[5] Examples of waiting passages include brief statements of the thematic material into which they lead.

Example	A Statement	B Development	C Waiting	D Closing
6.15				✓
6.16			✓	
6.17	✓			
6.18	✓			
6.19		✓		
6.20		✓		
6.21			✓	
6.22	✓			
6.23		✓		

CORRECT ANSWERS

Example	Composer, title, date	A Statement	B Development	C Waiting	D Closing
6.15	Beethoven, *Quartet,* Op. 18, no. 1, second movement, 1799				X
6.16	Beethoven, *Sonata for Violin and Piano,* Op. 30, no. 2, third movement, 1802			X	
6.17	Beethoven, *Quartet,* Op. 18, no. 1, fourth movement, 1799	X			
6.18	Mozart, *Symphony 40,* K. 550, first movement, 1788	X			
6.19	Mozart, *Symphony 40,* K. 550, first movement, 1788		X		
6.20	Beethoven, *Quartet,* Op. 18, no. 1, fourth movement, 1799		X		
6.21	Beethoven, *Quartet,* Op. 18, no. 1, fourth movement, 1799			X	
6.22	Haydn, *Symphony 96,* fourth movement, 1791	X			
6.23	Haydn, *Symphony 96,* fourth movement, 1791		X		

ADDITIONAL MATERIALS

I

Mozart, *Symphony 40,* K. 550, fourth movement, 1788
Haydn, *Symphony 97,* first movement, 1792
Beethoven, *Symphony 4,* Op. 60, first movement, 1806

These three works (and many others are possible) illustrate large, symphonic sonata-form movements. They exemplify some of the diverse possibilities created by these three composers, who wrote in a relatively similar style and within the same structural framework. Listen to each of the movements several times. First, on the immediate level of a series of events, consider the differences among them in overall character. Then, using the general model on pp. 252–253, compare the three movements in terms of structure, proportions, and the musical means used to generate these structural relationships. Consider the following questions:

1. Is there an introduction? How does it relate to the exposition? How would the piece sound without it?

2. What are the differences in character of the opening themes and what musical means are used to generate these differences? How are these differences related to the presence or absence of an introduction? Compare the differences in the proportions of these first theme statements.

3. How does the transition emerge out of the statement? What thematic material does it use? Is it immediately evident that you have left the stable statement? When and how does the composer move away from the first theme and key? What is the nature of the arrival at the new theme— is it delayed (the transition prolonged)? Is there a waiting passage, a pause, or a gradual emergence of the new theme? What is the difference in proportions among the transition passages, especially in relation to the first theme group?

Haydn, from autograph score of *Andante in F minor,* 1793

4. What is the nature of the contrast between the first and second theme groups in each piece? What means (such as instrumentation, melodic-rhythmic shape, or harmony) are used to generate this contrast? Are there similarities among the works?

5. What about the closing section? What proportion of the exposition does it occupy? Does it include a new (closing) theme? What means does each composer use to establish stability? Is the exposition repeated on your recording?

6. How does the development section begin? Are you aware at once that this is development—that is, is it immediately unstable, modulatory, or ambiguous in harmony? Do you hear manipulation and distortion of thematic material? What material from the exposition is developed in this section? Is new material introduced? What else does the composer do? Are there contrasts in texture and sonority? Is there a climax? Does the development fall into several sections? How does each composer "get back"? Through an extended waiting passage? Through the gradual emergence of stability and theme? At the climax, or after it? What about the length of the development in relation to the exposition and its parts?

7. Does the recapitulation begin exactly like the opening of the exposition? What differences are there between the recapitulation and the exposition?

8. Is there a coda? If so, how does it relate to the rest of the movement in proportions and function? Does it include, for example, further development? Does the movement end climactically or by "playing itself out"?

II

Sessions, *Piano Sonata 2,* first movement, 1946

Bartók, *Sonata for Two Pianos and Percussion,* second movement, 1937

Webern, *Concerto for Nine Instruments,* Op. 24, first movement, 1934

Schoenberg, *Quartet 4,* first movement, 1936

These works, all of them written within the last 45 years, are in the most general sense in sonata form. At the same time, the syntax of tonality operates, to some extent, only in the piece by Bartók. How, then, can we speak of sonata form, which depends for its very definition on tonal relationships? What is left of the form when the key relationships as well as the concepts of harmonic stability and instability associated with tonality are lacking?

Let us consider one of these movements more closely—Sessions's piano sonata. Listen to the movement several times to see if you can discover within it passages of relative stability. (Notice the opening, for example. It is a motive repeated with slight variation, elaborated to lead to a climax and the statement of another mo-

Bartók, from autograph score of *String Quartet No. 5,* 1934

tive.) Hearing these passages in terms of their relative stability is only possible, of course, when you can perceive the work on its own terms—without superimposing on it expectations which distort your perception. You will not hear, for example, stability generated by the resolution of dissonance (since resolution implies a triad) or by a dominant-tonic progression establishing a clear tonal center.

Remember, however, that in the works we have studied the stability of statement was generated by other means as well: a more homophonic texture or a more palpable melodic shape and rhythmic motives which together define a theme. Less stable sections were characterized not only by instability of key but also by a more active texture, conflicts in accent and rhythm, melodic fragmentation, and, in general, a more rapid rate of change. Conclusion was generated often by harmonic stasis but also by a braking action which slowed down the rate of events, reiterating rather than generating something new. From these characteristics we were able to perceive the function of a passage, and we described the particular set of relationships among these functions as sonata form.

In Sessions' sonata we hear the stability of statement generated by most of those attributes which we have associated with thematic statement in music of the past *except* that of tonal stability. Similarly, we hear transition, a contrasting second theme, and a closing passage. Development follows the exposition, leading then to a varied recapitulation of the opening material.

In the Brahms movement, we described the relationships of sonata form "almost more as essence"—and so it is with these twentieth-century pieces. Within styles which are radically different from the styles of the works studied earlier, the idea of sonata form is still operative. Consider the works suggested here simply as a group sharing a common organizing principle. As you listen to them, you should become aware of (1) the essential nature of the sonata form and its great flexibility as an organizing principle

and (2) the basic differences in style among these contemporaneous works, particularly as they influence the organization itself.

   With these considerations we are to some extent anticipating
Chapter 9, where we will focus on stylistic change at the beginning
of the twentieth century.

Vincent Van Gogh, *Starry Night,* 1889

CHAPTER 7
Continuous organization

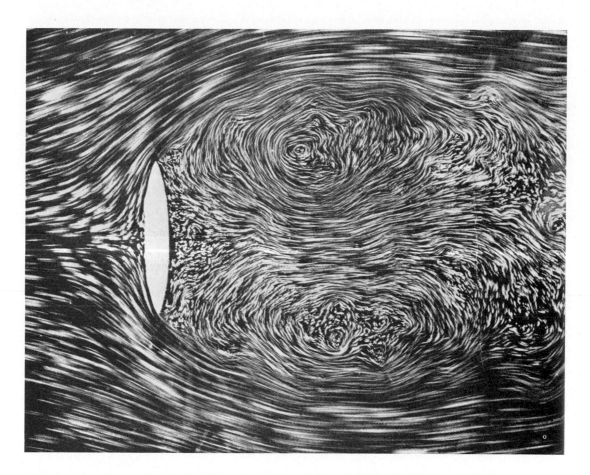

Flow of fluid passing an obstacle

Demonstration 7-1

SOME CONTINUOUS PIECES (Side 10)

Throughout this book we have emphasized the distinction between sectional and continuous organization as representing two distinct approaches to musical design. We first confronted the distinction on a rather small scale. In Chapter 3, for example, we differentiated between sectional melodies and continuous melodies. We noted that a prototypical tune in our culture tended to be a sectional one (like *Lassie*). Sectional tunes were characterized as having clear phrase structure and clearly articulated, often predictable, moments of arrival. Continuous melodies, in contrast, were different from our intuitive model of a tune especially in that they seemed, at least on first hearing, to go on and on, to be almost "serpentine" in their continuous "unwinding." The Vivaldi *Concerto Grosso* (Example 3.1) and the opening of the Liszt *Faust Symphony* (Example 3.2) were examples of continuous melodies.

In Demonstration 4-1, we focused on the contrast between sectional and continuous organization in larger-scaled structures. The minuet from Mozart's *Eine kleine Nachtmusik* (Example 4.10) was the initial illustration of a sectional piece, while a Chopin *Prelude* (Example 4.11) illustrated a continuous piece. We returned to the same Mozart minuet in Chapter 6 to begin the discussion of two basically sectional "forms," the minuet and the sonata form. We pointed out that sectional pieces are those which more easily lend themselves to schematic representation exactly because they fall into clearly defined sections to which we can give names. The discussion of sonata form, however, made it clear that sectional structures may include areas which are themselves more continuous than sectional. Indeed, it is the contrast between the more clearly sectional passages (statements) and the more continuous passages (development and transition) which contributes greatly to the variety and drama of the sonata form. And, interestingly, these more continuous sections are also apt to be more active in texture. Active texture will often create a more ongoing piece or section of a piece because the separate, independently moving strands tend to overlap.

But continuous organization is certainly not always generated by textural activity. The Chopin *Prelude* that you heard in Chapter 4 is quite inactive in texture, and yet it is fundamentally continuous—it does not fall into clearly distinguishable sections and thus defies schematic representation. In this chapter we will concentrate on the various factors that create continuousness and the ways in which continuous structure is organized. What, for example, does create this sense of ongoing movement in the Chopin *Prelude* you heard earlier? Go back and listen to Example 4.11 again. Your growing awareness of harmonic stability and instability will help you to account for its continuous onward movement. While there are "pauses" in the flow of sound, these cadences are never full cadences (on the tonic); they do not create stable points of arrival. The harmonic instability coupled with the continuous outpouring of notes propels you forward without stop. The piece seems to be a single, cumulative gesture, not only because of its brevity but also because of the tight unity of motivic and harmonic material. Notice how each impulse grows motivically out of the previous one—expanding or compressing it—to generate an improvisatory, impetuous character by the flexibility of pulse and rhythm. It is interesting to note Chopin's final "statement": two chords, V to I. Yet, because of the particular positioning of these last chords, the piece does not seem to come to a full stop. Still caught up in the continuous flow of the music, we listen on until the sound dies away.

Thinking back, then, over the pieces you have listened to and the various aspects of music they have illustrated, it becomes clear that the contrast between sectional and continuous organization encompasses nearly all of these aspects—texture, rhythm, melodic design, motivic development, and differences in formal structure as well. With this in mind, listen now to several pieces which are all continuous but in different ways and for different reasons. You might use them to review and refresh your listening skills as you shift your attention from one aspect of the music to another. As you listen, ask yourself: What, in each excerpt, creates its particular onward movement; what sorts of inner relations give each its particular coherence?

Example	Composer, title	Date
7.1	J. Farmer, *Fair Phyllis*	1599
7.2	Vivaldi, *The Four Seasons,* "Winter"	1725
7.3	Haydn, *The Seasons,* "Summer"	1801
7.4	Bruckner, *Mass in E Minor,* "Sanctus"	1882
7.5	Debussy, *Pelléas and Mélisande* Act IV, sc. 4	1902

You will notice that the five examples span a period of more than 300 years and that the pieces are ordered chronologically. Thus, as in previous chapters, you will want to pay attention to stylistic differences as you move through these three centuries of music.

John Farmer's *Fair Phyllis* is a late sixteenth-century *madrigal* —a secular work for voices based on a text in the "mother tongue" (rather than Latin). Like many English madrigals, the text is a jolly one and somewhat bawdy, but still more "polite" than many. The text concerns a shepherd who is looking for his fair love, Phyllis, and includes the words:

Up and down he wandered
Whilst she was missing,
When he found her,
Oh then they fell a-kissing.

Farmer creates a "catch" in both the music and the words by running the last line of the text above, around again to the first line. The piece thus "runs around" continuously both in words and music while the men and women sing the words "up and down" in quick imitation as if chasing one another in a game of "catch." No-

Madrigal singers
(sixteenth-century German print)

tice, too, Farmer's use of *word painting* as the pitch goes "up and down" along with the words.

In the excerpt from the fourth movement of *The Four Seasons*, Vivaldi expresses his impression of winter. Notice, for example, the "harsh" sonority of the opening section and later the rushing, downward-tumbling figures played by the violin, reminding the listener perhaps of blustering wind and snow. These imitations of nature in sound (somewhat like the "word painting" in Farmer's madrigal) are organized musically around sequential repetitions of just a few figures. Each figure creates the musical material—the pattern—for the various sections of the piece. Thus the piece is clearly partitioned into large sections, but within sections the music goes on continuously through sequential repetition of the particular figure. For example, the first "figure" is simply a single repeated chord played by the whole string orchestra. Notice that the repeated chord changes regularly every eight beats, the change creating a higher-level structural rhythm corresponding to the rate of harmonic change. The next section is marked by the introduction of the solo violin and a new *melodic* figure which is again repeated sequentially. And once again the length of the figure establishes the structural rhythm within the section. Each statement of the figure marks off a structural unit of time.

As the piece continues, Vivaldi builds up a kind of mosaic of pieces (sections), each heralded by the introduction of a new figure and each made up, in turn, of mosaic-like repetitions of this single, small figure. While the underlying pulse is always clearly present, rhythmic vitality is created by changes in the length of the sequential unit, the rate of the notes within the figures themselves, together with the changing length of the larger units of the mosaic —the sections. In this way Vivaldi creates a boldly hierarchic structure with each element delineated but then grouped together to form the next larger level of structure—notes are grouped into figures, figures are grouped into sequences, sequences are grouped into sections, and sections are grouped together to form the still larger divisions of the whole piece (notice that the excerpt ends with a return to earlier material). Continuousness, then, is contained by the boundaries of this structural hierarchy.

Haydn also composed a piece depicting the changing seasons. In this excerpt we find him in the middle of a summer storm which gradually fades away, ending with the sun breaking through the clouds. Haydn marvelously portrays the change by

Moorish arch
The elaborate figuration is contained by the broader architectural outlines . . . the excerpt ends with a return to earlier material.

gradually moving from imitative, texturally active, chromatic, and rhythmically agitated music to music which is texturally less and less active, more diatonic, and rhythmically straightforward. Following a cadence on the tonic and a pause, Haydn captures the sense of calm with a simple melody and accompaniment. The striking change occurs as the structure becomes sectional rather than continuous; the violins play and the tenor sings clearly articulated phrases, which characterize sectional organization. Thus the passage not only depicts the gradual dissipation of a summer storm but also the contrast between continuously organized music and sectionally organized music. Or, the contrast in musical means in fact *creates* the changes in pictorial and dramatic associations suggested by the text:

> Chorus: Furiously rages the storm.
> Heaven help us!
> The broad heavens are aflame.
> Woe to us wretches!
> Peal on peal crashes the heavy thunder.
> The earth totters, shaken
> to the depths of the sea.
>
> Tenor: The dark clouds scatter,
> the rage of the storm is stilled.

With the "Sanctus" from the Bruckner *Mass in F. Minor* (a setting of the Sanctus portion of the Catholic service; see the text on p. 161, Example 4.15), we move into the late nineteenth century and into a quite different musical world. The excerpt is certainly continuous but not simply because the slow-moving sound never stops to "breathe." What about the texture? It seems to be motionless and in motion at the same time. In fact, each voice of the eight-part chorus[1] is moving quite independently, and there is even a great deal of imitation among the parts. And yet the impression is one of a dense mass of sound which seems to contain

---

[1] The four usual voice sections in the chorus are each divided into pairs—Soprano I and II, Alto I and II, Tenor I and II, Bass I and II.

Detail of Spanish gold
and silk brocade
*An intricately woven,
animated fabric*

motion within it. Harmony, as well as the almost opaque texture, also contributes to this effect. The harmonic rhythm is basically very slow. However, while one basic harmony continues on, the many voices move inside of it, blurring the underlying triad. As a result, one harmony seems to merge into the next. How different from Haydn's use of the chorus, where his transparent texture and his sparkling rhythm allow us to hear each of the individually moving voice parts as a separate strand in an intricately woven, animated fabric! You may want to return to the Bruckner example when you get to Chapter 9, where we will have more to say about some of Bruckner's contemporaries and late-nineteenth-century musical style.

In the excerpt from his opera *Pelléas and Mélisande,* Debussy creates continuousness in a manner quite different from any of the other composers included in this group. We hear one voice at a time singing over a quiet, usually minimal accompaniment with a thin, almost fragile texture. The vocal lines are rhythmically more like speaking than like what we think of as a song. Compare them, for example, to the clearly articulated phrases of the song at the

Debussy, from autograph score of *Pelléas and Mélisande*, 1892–1902

end of the Haydn excerpt (Example 7.3) or to the duet from Mozart's *Don Giovanni* (Example 3.17). Certainly there are pauses—breaks in the flow of sound which at times give the lovers a breathless quality. But we move through these pregnant silences which carry the music dramatically onward rather than stopping it. Harmonically, Debussy combines pitches to create sonorities that are tonally ambiguous and ephemeral, and this too contributes significantly to the sense of continuous movement. This same excerpt is discussed again in Chapter 9, where we compare this love scene to one from Wagner's *Tristan and Isolde*. You may want to look ahead to that passage for further comments (see p. 362). Listen to the excerpt again, now following the text, below. Notice especially the extraordinary way that Debussy captures the mood and feelings of this climactic moment in the opera when the two secret lovers meet in the forest for the last time:

PELLÉAS

Ma pauvre Mélisande! J'aurais presque peur de te toucher. Tu es encore hors d'haleine comme un oiseau pourchassé. C'est pour moi que tu fais tout cela? J'entends battre ton coeur comme si c'était le mien. Viens ici, plus près de moi.

PELLÉAS

Poor Mélisande! I'm almost afraid to touch you. You're still out of breath like a hunted bird. Was it for me you did all that? I hear your heart beating as if it were my own. Come closer to me.

MÉLISANDE

Pourquoi riez-vous?

PELLÉAS

Je ne ris pas; ou bien je ris de
joie sans le savoir . . . Il y
aurait plutôt de quoi pleurer.

MÉLISANDE

Nous sommes venus ici il y a
bien longtemps. Je me rap-
pelle . . .

PELLÉAS

Oui . . . il y a de longs mois.
Alors, je ne savais pas. Sais-tu
pourquoi je t'ai demandé de
venir ce soir?

MÉLISANDE

Non.

PELLÉAS

C'est peut-être la dernière fois
que je te vois. Il faut que je m'en
aille pour toujours.

MÉLISANDE

Pourquoi dis-tu toujours que tu
t'en vas?

PELLÉAS

Je dois te dire ce que tu sais
déjà? Tu ne sais pas ce que je
vais te dire?

MÉLISANDE

Mais non, mais non; je ne sais
rien.

MÉLISANDE

Why do you laugh?

PELLÉAS

I'm not laughing; or perhaps
I'm laughing for joy, without
knowing it. There's really more
reason to cry.

MÉLISANDE

We came here a long time ago. I
remember . . .

PELLÉAS

Yes . . . months ago. I didn't
know then. Do you know why I
asked you to come this evening?

MÉLISANDE

No.

PELLÉAS

It's perhaps the last time I shall
see you. I must go away for ever.

MÉLISANDE

Why do you always say you are
going away?

PELLÉAS

Must I tell you what you already
know? Don't you know what I'm
going to say?

MÉLISANDE

No, no, I don't.

PELLÉAS
Tu ne sais pas pourquoi il faut
que je m'éloigne? Tu ne sais pas
que c'est parce que . . .

PELLÉAS
You don't know why I have to go
away? You don't know that it's
because . . .

(kissing her suddenly)

. . . je t'aime.

. . . I love you.

MÉLISANDE
Je t'aime aussi.

MÉLISANDE
I love you, too.

Demonstration 7-2

THE FUGUE (Side 10)

In Chapter 6 we dealt with two sectional forms, the minuet and
sonata form, which are perhaps unusual in recurring through
several centuries; yet each instance of these forms brings them to
life in a unique and particular way. In Demonstration 7-1 you
heard pieces which had a number of things in common—they were
all continuous rather than sectional in their organization, they
all were associated with a story or an impression of nature, and
all but one were written for voices. But unlike the examples in
Chapter 6, they were all quite different in their form. How, you
might ask, could there be a "form" that composers might use
to organize extended compositions which are continuous? The
fugue is just such a form; but exactly because it is more continuous than sectional, the working out of the fugal process varies
considerably from one example to another. Like sectional forms,
any one fugue is always the result of its particular germinal
motives, as well as the general stylistic characteristics common
to the time in which it was written and to the style of the particular

composer. But the differences among fugues go beyond this; in fact, the only part of the fugue really common to all of them is the opening procedure. Listen, for example, to the opening of the C-sharp Major fugue from the *Well-Tempered Clavier* by Bach.[2]

Example	Composer, title	Date
7.6	Bach, *Well-Tempered Clavier*, Book I, fugue no. 3 in C-sharp Major, opening	1722
7.7	Bach, *Well-Tempered Clavier*, Book I, fugue no. 3 in C-sharp Major, complete	1722

The fugue begins with a single unaccompanied melodic line called the *subject*. You will quickly discover that the entire fugue is concerned with it—a continuous exploration of its implications and possibilities. After the statement of the subject, the opening continues with the entrance in "imitation" of the two other participants, the middle and lower voices, which complete the texture. Notice that each voice enters with a complete statement of the subject. When the middle voice enters, however, the top voice continues on with a related melody, called the *countersubject,* which is played "against" the subject. As the third voice enters, the two higher voices continue; the texture grows progressively thicker and more complex. This opening portion of the fugue which introduces all the participants, each stating the subject, is called the *exposition*. It may be diagrammed as shown here:

---

[2] The *Well-Tempered Clavier,* Books I and II (two sets of preludes and fugues in all 24 major and minor keys), was written for the harpsichord or clavichord (the term *clavier* referred to stringed keyboard instruments). "Well-tempered" refers to a system of tuning which divides the octave into 12 equidistant tones, thus allowing for performance in all keys.

Example 7.6 Bach, *Fugue No. 3 in C-Sharp Major* (Exposition)

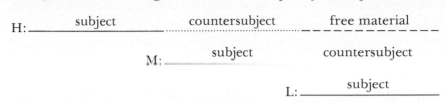

You have already heard a number of fugal expositions in previous demonstrations, for example, in Example 1.11, from the Bach *Suite in B Minor,* and Example 1.31, from the Handel *Concerto Grosso,* Op. 6, no. 2, where we discussed the procedure in terms of its texture and the embedding of a motive in "new sound environments." In Chapter 2 you heard the opening of a Mozart string quartet movement which we discussed in the context of "rhythmic complexity," pointing out that its active texture went together, in this case, with a slow-moving, nonactive subject. In Chapter 5 we used the exposition of the Bach fugue in B minor from his *Well-Tempered Clavier* to illustrate chromaticism. Finally, in Demonstration 7-1, the excerpt from Haydn's *The Seasons* begins with a fugal exposition, and though it is difficult to hear, the Sanctus from Bruckner's *Mass in E Minor* also begins with a fugal exposition.

To use the same word, *exposition,* to describe both the opening phase of the fugue and the first large section of the sonata form seems hardly appropriate. And in fact, a comparison of these two types of exposition will reveal some of the striking differences between the two approaches to musical design. You may want to consider these differences as you go on listening to the C-sharp Major fugue.

Listen to the whole fugue now. Following the diagram on the next page will help you pay attention to the contrast between moments when the subject is present and when it is not. Notice, for example, that after the exposition the piece continues with a passage that does not include the subject. These phases of the fugue, in which the subject does not appear in its entirety, are called *episodes.* The term conveys a sense of their freer, more continuous

Example 7.7 J. S. Bach, *Fugue No. 3 in C-Sharp Major* (Complete)

H: _____ .... _ _ _ _ _   _____

    M _____ ....   Episode 1   ....   Episode 2

        L: _____

        (sequential)   (subject   (modulates,
                     emerges   shifts to
                     out of   minor mode)
                     episode)

character. It is in the episodes of the fugue that Bach creates the greatest structural contrast. To do so, he uses the following compositional means:

1. The three voices are more equal in importance, since the fugue subject does not predominate.
2. The subject itself loses its integrity through fragmentation and other subtle transformations, such as the inversion of a melodic figure.
3. The harmony shifts in tonal center, often through the use of sequential passages.
4. The normative rhythmic unit (the length of the fugue subject) is disrupted.

This contrast between phases in which the subject is present and those in which it is not is crucial to the inner motion of the fugue. As the subject becomes submerged in the intricacies of the episodes, one feels a sense of instability and tension. The reappearance of the subject in turn creates a renewed stability in the otherwise continuous flow of the piece.

As you listen to the fugue, notice that in spite of these contrasts, the fugue seems a homogeneous whole; when the second voice and the countersubject have entered, all the material of the piece has been introduced. How different this procedure is from sonata form, with its clearly differentiated areas and dramatic contrasts! Your listening process must also be different: To expect from a fugue the kind of contrast that one finds in sonata form—

```
  ─ ─ ─ ─                                    ─ ─ ─ ─

              Episode 3                         ─────

  ─────                                       ............

(minor mode,    (sequential,    (subject rather submerged, minor mode,
  texture       modulating)            extended to cadence with
  thins)                                  less active texture)

              H:_____ ..........      ───── .......── ──        ───── ─ ─ ─ ┐
Episode 4     M:_ _ _ ___       Episode 5    ─── .......   Episode 6   ......... ─ ─ ─ │
              L:........._ _ _           ....... ─ _ ──                  ─ ─ ─ ─ ─ ─ ┘

(head of      (subject sneaks in)     (extended
subject in                            sequence—
sequence)                             ending with
                                       waiting
                                       passage)
```

contrasts in theme, character, texture, rate of events, and often instrumentation—could blind the listener to its pleasures. In listening to the fugue, you can become fascinated not only with the appearance and disappearance of the subject, but also with the subtle changes in texture and sonority. Enjoy the relative degrees of motion in the various strands of the texture and the changes in sonority that result from different voices playing the subject and from the surrounding activity.

The music of this fugue is printed on pages 280–283. However well (or poorly) you read music, you will be interested in following the music as you listen to the entire fugue. The episodes and reentries of the subject and countersubject are indicated in the music.

In a certain sense the fugue is player's rather than listener's music; the player, with the music before him or her, is extremely aware of the texture and its component lines. Yet in a work which

J. S. Bach, *Fugue No. 3 in C-Sharp Major*

Episode 5

Waiting passage (dominant pedal = x)

Episode 6

50

Cadential

may at first sound much the same all the way through—which is, indeed, monothematic (and might even be termed monochromatic)—the listener too can come to hear the subtle changes within its homogeneous, continuous structure—to perceive the art in the midst of artifice.

Example	Composer, title	Date
7.8	Handel, *Messiah,* "And with His stripes we are healed"	1742
7.9	Telemann, *Trio Sonata in D Minor,* fourth movement	1740
7.10	Beethoven, *Symphony 7,* Op. 92, second movement	1811–1812
7.11	Hindemith, *Mathis der Maler* (symphony)	1934

In the next group of examples you will hear two more fugues from the Baroque Period by composers who were contemporaries of Bach, and *fugatos* from a Beethoven symphony and a twentieth-century symphony. The fugue was at its height during the Baroque Period. Essentially a procedure rather than a fixed form like the minuet in the Classical Period, the fugue could assume a variety of characters in both vocal and instrumental music. Bach's contemporary Handel wrote a fugue in his oratorio *Messiah* on the words "And with His stripes we are healed" (Example 7.8). The wide

Detail from "Ecce Homo" by Pedro de Mena
"And with His stripes we are healed."

Flute players

leap on "His stripes" (i.e., his lacerations) contrasts with the *melisma* (many tones on one syllable) on "healed"—both are examples of Handel's word painting. The voices enter successively from highest to lowest—sopranos, altos, tenors, and basses.

Another contemporary of Bach, not nearly as well known today yet quite famous in the eighteenth century, is Georg Phillip Telemann. In fact, when the important position of Cantor (director of music) at St. Thomas's Church in Leipzig became vacant in 1722, Telemann was the first choice, over Bach, of the Church authorities. Only when Telemann declined the position was Bach chosen for the post the following year. Example 7.9 is the last movement of the *Trio Sonata* by Telemann for flute, oboe, and basso continuo (the second movement of which you heard previously, Example 2.18), and it is a fugue. Since this is only a three-voiced fugue, and each of the instruments has a distinctive timbre, you should be able to follow the course of the fugue very clearly. The three parts (basso continuo actually includes cello and harpsichord) enter in the order flute, oboe, and basso continuo. After a short episode, we hear a statement of the subject in the major mode by the flute followed by a cadence which marks the end of the first large section of the fugue. Notice that unlike Bach in the

C-sharp Major fugue, Telemann marks off boundaries which contain the otherwise continuous motion. The next large section begins with an episode followed by statements of the subject by oboe and then flute, separated by an episode which is again marked by a cadence. Finally, in the last section we hear statements by continuo and flute in close imitation, called *stretto*—that is, the flute begins its statement before the continuo has completed its statement. A ritardando, a rather surprising unison passage (in the midst of all this activity), and then a last cadential passage complete this brief, spirited fugue.

Example 7.10 is a *fugato,* that is, a long fugal section, often climactic in effect, in a larger composition, as opposed to a fugue as an independent movement. Here Beethoven uses the theme of a theme-and-variations movement as a fugue subject, and uses the cumulative aspect of the fugal exposition to build to a climax. The passage begins softly in the strings with the subject (♩ ♫ | ♩ ♩ ♪) combined with a countermelody in faster-moving notes. After all the strings have entered, the winds enter quickly in succession with a crescendo leading to a thunderous *fortissimo* statement of the subject and countermelody by the entire orchestra.

The practice of fugal writing continued into the twentieth century. Hindemith, somewhat analogously to Beethoven, wrote a *fugato* in the first movement of his symphony derived from his opera *Mathis der Maler* (*Matthias the Painter*). Like earlier classical symphonies, this first movement is in sonata form. And like the Beethoven excerpt, Hindemith's fugato occurs in the development section: Near the beginning he uses the second theme from the exposition, where it had a more lyrical, romantic character, as a more angular fugue subject. How do you know this is not a nineteenth-century piece?

While this chapter has been concerned with continuously organized music, the examples themselves should make it clear that "continuous" and "sectional" represent the extremes of a continuum rather than a simple dichotomy. That is, any particular piece might be described as more or less continuous or sectional, each one falling somewhere along this continuum. More important, as we have suggested earlier, pieces which are, say, primarily sectional in their organization will most likely include significant contrasting passages which are themselves continuous. Indeed, such passages will then take on a particular *functional* significance (as transition, development, dramatic climax, etc.) within the context of an otherwise clearly sectional structure. In a similar way, pieces which are primarily continuous will include passages that clearly delimit sections; within these sections, though, the music is continuous. For example, we noted that Vivaldi, in the "winter" excerpt from *The Four Seasons,* created a hierarchy of mosaics with the musical "content" of these mosaics made up of continuously related sequences and groups of sequences. The fugue, while at first seemingly continuous in its general procedure, was found to fall into phases (if not sections) characterized by the statement of the fugue subject in one voice or another in contrast to episodes where motives from the subject were treated more freely. Furthermore, each of the fugues you heard differed in their relations between subject statements and episodes—depending on the length of the fugue subject itself, the number of voices involved, and the proportion of time devoted to statements of the subject in contrast to the manipulation of subject motives in the episodes. Finally, in the Telemann fugue we found that, somewhat like Vivaldi, the larger architectural design was defined by periodic cadences which bound together into sections the continuousness of fugal imitation and freer episodes.

But the distinction is perhaps most important as it contributes to the art of listening. We pointed out earlier that an awareness of the differences between the two approaches to musical design in fact involves nearly all the aspects of music which we have discussed throughout the book. Thus, growing more sensitive to this general contrast between two ways of shaping music and hence of *listening to music* means at the same time growing more appreciative of the many dimensions of music and the multiplicity of ways composers can interrelate them. In the end, then, this thread which we have woven through all the sections of the book is perhaps as much a way of unifying *its* concerns as it is a way of helping you toward the art of listening.

ADDITIONAL MATERIALS

One aspect of our initial distinction between sectional and continuous organization remains to be clarified. We indicated that works described as continuous in organization "defy schematic representation"; that is, they cannot be meaningfully described in terms of some combination of letters (A, B, *a, b,* etc.). What, then, can be said of the fugue? Is it not a "form"?

Listen to the following pieces, all of which are fugues. Think about the concept *fugue* as a generalization applicable to these works, compared with the concept *sonata form* as a generalization applicable to the works discussed in Chapter 6.

Bach, *Cantata 21,* final chorus, 1714
Mozart, *Requiem,* Kyrie, K. 626, 1791
Beethoven, *String Quartet,* Op. 133 (*Grosse Fuge*), 1825 (Example 5.17)
Liszt, *Faust Symphony,* "Mephistopheles" (fugue exposition only), 1854
Brahms, *Variations and Fugue on a Theme by Handel,* fugue, 1861
Bartók, *Music for Strings, Percussion, and Celesta,* first movement, 1936
Hindemith, *Ludus Tonalis,* first fugue, 1942

While we emphasized in Chapter 6 that the sonata form is an abstraction which each piece realizes uniquely, the design nevertheless does describe the whole work. It includes a basic *ordering* of functional relationships: exposition (statement, transition, statement, closing), development, recapitulation, coda.

Whatever the common attributes of fugues, however, their continuous nature precludes (except in the exposition) such a generalized ordering of events. The course or design of each fugue is unique. Tovey makes the distinction clear in his definition of fugue: "Fugue is a texture the rules of which do not suffice to determine the shape of the composition as a whole."[3]

For example, notice that in the fugue from Bach's *Cantata 21* the subject is nearly always present, one statement following immediately upon another. Only once before the freer coda do we find an episode. In this piece a normative structural rhythm is established by the length of the subject and is maintained almost throughout. How different from Bach's fugue no. 3 in C-sharp Major (discussed in Demonstration 7-2), in which the play between subject statements and episodes is an ever-present source of structural tension! In the fugue from the cantata, the omnipresence of the subject itself transfers our attention to the tone color of the particular voice or instrument playing it, the contrasts in density and complexity of texture, and the fashion in which each subject statement emerges out of the total sound fabric.

While the different effects of the two Bach fugues stem primarily from the spectacular use of chorus and orchestra (with prominent trumpets) in the cantata, as opposed to the solo harpsichord or piano used in the C-sharp Major fugue, the particular ordering of events in each fugue is also a contributing factor. Certainly the cantata fugue seems, in our continuum of sectional-continuous organization, much nearer the sectional pole, while the C-sharp Major fugue seems much more continuous.

In listening to the other fugues listed above, notice the following aspects: (1) the relative proportions of subject statements and episodes; (2) the character of the subject itself and how this influences other events in the fugue; (3) the effect of harmonic style (for example, whether the piece is tonal or not); (4) consistency of texture and textural contrasts (in density, complexity, and activity); and (5) the importance of thematic material other than the subject and, indeed, whether more than one subject is developed.

---

[3] Donald Tovey, *The Forms of Music* (New York: New American Library, Meridian Books, 1957), p. 36.

PART FOUR
The historical context

Rembrandt, *Three Crosses* (2nd state)
Courtesy Museum of Fine Arts, Boston. Katherine E. Bullard Fund in Memory of Francis Bullard and Bequest of Mrs. Russell W. Baker.

The "chronology" of an etching: two states of a single work.

CHAPTER 8
A chronology

Rembrandt, *Three Crosses* (4th state)
Courtesy Museum of Fine Arts, Boston. Harvey D. Parker Collection.

At this juncture we add another dimension to your listening—that of style and music history. The works you have studied so far include music written over a period of perhaps eight centuries, including a few examples of African and Asian music, but mostly concentrating on Western music. While we have asked you to listen for and think about stylistic differences as you went along, only now do we focus directly on the question of style or the significance of historical context.

In this chapter the examples that you heard previously are rearranged chronologically to suggest some generalizations about the style of each period. The chronological reordering should give you a skeletal outline of music history. With this larger context in mind, in Chapter 9 we will propose a model of procedure by studying in depth the period from 1860 to 1913. Together these two chapters should provide you with the tools to analyze works within their historical frameworks.

Nevertheless, the chronological regrouping of examples calls for a cautionary note. In keeping with the fundamental approach of this book, our aim here is for your *experience* of the pieces themselves to precede the discussion and acquisition of facts about the music. Because the examples you have heard have been for the most part excerpts from larger works, you should now listen as much as possible to entire works in order to hear them as a whole. On the other hand, even rehearing the excerpts in this new chronological context should give you some sense of the style of the various eras. Go back and listen to the examples, and reread the discussions of them. Consider where each example occurred and what it illustrated.

The stylistic generalizations we make about a period are based primarily on these excerpts. Since the various musical works in those earlier chapters were chosen with other purposes in mind, it follows that they may not be the most "representative" works— that they may not give a complete picture of the period (if this were even possible within our limited time and space, and without superficiality). This problem is particularly evident in the earlier periods. To overcome it, we will suggest additional listening which will help you "cover" a period more adequately. As mentioned above, the detailed discussion of the period from 1860 to 1913 which is presented in Chapter 9 should serve as a model for your study of other periods.

We know little about ancient Greek and Roman music. About a dozen fragments of Greek music have been discovered, but the notation is so sketchy it is difficult to know how the music actually may have sounded. No Roman examples seem to have survived. We have learned a certain amount about the music from writings by theorists like Pythagoras and Ptolemy, and philosophers like Plato and Aristotle, as well as from Greek vase paintings and Roman frescoes. The music was primarily monophonic, improvised, vocal, and associated with drama or dance. The most obvious indebtedness of the West to ancient Greek music is in the mode names (see p. 143) adopted by medieval theorists based on their readings of Greek treatises.

Suggested Reading

The three general histories of music listed below are all highly recommended for their comprehensive coverage. The books differ somewhat in approach: The first two contain more analyses of individual works; the third provides a broader cultural background.

Crocker, Richard L., *A History of Musical Style,* New York: McGraw-Hill, 1966.

Grout, Donald, *A History of Western Music,* rev. ed., New York: Norton, 1973.

Lang, Paul Henry, *Music in Western Civilization,* New York: Norton, 1941.

MEDIEVAL: C. 400 TO C. 1400

The Medieval Period (Middle Ages) spans the era from the fall of the Roman Empire through the fourteenth century. It is sometimes divided into the Early Middle Ages (400 to 1100) and Later Middle Ages (1100 to 1400), or the Romanesque and Gothic periods. There are few extant sources for music history before 1100—far fewer than the surviving sources for art and literature.

A CHRONOLOGY OF COMPOSERS AND GENRES

MEDIEVAL (c. 400 to c. 1400)   Genres

Composers anonymous until Later Middle Ages		Chant	Caccia
Leonin	(late twelfth century)	Organum	Ballata
		Conductus	Virelai
Perotin	(c. 1200)	Madrigal	Ballade
Guillaume de Machaut	(c. 1300–1377)	Motet	Rondeau
Francesco Landini	(1325–1397)	Mass	

RENAISSANCE (c. 1400 to c. 1600)

John Dunstable	(c. 1385–1453)	Motet	Anthem
Guillaume Dufay	(c. 1400–1474)	Mass	Ricercare
Johannes Ockeghem	(c. 1430–1495)	Madrigal	Fantasia
Jacob Obrecht	(1452–1505)	Chanson	Toccata
Heinrich Isaac	(c. 1450–1517)	Canzona	Dance music
Josquin *des Prez*	(c. 1450–1521)	Magnificat	
Adrian Willaert	(c. 1490–1562)		
Giovanni Pierluigi Palestrina	(c. 1525–1594)		
Orlandus Lassus	(1532–1594)		
William Byrd	(1543–1623)		
Thomas Morley	(1557–1602)		
Orlando Gibbons	(1583–1625)		

BAROQUE (c. 1600 to c. 1750)

Giovanni Gabrieli	(c. 1557–1612)	Opera	Passion
Claudio Monteverdi	(1567–1643)	Cantata	Fugue
Girolamo Frescobaldi	(1583–1643)	Prelude	Sonata
Heinrich Schütz	(1585–1672)	Concerto	Suite
Giacomo Carissimi	(1605–1674)	Overture	Chorale-prelude
Jean-Baptiste Lully	(1632–1687)	Oratorio	
Arcangelo Corelli	(1653–1713)		
Henry Purcell	(c. 1659–1695)		
Alessandro Scarlatti	(1660–1725)		
François Couperin	(1668–1733)		
Antonio Vivaldi	(c. 1678–1741)		
Jean-Philippe Rameau	(1683–1764)		
Johann Sebastian Bach	(1685–1750)		
Domenico Scarlatti	(1685–1757)		
George Frideric Handel	(1685–1759)		

CLASSICAL (c. 1750 to c. 1827)

Christoph Willibald Gluck	(1714–1787)	Sonata	String quartet
Carl Philipp Emanuel Bach	(1714–1788)	Symphony	Oratorio
Franz Josef Haydn	(1732–1809)	Opera	Mass
Johann Christian Bach	(1735–1782)		
Wolfgang Amadeus Mozart	(1756–1791)		
Ludwig van Beethoven	(1770–1827)		

ROMANTIC (c. 1827 to c. 1900)

Carl Maria von Weber	(1786–1826)	Sonata	Symphony
Gioacchino Rossini	(1792–1868)	Symphonic poem	Concerto
Franz Schubert	(1797–1828)	String quartet	Nocturne
Hector Berlioz	(1803–1869)	Étude	Ballade
Felix Mendelssohn	(1809–1847)	Song (lied)	Opera
Robert Schumann	(1810–1856)	Oratorio	Ballet
Frederic Chopin	(1810–1849)		
Franz Liszt	(1811–1886)		
Richard Wagner	(1813–1883)		
Giuseppe Verdi	(1813–1901)		
Johannes Brahms	(1833–1897)		
Georges Bizet	(1838–1875)		
Modest Moussorgsky	(1839–1881)		
Peter Ilyitch Tchaikovsky	(1840–1893)		
Giacomo Puccini	(1858–1924)		
Gustav Mahler	(1860–1911)		

TWENTIETH CENTURY (c. 1900 to present)

Claude Debussy	(1862–1918)	Sonata	Concerto
Richard Strauss	(1864–1949)	String quartet	Opera
Erik Satie	(1866–1925)	Overture	Oratorio
Arnold Schoenberg	(1874–1951)	Ballet	Electronic music
Charles Ives	(1874–1954)	Symphony	
Maurice Ravel	(1875–1937)		
Béla Bartók	(1881–1945)		
Igor Stravinsky	(1882–1971)		
Anton Webern	(1883–1945)		
Alban Berg	(1885–1935)		
Edgard Varèse	(1885–1965)		
Serge Prokofiev	(1891–1953)		
Darius Milhaud	(1892–1974)		
Paul Hindemith	(1895–1963)		
Roger Sessions	(1896–)		
Aaron Copland	(1900–)		
Elliot Carter	(1908–)		

Date	Composer, title	Source
Middle Ages	*Veni Creator Spiritus* (Gregorian chant)	1.3, 2.5
Middle Ages	*Offertory* (Gregorian chant from the Christmastide Midnight Mass)	3.19

Too few to allow for any generalizing, these two Gregorian chants illustrate unaccompanied melody (monophony). Chant and its secular counterpart (music of the troubadours and trouvères) prevailed in the earlier period as polyphonic music began to develop. Parallel with this development composers emerged from anonymity: Among the more famous were Leonin and Perotin in Paris around the year 1200 and Machaut and Landini in the fourteenth century.

Most medieval music is *modal* (e.g., Dorian, Phrygian—see the Ancillary Reading to Chapter 3) rather than *tonal* (major-minor); one does not feel the strong pull of dominant to tonic movement as in functional harmony. Also, most of the music that has come down to us (in manuscript only, of course) is sacred vocal music. Idiomatic instrumental music develops at a later date.

Suggested Listening

Anonymous, Gregorian Chant, *The Play of Daniel* (a liturgical drama)

Adam de la Halle, *Le Jeu de Robin et Marion* (a musical play)

Leonin, *Viderunt Omnes*

Perotin, *Sederunt Principes, Alleluya Nativitas*

Guillaume de Machaut, Mass and secular works

Francesco Landini, secular works

Suggested Reading

Reese, Gustave, *Music in the Middle Ages*, New York: Norton, 1940. The most comprehensive, scholarly work in English on medieval music; a new edition is forthcoming.

Seay, Albert, *Music in the Medieval World,* 2nd ed., Englewood Cliffs, N.J.: Prentice-Hall, 1975.

Strunk, Oliver, *Source Readings in Music History,* New York: Norton, 1950, pp. 59–190. Translations of writings by theorists and composers from ancient Greece through the Romantic Period. The readings for each period are also available in separate paperbound volumes.

RENAISSANCE: C. 1400 TO C. 1600

The Renaissance—literally, a "rebirth,"and a new era as those at the time saw it—went for its inspiration back past the "Dark Ages" (as they considered the Middle Ages) to the glories of the classical civilizations of Greece and Rome. At the same time, with the development of humanism, life and culture became increasingly secularized. The Renaissance was a period of great expansion in every area—geographical, economic, scientific, and cultural. The arts flourished at the many courts throughout Europe. Though the impetus for the Renaissance came from Italy, most of the greatest music of the period was the product of Franco-Flemish composers who traveled throughout Europe. The sense of the age as being new and important is well illustrated by the following statement, made in 1477 by the Flemish theorist and composer Johannes Tinctoris: "There does not exist a single piece of music, not composed within the last forty years, that is regarded by the learned as worth hearing."[1]

---

[1] *Liber de Arti Contrapuncti,* as quoted in Friedrich Blume, *Renaissance and Baroque Music* (New York: Norton, 1967), p. 15.

Date	Composer, title	Source
c. 1531	C. Gervaise, *Bransle de Poictou*	2.16
c. 1580	Gabrieli, *Ricercare*	1.26
1590	Palestrina, *Missa Aeterna Christi munera,* Sanctus	4.15
1594	Morley, *Ho! Who comes here*	1.36
1599	J. Farmer, *Fair Phyllis*	7.1
c. 1608	Gibbons, *Fantasia a 4*	Ch. 1 AM[2]
c. 1608	Gibbons, *Fantasia a 2*	1.23
1611	Gesualdo, *Dolcissima mia vita*	5.4

All but two of the Renaissance excerpts listed here served earlier to illustrate either aspects of texture (active) or continuous organization. *Imitation* permeates the Gabrieli *Ricercare,* while the Gibbons *Fantasia a 2* and the Morley excerpt showed polyphony in which the parts are of equal importance. As you rehear these last two examples, you will note immediately that they are also, like the Gabrieli and the Palestrina as well, characterized by initial imitation. While Renaissance music was generally polyphonic, it also showed great textural variety (see the Suggested Listening).

The vocal pieces (Palestrina, Farmer, Gesualdo, Morley) are performed *a cappella,* that is, by voices alone. Instruments might have been added, however, for the performance practice of the period was flexible, and composers did not indicate instrumentation. The Gabrieli *Ricercare,* which also did not specify instrumentation, is performed in the recorded example on modern brass instruments; the Gibbons and Gervaise pieces, on the other hand, use recorders, which were common instruments in the Renaissance.

The Farmer and Palestrina examples were discussed earlier as illustrating the continuous structure generated by polyphony. The Palestrina, in particular, was described in terms of its so-called

---

[2] "AM" refers to Additional Materials. "Ch. 1 AM" indicates that the excerpt originally was given in the Additional Materials section of Chapter 1. This form of abbreviation is used throughout this chapter.

sixteenth-century motet style. The piece proceeds through imitative "points of arrival" at each new line of text, the new imitation overlapping the cadence which concludes the previous "section."

Our eight examples hardly give a complete picture of Renaissance music. None is from the fifteenth century, two are by Gibbons, and three are from the early seventeenth century (the late Renaissance in Elizabethan England). To gain a better sense of the style of the period, listen to works from the following list.

Suggested Listening

Dunstable, *Veni sancte Spiritus, O Rosa bella*
Dufay, secular works, *Missa Se le face ay pale*
Ockeghem, secular works, *Missa Prolationum, Missa Fors seulement*
Obrecht, *Parce Domine* (motet), *Missa Fortuna desperata*
Isaac, *Innsbruck ich muss dich lassen, Quis dabit capiti meo aquam*
Josquin des Prez, secular works, *Missa Pange lingua,* motets
Willaert, madrigals, instrumental *ricercare*
Palestrina, *Missa Papae Marcelli, Stabat Mater* (motet)
Lassus, secular works, *Missa Puisque j'ay perdu, Tristis est anima mea*
(motet)
Madrigals of Marenzio, Morley, Gesualdo, and Monteverdi
Instrumental pieces for lute, organ, and virginals

Suggested Reading

Blume, Friedrich, *Renaissance and Baroque Music,* New York: Norton, 1967.
Brown, Howard M., *Music in the Renaissance,* Englewood Cliffs, N.J.: Prentice-Hall, 1976.
Reese, Gustave, *Music in the Renaissance,* New York: Norton, 1959. An exhaustive, scholarly study of the period; almost more of a bibliographical reference work than a readable survey of Renaissance music.
Strunk, Oliver, *Source Readings in Music History,* New York: Norton, 1950, pp. 193–359.

BAROQUE: C. 1600 TO C. 1750

The Baroque Period, which extends from the first year of the seventeenth century until the death of Johann Sebastian Bach in 1750, borrows its name from art history. As with all eras, the beginning and ending dates are conveniences rather than precise moments of historical change. Aspects of the new Baroque style began to emerge before 1600, and younger composers began to move away from the Baroque style during Bach's lifetime. Also, within this century and a half—the period from Monteverdi through Bach—there were so many significant changes and developments that writers have difficulty defining the period as one era.

The examples from this period heard previously can hardly be considered a representative sample. Half of them are by a single, late-Baroque composer, Johann Sebastian Bach (1685–1750). The generalizations that follow, therefore, apply primarily to late Baroque music. For a fuller appreciation of additional facets of the Baroque style, listen to works by the seventeenth-century composers listed in the Suggested Listening.

As can be seen in the list of excerpts that follows, most of the Baroque examples were used to illustrate varieties of texture

Bach, from autograph score of *Clavierbüchlein vor Wilhelm Friedemann Bach,* 1720

(Chapter 1) and aspects of continuous organization (Chapters 3, 4, and 7). In addition, some examples illustrated sequence, imitation, or the fugue. Indeed, a description of late Baroque music would focus on these areas. Many of the examples illustrate late Baroque polyphony, in which the independence of the parts which existed

Date	Composer, title	Source
1686	Lully, *Armide,* overture	Ch. 1 AM
1689	Purcell, *Dido and Aeneas,* Dido's Lament	Ch. 4 AM
1690	Jacchini, *Sonata with Two Trumpets*	2.17
c. 1712	Vivaldi, *Concerto Grosso,* Op. 3, no. 11	1.32
c. 1712	Vivaldi, *Concerto Grosso,* Op. 3, no. 6	3.1
c. 1712	Vivaldi, *Concerto Grosso,* Op. 3, no. 7	4.6
c. 1715	Bach, *Cantata 31*	1.38, 2.19
1720	Bach, *Partita 2 for Unaccompanied Violin*	1.13, 3.12
c. 1720	Bach, *Concerto in E Major for Violin and Orchestra*	4.3
c. 1720	Bach, *Two-Part Invention in F Major,* no. 8	4.16
c. 1721	Bach, *Suite in B Minor*	1.11, 5.31
c. 1721	Bach, *Brandenberg Concerto 5*	5.10, Ch. 3 AM
1722	Bach, *Well-Tempered Clavier,* Book I, prelude no. 2 in C minor, fugue no. 24 in B minor, fugue no. 3 in C-sharp Major	4.2, 5.16, Ch. 3 AM, 7.7
c. 1723	Bach, *St. John Passion*	1.28, 1.41
1724	Rameau, *Suite in E*	4.17
1725	Vivaldi, *The Four Seasons*	7.2
1729	Bach, *St. Matthew Passion*	1.18, 3.20
c. 1730	Bach, *Concerto in D Minor for Harpsichord and Orchestra*	1.2, 1.15, Ch. 2 AM
c. 1734	Handel, *Concerto Grosso,* Op. 6, no. 2	1.31, Ch. 3 AM
1740	Telemann, *Trio Sonata in D Minor*	2.18, 7.9
1742	Handel, *Messiah*	7.8

in earlier periods yielded somewhat to a polarity between the outer voices. The lowest part (the *basso continuo,* played by a bass instrument and a keyboard instrument playing chords) was combined contrapuntally with the top part within the context of the newly developed functional harmony.

The Bach two-part invention (c. 1720, Example 4.16) illustrated continuous organization—the polyphonic interrelationship of the two parts generated a nonperiodic structure in which caesuras (and "predictable" phrase lengths) occurred infrequently. This kind of "spinning out" or unraveling of the rhythmic and melodic movement can be heard in most of the pieces listed on p. 303. The effect of continuous unraveling is heightened by the prominent use of sequence, which functions rhythmically, melodically, and harmonically in building up the structure. One also feels a very strong pulse—but one which is not obviously broken up into metrical units.

You also may have noticed how many instrumental works there were among the excerpts—many more than in the earlier periods. In the Baroque Period instrumental music developed at a rapid pace. In fact, many of the instrumental genres still in existence today (such as the sonata, concerto, and overture) originated then. Toward the end of the seventeenth century, major-minor tonality became established, and it enabled composers to create more extended structures without relying on a text. This development helped instrumental music to flourish. Within this new harmonic framework chromaticism was often used, both as an expressive means and as a basis for harmonic contrast.

Suggested Listening

J. S. Bach, *Cantata 78,* Jesu der du meine Seele
  B Minor Mass
  Brandenburg Concerto 5
  English Suite No. 3
  Toccata and Fugue in D Minor

Carissimi, *Jephtha* (oratorio)
Corelli, *Concerto Grosso,* Op. 6, no. 8 ("Christmas Concerto")
F. Couperin, *Suites* for harpsichord
Frescobaldi, *Toccatas* for organ
Handel, *Julius Caesar* (opera)
    Messiah (oratorio)
    Concerto, Op. 6, no. 12
Lully, *Alceste* (opera)
Monteverdi, *Orfeo* (opera)
Purcell, *Dido and Aeneas* (opera)
Rameau, *Les Indes Galantes* (opera-ballet)
D. Scarlatti, *Sonatas* for harpsichord

Suggested Reading

Bukofzer, Manfred, *Music in the Baroque Era,* New York: Norton, 1947. This is the most comprehensive study of the entire period; it includes a very large list of Baroque books on music.

Grout, Donald, *A Short History of Opera,* 2nd ed., New York: Columbia University Press, 1956, pp. 1–215.

Newman, William S., *The Sonata in the Baroque Era,* Chapel Hill: University of North Carolina Press, 1959.

Palisca, Claude, V., *Baroque Music,* Englewood Cliffs, N.J.: Prentice-Hall, 1968.

Strunk, Oliver, *Source Readings in Music History,* New York: Norton, 1950, pp. 363–615.

CLASSICAL: C. 1750 TO C. 1827

As with all periods, the dates defining the Classical Period are almost impossible to fix. The era is generally marked off by the dates of the deaths of two composers—Bach in 1750 at one end and Beethoven in 1827 at the other. Aspects of the classical style in music roughly parallel "neoclassical" developments in the other arts, which were inspired by the classical civilizations of Greece and Rome. To oversimplify, we might describe the style as characterized by the predominance of form over content, reason over emotion, manner over matter. Music, however, through three great composers—Haydn, Mozart, and Beethoven, all born within a 40-year period—reached greater heights than the other arts. In the works of these three composers we hear the general characteristics of the style so integrated and expanded as to create music of intense personal expressiveness and meaning.

Date	Composer, title	Source
c. 1761	Haydn, *Symphony 8*	1.5, Ch. 1 AM, Ch. 5 AM
1778	Mozart, *Sonata for Piano in A,* K. 331	3.5, 5.22, 5.23
1778	Mozart, *Variations on "Ah, vous dirai-je, maman,"* K. 265	4.13
1778	Mozart, *Sonata for Piano in F*, K. 332	Ch. 4 AM
1782	Mozart, *Quartet in G Major*, K. 387	Ch. 1 AM, 2.20, 6.14
1782	Mozart, *Serenade in C Minor*, K. 388	5.46
1783	Mozart, *Duo for Violin and Viola*, K. 424	1.24
1783	Mozart, *Concerto for Horn and Orchestra*, no. 2, K. 417	4.1
1787	Haydn, *Symphony 88*	2.1
1787	Mozart, *Eine kleine Nachtmusik*, K. 525	Ch. 3 AM, 4.10, 6.1
1787	Mozart, *Don Giovanni*	3.17
1788	Mozart, *Symphony 39*, K. 543	Ch. 3 AM
1788	Mozart, *Symphony 40*, K. 550	6.7–10, 6.18, 6.19, Ch. 6 AM
1791	Mozart, *The Magic Flute*	3.10, Ch. 5 AM
1791	Haydn, *Symphony 96*	4.5, 6.22, 6.23
1791	Haydn, *Trio in G*, Rondo all' Ongarese	4.18

1791	Mozart, *German Dance,* K. 605, no. 1	Ch. 4 AM
1792	Haydn, *Symphony 97*	Ch. 6 AM
1793	Haydn, *Symphony 99*	1.29, 6.2, Ch. 3 AM
1794	Haydn, *Symphony 100*	5.33–5.39
1795	Haydn, *Symphony 104*	5.28
1796	Haydn, *Concerto for Trumpet and Orchestra*	1.21
1797	Haydn, *String Quartet,* Op. 76, no. 5	2.23
1798	Beethoven, *Trio,* Op. 11	Ch. 1 AM
1799	Beethoven, *Quartet,* Op. 18, no. 1	6.3, 6.11–6.13, 6.15, 6.17, 6.20, 6.21
1800	Beethoven, *Septet,* Op. 20	5.29
1801	Haydn, *The Seasons*	1.42, 7.3
1802	Beethoven, *Sonata for Violin and Piano,* Op. 30, no. 2	6.16
1802	Beethoven, *Sonata for Piano,* Op. 31, no. 3	5.11
1803	Beethoven, *Symphony 3,* Op. 55	1.43, 5.9, Ch. 1 AM
1804	Beethoven, *Variations on "God Save the King"*	2.21
1806	Beethoven, *String Quartet,* Op. 59, no. 3	1.33
1806	Beethoven, *Symphony 4,* Op. 60	Ch. 6 AM
1808	Beethoven, *Sonata for Cello and Piano,* Op. 69	2.22
1808	Beethoven, *Symphony 5,* Op. 67	Ch. 3 AM
1809	Beethoven, *Violin Concerto,* Op. 61	5.24
1811–1812	Beethoven, *Symphony 7,* Op. 92	7.10
1823	Beethoven, *Symphony 9,* Op. 125	1.9, Ch. 2 AM
1825	Beethoven, *String Quartet,* Op. 133 *(Grosse Fuge)*	5.17
1826	Beethoven, *String Quartet,* Op. 131	Ch. 3 AM

Beethoven, from autograph score of *Sonata for the pianoforte in E major*, Op. 109, 1820

A glance at our list of Classical Period pieces shows that the examples occur in almost every demonstration and exercise. They reveal the great diversity of the style—diversity in almost every dimension of music. In a sense, this variety—this freedom—demands the delimiting of form as we have found it in Classical Period music; but at the same time the wealth of possibilities makes the more rigorous structure come alive as process. Recall, for example, how our explanations of fundamental musical procedures, as well as of sectional and continuous organization, fed into our discussion of sonata form in Chapter 6. Because of the clarity of the style and the variety of musical possibilities it utilizes, isolating and demonstrating many of the facets of music becomes easier in works of this period than in those of any other.

In Chapter 1 we discussed aspects of the classical orchestra and of its function in articulating musical events. Later, a Mozart aria (1787, Example 3.17) illustrated balanced, clear phrase structure, and a Mozart minuet (1787, Example 4.10) served as a model of sectional organization. The discussion of functional harmony (the foundation on which nearly all aspects of the style rest) also drew numerous examples from the Classical Period.

Demonstration 6-1 set forth the notion of listening in terms of a structural norm—in this case a schema derived from the Classical minuet. Perhaps the fundamental tenet of Classical style is this establishment of norms (and consequently expectations). Deviations from the norm become highly significant. The integrity of the theme is violated in development, the predominant homophonic texture yields to polyphony at crucial points in the structure, harmonic stability is broken by modulation, and even metrical regularity is upset by syncopation. The term *balance* becomes important here, as composers succeeded in integrating and coordinating all facets of music into a balanced, unified style. If you reconsider Chapters 5 and 6 now, the essentials of Classical style should become clear.

Suggested Listening

The pieces above would constitute an excellent listening list for this period. Missing, however, are some works by lesser masters. If time permits, it would be especially instructive to listen to works by composers other than the three greats in the list above—two sons of Bach, Johann Christian and Carl Philipp Emanuel, as well as Clementi, Boccherini, Cherubini, and Paisiello, to name only a few of the many good composers in this fertile period.

Suggested Reading

Grout, Donald, *A Short History of Opera,* 2nd ed., New York: Columbia University Press, 1965, pp. 215–314.

Newman, William S., *The Sonata in the Classic Era,* Chapel Hill: University of North Carolina Press, 1963.

Pauly, Reinhard G., *Music in the Classic Period,* 2nd ed., Englewood Cliffs, N.J.: Prentice-Hall, 1973.

Rosen, Charles, *The Classical Style: Haydn, Mozart, Beethoven,* New York: Norton, 1972.

Strunk, Oliver, *Source Readings in Music History,* New York: Norton, 1950, pp. 619–740.

ROMANTIC: C. 1827 TO C. 1900

In the nineteenth century, music occupied a unique position. According to the writer-composer E. T. A. Hoffman, music was *the* romantic art; and during the period the critic Walter Pater wrote that "all art constantly aspires toward the condition of music." A period which witnessed an increasing interrelationship among the arts and among artists themselves, the nineteenth century saw music push toward extremes in all its dimensions—dynamics, length, and emotional expression, to mention only the most obvious. It is a regrettable fact that the Romantic and Classical periods together provide the great majority of works in the standard concert repertory—regrettable certainly not because this music is inferior to that of any other period, but because in our time, for the first time in history, contemporary music does not constitute the bulk of the repertory.

The second half of the Romantic Period is treated in detail in the model of procedure in Chapter 9, where nine of the nineteen composers on this list are discussed. In this period color in harmony and instrumentation becomes a significant end in itself rather than a means to some structural end. (See, for example, Mahler, *Symphony 1,* Example 6.5, or Liszt, *Faust Symphony*, Example 3.2. On the use of the orchestra in this respect, see Chapter 1.)

The piano, which had recently undergone a number of technological improvements, was also exploited for its coloristic possibilities, and the orchestra grew in size. To the standard orchestra were added more and different winds (English horn, trombones, horns and trumpets with valves), harp, and many more percussion instruments.

Date	Composer, title	Source
1819	Weber, *Invitation to the Dance*	5.7
1823	Schubert, *Ländler,* Op. 171, no. 4	4.12
1823	Schubert, songs from *Die schöne Müllerin*	Ch. 3 AM, 5.26, 5.32
1827	Schubert, *Impromptu,* Op. 90, no. 2	4.20
1828	Schubert, *Quintet in C,* Op. 163	2.24, 5.12, 6.4
1829	Rossini, *William Tell,* overture	2.15
1832	Chopin, *Étude,* Op. 10, no. 3	5.20
1832–1833	Chopin, *Mazurka,* Op. 17, no. 4	2.25
1838	Chopin, *Prelude,* Op. 28, no. 18	4.4, 4.11

1848	Schumann, *Album for the Young,* "The Wild Horseman"	5.25
1853	Verdi, *La Traviata*	1.20
1854	Liszt, *Faust Symphony*	3.2, 5.18
1854	Wagner, *Das Rheingold,* prelude	5.0
1855	Bizet, *Symphony in C*	4.9
1857–1859	Wagner, *Tristan and Isolde,* Liebestod	3.21, Ch. 4 AM, Ch. 5 AM
1868	J. Strauss, *Voices of Spring*	5.14
1868–1872	Moussorgsky, *Boris Godunov*	Ch. 9
1869	Brahms, *Alto Rhapsody,* Op. 53	Ch. 9
1869–1887	Borodin, *Prince Igor,* Polovtsian Dances	Ch. 9
1872	Bizet, *L'Arlésienne Suite 2*	1.39
1873	Brahms, *Variations on a Theme by Haydn,* Op. 56a	5.27
1873–1881	Moussorgsky, *Khovantchina*	Ch. 1 AM, 3.18
1874	Moussorgsky, *Pictures at an Exhibition*	1.16, Ch. 2 AM, Ch. 9
1876	Tchaikovsky, *Marche slave*	2.10
1877	Tchaikovsky, *Symphony 4*	5.15
1882	Bruckner, *Mass in E Minor,* Sanctus	7.4
1877	Rimsky-Korsakov, *Capriccio espagnol*	Ch. 9
1888	Mahler, *Symphony 1*	1.6, 5.13, 6.5, Ch. 1 AM
1888	Sousa, *Semper Fidelis*	1.8, 2.13
1888	J. Strauss, *Emperor Waltz*	2.9
1888	R. Strauss, *Don Juan*	Ch. 9
1891	Brahms, *Trio for Piano, Cello, and Clarinet,* Op. 114	2.26
1893	Debussy, *String Quartet in G Minor*	Ch. 9
1894	Debussy, *Prélude à l'Après-midi d'un faune*	Ch. 9
1896	Sousa, *Stars and Stripes Forever*	2.7
1898	R. Strauss, *Ein Heldenleben*	3.8

In Chapter 5, in Demonstration 6-1 on the minuet and the scherzo, and in the discussion of the first movement of Brahms's *Symphony 3* in Demonstration 6-2, we gained a sense of the increasing chromaticism in harmony and the changes in structural procedure that characterize the music of the Romantic Period. But one more significant difference between this music and that of earlier periods should be mentioned.

Before the nineteenth century, composers often borrowed freely from preexisting musical sources—either their own works or the works of others. As a result, the style in these earlier periods is more generalized; there is a kind of community of composers and compositions within which the "beacons" of each era stand out. With Romanticism, the "art of the ego," individuality becomes increasingly important, and a composition almost self-consciously tends to take on the particular stamp of its composer.

Suggested Listening

Berlioz, *Symphonie fantastique*
Brahms, *Symphony 3*
   Concerto 2 for Piano and Orchestra
   songs
   Clarinet Quintet
Chopin, piano music
Liszt, piano music
   Faust Symphony
Mahler, *Symphony 1*
Mendelssohn, overture and incidental music to Shakespeare's *A*
   Midsummer Night's Dream
Moussorgsky, *Boris Godunov*
   Pictures at an Exhibition
Puccini, *La Bohème* (opera)
Schubert, songs
Schumann, songs
   Concerto for Piano and Orchestra
R. Strauss, *Till Eulenspiegel* (tone poem)

Tchaikovsky, *Symphony 4*
Verdi, *La Traviata* (opera)
Wagner, *Tristan and Isolde* (opera)

Suggested Reading

Abraham, Gerald, *A Hundred Years of Music,* 3rd ed. Chicago: Aldine, 1964.

Einstein, Alfred, *Music in the Romantic Era,* New York: Norton, 1947.

Grout, Donald, *A Short History of Opera,* 2nd ed., New York: Columbia University Press, 1965, pp. 315–493.

Longyear, Rey M., *Nineteenth Century Romanticism,* 2nd ed., Englewood Cliffs, N.J.: Prentice-Hall, 1973.

Strunk, Oliver, *Source Readings in Music History,* New York: Norton, 1950, pp. 743–902.

TWENTIETH CENTURY

The Romantic and Modern periods overlap. In a sense the twentieth century in music does not begin until about 1910, and the characteristics of Romanticism linger on in music written far into the century. In the first decades of the century, however, avant-garde composers were self-consciously concerned with freeing themselves from the shackles of Romanticism; and the term *new music* became significant.

The first 13 years of the twentieth century and all of the composers represented in the chronology up to 1913, except for Webern, are discussed at some length in the following chapter. But what has happened since then? It is nearly impossible to give a cursory account of the music which developed after this date—partly because it has been a period of intensive experimentation, but mostly (and perhaps refreshingly) because we have no historical perspective from which to view the present.

Date	Composer, title	Source
1899	Schoenberg, *Transfigured Night*	Ch. 9
1902	Debussy, *Pelléas and Mélisande*	7.5
1902–1903	Ravel, *String Quartet in F Major*	Ch. 9
1903–1905	Debussy, *La Mer*	Ch. 1 AM
1906	Schoenberg, *Chamber Symphony 1 in E Minor*, Op. 9	Ch. 9
1906–1909	Debussy, *Rondes de printemps*	1.7
1906–1909	Debussy, *Iberia*, "Parfums de la nuit"	Ch. 9
1907	Ravel, *Rhapsodie espagnole*, "Prélude à la nuit"	Ch. 9
1908	Mahler, *The Song of the Earth*, no. 2	Ch. 9
1909	R. Strauss, *Elektra*	Ch. 9
1909	Schoenberg, *Five Pieces for Orchestra*, Op. 16, no. 1	Ch. 9
1909–1912	Ravel, *Daphnis and Chloé*	2.2
1910	Stravinsky, *Firebird Suite*	1.10, Ch. 1 AM
1910	Schoenberg, *Quartet 2 in F-Sharp Minor*	Ch. 9
1910–1913	Debussy, *Préludes*, Book II, no. 1	Ch. 9
1911	Stravinsky, *Petrouchka*	2.27, 4.7
1911	Schoenberg, *Herzegewächse*	3.11, Ch. 5 AM
1911	Schoenberg, *Six Little Piano Pieces*	4.21, Ch. 5 AM
1912	Schoenberg, *Pierrot lunaire*	Ch. 3 AM
1913	Webern, *Five Pieces for Orchestra*, Op. 10, no. 2	2.29, 4.8
1913	Stravinsky, *Le Sacre du printemps*	1.1, 4.23, Ch. 1 AM, Ch. 2 AM
1916	S. Joplin, *Maple Leaf Rag* (played by S. Joplin)	2.30
1922	Hindemith, *Kleine Kammermusik*, Op. 24, no. 2	2.8
1922	Ravel, *Orchestration of Moussorgsky's Pictures at an Exhibition*	Ch. 9
1923	Milhaud, *La Création du monde*	1.37
1923–1924	Stravinsky, *Octet for Wind Instruments*	2.6, 3.9
1925	Berg, *Wozzeck*	3.3

1925	Schoenberg, *Suite for Piano*, Op. 25	6.6
1927	J. Wood, *Mean Old Bedbug Blues* (sung by Bessie Smith)	5.41
1928	L. Armstrong, *Muggles*	5.43
1929	Stravinsky, *Four Études for Orchestra*	1.30
1930	Gershwin, *I Got Rhythm*	3.6, 3.13
1932	S. Reese, *Which Side Are You On?*	4.19
1934	Hindemith, *Mathis der Maler*	1.34, 1.35, 7.11
1934	Webern, *Concerto for Nine Instruments*	Ch. 6 AM
1936	Varèse, *Density 21.5*	1.12
1936	Schoenberg, *Quartet 4*	Ch. 6 AM
1937	Bartók, *Sonata for Two Pianos and Percussion*	2.28, Ch. 6 AM
1938	Gordon, Roberts, and Kaufman, *Me, Myself and I* (sung by Billie Holiday)	1.25
1938	S. Joplin, *Maple Leaf Rag* (played by Jelly Roll Morton)	2.31
1939	B. Holiday, *Fine and Mellow*	5.42
1943	J. Yancey, *How Long Blues*	5.40
1945	J. Gillespie and C. Parker, *Shaw 'Nuff*	3.14
1946	Sessions, *Piano Sonata 2*	Ch. 6 AM
1947	C. Parker, *Relaxin' at Camarillo*	5.44
1955	Boulez, *Le Marteau sans maître*	5.5
1956	S. Rollins, *Valse Hot*	2.12
1959	Coltrane, *Giant Steps*	5.19
1960	J. Lewis, *Django* (played by the Modern Jazz Quartet)	4.22
1962	M. Reynolds, *Little Boxes* (sung by Pete Seeger)	4.14, 5.30
1966	Babbitt, *Philomel*	1.22
1969	King and Josea, *Be Careful with a Fool* (sung by Johnny Winter)	5.45
1976	Ward, *America the Beautiful* (played by the Al Cohn Quartet)	2.14

We will not attempt, then, to survey all the music written since 1913; you can gain a more complete view of twentieth-century music by reading some of the books listed in the Suggested Reading for the period or, even better, by listening to music written during the last 70 years. For, after all, it is the works composed during this period that make up its musical history. We will, however, comment on some of the experimentation which has occurred since 1945. Our goal is to provide you with both a larger framework for the pieces included in previous chapters and at least a partial sequel to the period from 1860 to 1913, discussed in Chapter 9.

The two contrasting trends described in Chapter 9—music of Austro-Germany and music of Russia and France—continued to provoke stylistic (and sometimes personal) differences well into the twentieth century. Schoenberg in Germany—along with his students, Webern and Berg—found followers among composers both in Europe and in America. Stravinsky in France became the hero and moving spirit in the opposing camp. Interestingly, both composers lived the last years of their lives in the United States.

The kinds of musical experimentation that have occurred since 1945 are in many ways a spin-off from the expansion of possibilities that is found in the music of Schoenberg and Stravinsky. We will focus on three areas: experimentation with sound(s), experimentation with various kinds of limiting forces, and experimentation with chance. The categories are not mutually exclusive. Indeed, while any one of these concerns may be a focal point for a composer, each in some way requires the others. In fact, the interrelationships among these factors often define the particular differences among specific works.

The challenge of new sound or new sound sources brings with it, for example, the search for limits—for ordering principles. But the kinds of limits a composer chooses—his or her means of defining order, may also generate new sounds. (See, for example, the discussion of the blues in Demonstration 5-4.) And even experimentation with chance, which has led to *aleatoric* music (from *alea,* "dice," and by extension, "chance"), can bring forth not only innovative sound combinations but also new structure. In the earlier works of Stravinsky and Schoenberg we already hear the expansion of sound possibilities as well as new kinds of structure. Stravinsky emphasized the use of sonorities—a particular collection of pitches sounding together—which he extended in time and animated through rhythmic, textural, and instrumental transformations. (Listen, for example, to *Le Sacre du printemps,* "Rondes printanières," or to the "Dance of the Adolescents" in Example 1.1.) In later experimental music, sound became something to be made and molded almost as a thing in itself. Edgar Varèse in his *Ionization* (1931) used percussion instruments including sirens, chains, anvils, and a whip as the material for a tightly organized work which was highly influential. Examples of later experimentation with sound can be heard in Example 1.22, *Philomel,* by Milton Babbitt (1966), and Example 5.5, *Le Marteau sans Maître,* by Pierre Boulez (1954). Both works feature a very difficult soprano part with an accompaniment rich in colorful sounds, electronically generated in the Babbitt work. John Cage, who might be described as writing music which is philosophy (music which comments on music) has said, "As contemporary music goes on changing in the way I am changing it, what will be done is to more and more completely liberate sounds."[3]

The development of electronic means for generating sound (the various kinds of synthesizers, some coupled with computers)

[3] John Cage, *Silence* (Middletown, Conn.: Wesleyan University Press, 1961), p. 161.

Arp music synthesizer

encouraged composers to play with sounds (and silence) almost as if the sounds were as tangible and as material as the tape on which they are recorded. Large and complex computer laboratories (mostly at universities—Princeton, Columbia, Stanford, and M.I.T., among others) provide composers with the tools for building sounds and also for experimenting with the nature of sound. Advanced computer programming languages permit composers to manipulate each attribute of a sound separately. Many systems are "interactive"—that is, composers can type in their instructions to the computer, listen to the results, and then immediately make any changes they want. These possibilities have also expanded the field of psychoacoustics—the development of theoretical *descriptions* of sounds which account for the *perception* of sounds as our minds make sense of them.

Still other composers have developed theoretical systems sufficiently generalized to enable them to program a computer to "compose" pieces. Using complex and powerful computer languages, composers can describe structural relations of a composition. The descriptions are in terms of computer procedures which when computed generate the sound events (pitch-time-timbre) which meet the composer's structural specifications.

For Schoenberg, sound, as a generalized quality, was more closely integrated with sound in its most specific aspect: *pitch.* Indeed, it was the orderings of pitch relationships conceived of as a set of linear intervals—a row—that, more as a by-product, generated new sounds in his music. Out of his early, highly chromatic music emerged not only the "emancipation of the dissonance" (see Chapter 9) but also Schoenberg's compositional procedure, the 12-tone technique, or as he preferred to call it, "composition with twelve notes related only to one another." Schoenberg added, "Personally, it is on the word *composition* that I place the emphasis. Unfortunately most would-be followers of this method do something removed from the idea of composing music."[4] This idea of "serializing" pitches involved establishing an initial ordering of the

---

[4] As quoted in J. Rufer, *Composition with Twelve Notes,* translated by Humphrey Searle (London: Barrie and Rockliff, 1965), p. 2.

12 pitches, which then became the normative "pitch set" for an entire work. From this possibility grew procedures for "totally ordering" other aspects of music, such as rhythm or timbre.

But the bases for so organizing the various dimensions or parameters of music—timbre, rhythm, pitch—have varied greatly among recent composers. Some composers have used varieties of arithmetic or statistical manipulations as a basis for determining the succession of events—permuting and interrelating numerical series, for example. At the opposite extreme, some composers have allowed chance to make their decisions. They have tried tossing coins, using random number tables, or even, in the case of John Cage, using the *I Ching*, the classic Chinese Book of Changes, to predetermine events in various dimensions. Xenakis has combined chance and determinacy by using the kinetic theory of gases, for example, to control the density and structure of his "clouds" of sound.

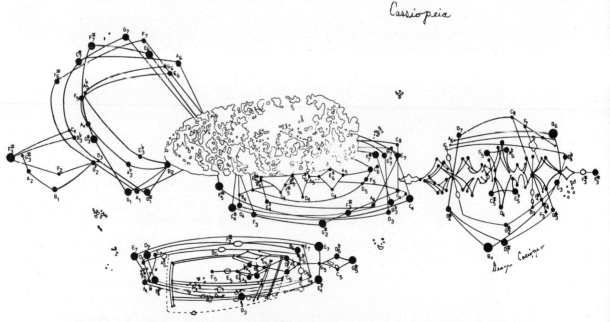

Reproduction of the autograph manuscript of the composition *Cassiopeia*, George Cacioppo. (From *Notations*, by John Cage, editor. Copyright © 1969 by John Cage. All rights reserved. Reprinted by permission of Something Else Press.)

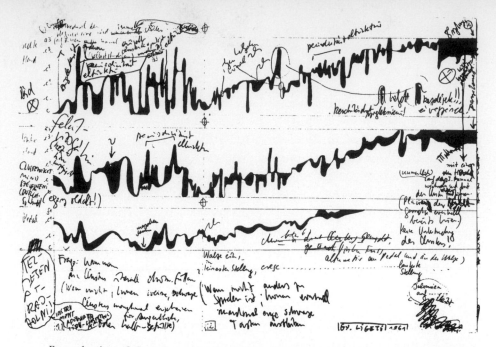

Reproduction of the autograph manuscript of the composition *Volumina*, György Ligeti, 1961. (Copyright © 1967 by Henry Litolff. Reprint permission granted by C. F. Peters Corporation.)

Experimentation has also led to new kinds of music notation —computer-programming languages, languages which describe acoustical phenomena, or even a language of inches of prerecorded tape. In the more aleatoric notations, performers are free to improvise around a few indicated pitches, a graphic design (see pp. 319–320), or some preexisting bit of music (see, for example, Stockhausen's *Hymnen*).

But one should not confuse a technique or a sound surface with the composition itself. For example, Stravinsky, in his later works, used serial techniques as Schoenberg and his students did, but he still maintained his personal rhythmic and textural "gesture" (see, for example, Stravinsky's *Movements for Piano and Orchestra*, 1960, and *Threni*, 1958). Aaron Copland, who was influenced both by his years of study in France and by his American heritage, incorporated the 12-tone approach with quite different effect, for example, in his *Piano Fantasy* (1957).

In similar fashion, the use of electronically generated sounds can be a vehicle—a medium—for pieces as different from each other as the composers themselves. Composers and performers use their instruments—electronic or otherwise—only as a means. Their composition, design, and expressive gesture depend ultimately upon their intent, their creative imagination, and their skill as musicians—that is, upon their artistic choices.

The last ten years have seen a change in the general attitude among composers. While the time up to the mid-1960s was marked by "schools" to which young composers were drawn or to which they expressed antagonism, more recently these "isms" have tended to fade. Composers strive to find their own "voice," taking what they like from the past and present and melding it with their own sense of structural constraints as these shape their creative expression.

Our jazz examples have their own history. They span more than half a century, from Scott Joplin's performance of his own *Maple Leaf Rag* in 1916 to Al Cohn's *America the Beautiful* in 1976. Since jazz is an improvisational art, its history is allied with that of recording techniques. We have a body of recordings rather than a body of manuscripts or printed music; we have no trace of the earliest jazz, before 1916.

Joplin's *Maple Leaf Rag* (Example 2.30) was done on a piano roll the year before his death (and probably when he was past his prime as a performer). Our next examples are from 1927 (Bessie Smith) and 1928 (Louis Armstrong), when electrical recording was in its infancy. Obviously the sound leaves much to be desired in terms of fidelity. Furthermore, until the development of tape, recorded pieces were restricted in length to three minutes; we thus have no idea of what a live, inspired jazz performance at that time was really like. While both are blues, Louis Armstrong's piece exemplifies late New Orleans style. The blues have followed a parallel but independent course with jazz, which continuously nourishes itself on the blues.

Bessie Smith's *Mean Old Bedbug Blues* (Example 5.41) illustrates a type of blues characterized as classic blues, as differentiated from country blues, which were freer and rougher, and rarely recorded in the 1920s. Bessie Smith was the most popular (she was known as the "Empress of the Blues") of a number of women blues singers who performed in theaters before almost exclusively black audiences.

Louis Armstrong's *Muggles* (5.43) while also a blues, represents a final stage of development of New Orleans style. New Orleans, a most cosmopolitan center at the turn of the century, was a focal point in the origins of jazz. After 1917, when Storyville (the red-light district of New Orleans, where many jazz musicians found employment) was closed, many New Orleans musicians moved north to Chicago, which became a jazz center in the 1920s. The traditional New Orleans jazz ensemble (in later manifestations the style was referred to as "Dixieland") comprised trumpet, clarinet, and trombone plus rhythm section (in this Louis Armstrong example, piano, banjo, and drums). In the very early days jazz musicians often did not know how to read music; they played well-known tunes ("rags" or marches) with occasional solos but primarily together—trumpet leading, clarinet with a countermelody, and trombone on the bass line. The resultant polyphonic ensembles were unique in that they were a product of collective improvisation. Improvisation flourished in "classical" music in earlier centuries (Bach, Mozart, and Beethoven, for example, were famous improvisers) but usually done by a soloist, not an ensemble. The Louis Armstrong example represents the dissolution of New Orleans style, for instead of a final ensemble with relative equality among trumpet, clarinet, and trombone, the trumpet (played by Louis Armstrong, the leader and "star") completely dominates the final two choruses.

The two Billie Holiday excerpts (1938, 1939) are from the so-called *swing* period: saxophones are now prominent, the double bass plays pizzicato on every beat, and the music is more tightly arranged. In addition, recording techniques were much improved. *Me, Myself and I* (Example 1.25), in its duet of singer and tenor sax above a subordinate accompaniment, has an analogue in Bach arias in which a singer and a solo woodwind or violin create a polyphonic texture above a minimal accompaniment.

Two examples from 1945 and 1947 (3.14 and 5.44) featuring Charlie Parker ("Bird") on alto sax are prime examples of *bebop*, the style of jazz which succeeded swing in the early 1940s. Some of its characteristics can be heard in these two examples: highly syncopated piano chords and unsettling drum accents, more chromatic harmonies with a prominent use of the interval of the diminished fifth, and in *Shaw 'Nuff*, a dazzlingly fast tempo requiring virtuosic performance by the soloists.

Sonny Rollins's *Valse Hot* (1956, Example 2.12) is a rare example of a jazz waltz. Until recently most jazz has been in duple meter (probably a function of the early influence of the New Orleans marching bands), though currently more complex meters are often used.

The last examples reveal further innovations in jazz history. In John Coltrane's *Giant Steps* (1959, Example 5.19) we find an unprecedentedly complex chromatic harmony in which chords change at a very rapid rate; this consequently demands great facility on the part of the improviser, as is demonstrated by Coltrane in this example. In *Django* (1960, Example 4.25) we have an unusual structure. While most previous jazz either followed the 12-bar blues format or a 32-bar *a a b a* or *a + a'*, here we have *a a b a' c* in which the first two *a* segments are 6 bars in length rather than the usual 4 or 8.

Be Careful With a Fool (1969, Example 5.45) shows the significant blues and jazz influence on rock. More recently there has been a type of "fusion music" seeking a reconciliation of jazz and rock. In Al Cohn's unusual treatment of *America the Beautiful* we hear, among other things, evidence of the recurrent Latin American influence on jazz—in this case the *bossa nova* from Brazil. Another fairly recent development is "free jazz," that is, a kind of collective improvisation (an echo of old New Orleans jazz), often atonal, without a regular periodic structure, and often without a pulse, or in an unusual meter. Limitations of space have prevented the inclusion of some of these recent examples on the records.

In considering the wide range of styles within our own time—including the seemingly great differences between music composed and written down to be played in the concert hall as opposed to mostly improvised jazz—we should bear in mind that the composer (or composer-performer) in searching for personal expression must always make choices. In many ways the nature of these choices defines his or her style, but choosing always involves a struggle between the challenge of possibility and the search for limits. This struggle may seem more poignant today, but as we have tried to demonstrate throughout this book, it seems to be a universal, pervading all aspects of artistic creation: "Well, of course the dialectic of freedom is unfathomable. . . ."[5]

Suggested Listening

Works by composers on the list on p. 297 and mentioned in the preceding pages, as well as works by others such as Babbitt, Berger, Berio, Boulez, Britten, Crumb, Dallapiccola, Davidowsky, Davies, Gideon, Kim, Kirchner, Ligeti, Messaien, Perle, Shapey, Shifrin, Weinberg, Weisgall, Wolpe, and many more.

Suggested Reading

Austin, William A., *Music in the 20th Century,* New York: Norton, 1966. This is a thoughtful and very thorough book on the period, particularly the earlier years.

Boretz, Benjamin, and Edward T. Cone, eds., *Perspectives on American Composers,* New York: Norton, 1972.

Boretz, Benjamin, and Edward T. Cone, eds., *Perspectives on Schoenberg and Stravinsky,* New York: Norton, 1972.

Boulez, Pierre, *Boulez on Music Today,* Cambridge, Mass.: Harvard University Press, 1971. A rather technical but very insightful discussion of analytical procedures applicable to many musical periods but especially appropriate to the twentieth century.

Boulez, Pierre, *Notes of an Apprenticeship,* New York: Knopf, 1968.

Cage, John, *Notations,* New York: Something Else Press, 1969.

Cage, John, *Silence,* Middletown, Conn: Wesleyan University Press, 1961. Nontechnical, free-flowing comments on music and contemporary life.

---

[5] Thomas Mann, *Doctor Faustus* (New York: Knopf, 1948), p. 193.

Forte, Allen, *The Structure of Atonal Music,* New Haven: Yale University Press, 1973.

Griffiths, Paul, *A Concise History of Avant Garde Music from Debussy to Boulez,* New York, Toronto: Oxford University Press, 1978

Jones, Le Roi, *Blues People,* New York: Morrow, 1963.

Lincoln, Harry B., ed., *The Computer and Music,* Ithaca, N.Y.: Cornell University Press, 1970. A collection of essays by many of the most prominent people in the field of computer-related musical activity.

Perle, George, *Serial Composition and Atonality,* 4th ed., Berkeley: University of California Press, 1978.

Reynolds, Roger, *Mind Models: New Forms of Musical Experience,* New York: Praeger, 1975.

Rufer, Josef, *Composition with Twelve Notes.* trans. Humphrey Searle, London: Barrie and Rockliff, 1965. The most authoritative book on Schoenberg's compositional procedures.

Salzman, Eric, *Twentieth Century Music: An Introduction,* 2nd ed., New York: Norton, 1974.

Schwartz, Elliott, and Barney Childs, eds., *Contemporary Composers on Contemporary Music,* New York: Holt, Rinehart & Winston, 1967.

Sessions, Roger, *Questions About Music,* Cambridge, Mass.:Harvard University Press, 1970. A series of lectures concerning current questions on both contemporary music and the music of the past.

Shapiro, N., and N. Hentoff, *Hear Me Talkin to Ya: The Story of Jazz by the Men Who Made It,* New York: Dover, 1966.

Slonimsky, Nicholas, *Music Since 1900,* 4th ed., New York: Scribners, 1971.

Stearns, Marshall W., *The Story of Jazz,* London, New York: Oxford University Press, 1958.

Stevens, Halsey, *The Life and Music of Béla Bartók,* 2nd ed., New York: Oxford University Press, 1963.

Stravinsky, Igor, and Robert Craft, *Retrospectives and Conclusions,* New York: Knopf, 1969.

Stuckenshmidt, H. H., *Twentieth Century Music,* trans. Richard Daveson, New York: World University Library, McGraw-Hill, 1969.

Tirro, Frank, *Jazz: A History,* New York: Norton, 1977.

Arnold Schoenberg

CHAPTER 9

Style and music history: a model of procedure

Igor Stravinsky
by Pablo Picasso

On several occasions in the course of this book we have asked you to think about questions of musical style, but usually within the context of some particular aspect of music. In Demonstration 1-1, The Variety of Sound, for example, we asked questions concerning different "sound worlds," uses of the orchestra—even different uses of music in varying social contexts. Each of these characteristic aspects of a piece, in fact, helps to define its particular style. In Chapter 2 we made a quick sweep through music history, considering the varying uses of rhythmic complexity in works written over a period of 400 years. In Chapter 3 we drew attention to your intuitive "model of a sensible tune," contrasting this with melodies that seemed to derive from a different set of norms for melody making. This was another way of pointing to differences in style. Chapter 5 included not only a discussion and illustrations of possibilities other than functional harmony, that is, differing *harmonic* styles, but also contrasting examples of the twelve-bar blues, showing stylistic change within a single structure. This idea was carried further in the historical trip through the minuet and sonata forms in Chapter 6. Finally, in Chapter 7 we illustrated stylistic differences within continuously organized music generally and within fugues specifically. In Chapter 8 we confronted historical questions through a general survey of the history of Western music, but we did not deal directly with how the words *style* and *history* relate to a given work or composer or how various styles interact within one musical era. It is to these more specific historical questions that we now turn.

Style, as we shall use the term, refers to the collection of musical attributes that characterizes the music of a particular composer or era. A composer's style is, in fact, his or her set of implicit norms, assumptions, and unique characteristics which allows you to say, even when you turn on the radio in the middle of a work, "Ah, Bach!" or "That's Brahms!" How do you know?

We are not concerned here merely with identification, which can become a game substituting for, or at least interfering with, the experience of the unique work in its totality. Rather we are concerned with a kind of flexibility in listening, at times approaching virtuosity, which allows you to shift your focus—to move freely from one period of music to another, perceiving as configurations and events those which are appropriate to the piece in question. In short, we are concerned with your ability to involve yourself with the work on its own terms.

A discussion of style necessarily involves the many problems and questions of music history, most especially the changes in style that have taken place over a period of time. We can, in the context of this book, merely enumerate some of these problems (see the following questions) and, in the detailed model of procedure beginning on page 331, touch on some of the answers.

1. What is the relationship between the style of an individual composer and the general style of his or her era? In earlier periods are individual differences fewer—that is, can we truly speak of a "common practice?" Or do the apparent similarities in style result only from chronological distance?

2. How important is critical evaluation, during and after their times, of composers within a specific era? For example, our excerpts from the Classical Period are drawn only from Haydn, Mozart, and Beethoven; what about the music of their "lesser" contemporaries and its relationship to the style of the period? In the late Baroque Period, Telemann was generally held in higher esteem than J. S. Bach, yet today we hear relatively little of Telemann's music.

3. Can we or should we try to listen with, let us say, "eighteenth-century ears" to eighteenth-century music? Our understanding of a period means that we have determined and are in some respects sensitive to its normative procedures—for example, the function of passages within a sonata-form movement of the late eighteenth century. But how can we shut out the sounds of two subsequent centuries of music? Could we possibly hope to recapture the feeling that a sensitive listener must have experienced hearing for the first time the beginning of the development section of the last movement of Mozart's *Symphony 40*? Our reaction

to this tremendous shock to the tonal system is of course tempered by our experience of the subsequent expansion and ultimate dissolution of tonality as a fundamental force.

4. How do styles change from one period to another, and can we determine causal factors?

5. Can we speak meaningfully of interrelationships among the arts at a particular time? Can we transfer our generalizations about music to contemporaneous activities in art and literature? And how do we make this kind of transfer to a very different art? Is there a "time lag" between one art and another? If so, when and why?

6. Finally, what is the relationship between music and society? What role do sociological and economic factors play in the history of an art? What is the relationship between the artist and his or her audience? Do the attitudes and tastes of the audience influence the composer's work? For example, we might ask here: What about music written on the turbulent eve of the French Revolution? Mozart and Haydn were the leading composers!

While we are posing fundamental questions about the interpretation of history, its events, and their resultant "objects," partial answers can be found within your own experience. In previous sections we have usually discussed works irrespective of their dates of composition, often to demonstrate *similarities*. When we have proceeded chronologically, it was often to demonstrate change within a framework of certain structural *constants*. By regrouping all the musical excerpts chronologically in Chapter 8, we added another dimension—that of a composition as a historical "object" existing within a body of other objects bearing some relation to it.

From your own experience of these works it should be clear, then, that flexibility of perception does not imply assuming a totally new stance when listening to pieces written at different times and in different styles. Some aspects of musical organization are relevant to all music; the questions are which and when.

Listening to a work *on its own terms*, then, assumes both the ability to perceive the various possibilities we have discussed earlier in this book and an awareness of the particular manner in which a composer manipulates and plays with these possibilities. Expanding and using this awareness in reference to works written within a given period will create a sense of historical context.[1]

A MODEL FOR THE STUDY OF MUSICAL STYLE AND HISTORY: 1860 TO 1913

The study of a specific period in music history can require a year-long course, a week or two in a survey course, or the lifetime of a musicologist. Here we present a model for procedure in such a study. Our discussion will be confined to music written during the latter half of the nineteenth and the early part of the twentieth century, and we will focus on only a few significant works, pointing out what we take to be the two main trends during this period. We continue to emphasize personal experience—this time your experience of specific works as you hear them within their historical context. To gain a broader perspective on the period under discussion, you should, in addition to "immersing" yourself in the music of the period, read selectively from among the books listed in the Suggested Reading at the end of this chapter.

We have chosen the period from about 1860 to the outbreak of World War I because it includes marked stylistic contrasts. Indeed, a sensitivity to stylistic change becomes important in listening to the music of this time precisely because of its growing diversity. In some senses, also, this period provides guides to the music of our own era.

---

[1] The musical examples discussed in this chapter usually are not included on the records. Since the discussion in most cases is more general than in previous chapters (referring, for example, to sections of an entire movement of a symphony or to a scene from an opera), you will find it helpful to use a recording of the complete work. But remember that the discussion here, as elsewhere in the book, will have little meaning if the reader is not also a listener.

Listen first to two works written at either end of the period.

Wagner, *Tristan and Isolde,* Act II, scene 2, 1857–1859 (first performance, 1865)
Schoenberg, *Pierrot lunaire,* "Mondestrunken" ("Moondrunk"), 1912

How would you describe the fundamental differences in style
between these two works? Implicit in this question is another:
What fundamental means does each composer use to make his
work comprehensible? Or, more important for our purposes,
what specific assumptions must listeners make if they are to respond appropriately to each work?

You must shift your focus—must use the kind of listening
flexibility we have emphasized—if you are to understand both the
Wagner and the Schoenberg works. If you cling to the assumptions
inherent in the Wagner piece, you may find the Schoenberg work
incomprehensible (consider only the harmonic assumptions, for
example). Certainly, two more questions arise: (1) How do you
achieve this essential flexibility and (2) what sort of historical
process occurred between Wagner and Schoenberg?

Can the first question be resolved by listening to the earlier
work first? Will listening to Wagner's *Tristan* then make the
Schoenberg piece more intelligible? In other words, is there a natural stylistic evolution which, if experienced, makes the various
phases of music history understandable? Can the history of music
be described in terms of influences and orderly transformations?
And if it can, how important is the individual composer (with his
or her own history and own private consciousness) or the individual composition (with its own history and its own set of internal
events)?

To emphasize these problems, consider two more works also
written at the limits of our selected time span.

Moussorgsky, *Boris Godunov,* coronation scene, 1868–1872 (first
performance, 1874)
Stravinsky, *Le Sacre du printemps,* "Dance of the Adolescents,"
1913 (Example 1.1)

Then listen to the four examples again and consider how you would pair them, using similarity of style as a basis. Will you pair them by date of composition: the two nineteenth-century works and the two twentieth-century works? Or by nationality: two German (or, in the case of Schoenberg, Austro-German) composers and two Russian composers?

It seems clear that the greatest similarity is between the last two works—both by Russian composers. What characteristics do these pieces have in common? Listen to them again, noticing the following similarities:

1. An insistent sonority (particular combination of pitches) which pervades the "pitch atmosphere." In Moussorgsky's work, the characteristic sonority is generated by the alternation of two chords from the traditional tonal repertoire, here no longer functionally (tonally) related; and in Stravinsky's, we hear a single chord which is nonfunctional in the traditional sense.
2. A persistent beat, metrically regular in Moussorgsky's piece but much less so in Stravinsky's.
3. An exploitation of instrumental color for its own sake.
4. *Juxtaposition* of sections rather than *transition* between them.
5. Folklike melodies which are modal rather than tonal in their pitch organization and which are often simply repeated with different orchestration (or voices) rather than developed.

While the Wagner and Schoenberg examples are less strikingly similar, they are more like each other than like either of the other pieces. For example, they share the following traits:

1. An effect of charged intensity.
2. The use of melodic motives as the basic source of unity (rather than the persistent sonority used by Moussorgsky and Stravinsky).
3. The transformation of these motives through sequence, imitation, and other techniques.
4. A sense of continuous development achieved in part by motivic transformation and including transition rather than juxtaposition as a means of moving from one section to another.
5. An absence of clear phrases resulting from the motivic nature of the melodic lines and from overlapping among the parts.

6. An active texture, with parts struggling against one another to be heard.
7. A large range in both the instrumental and the vocal parts.
8. A sense of *structural rhythm,* generated by chord changes, the length of the motives, and the pace of motivic repetition rather than prominence of the beat per se. (The sense of pulse, in fact, is quite subordinate in Wagner's and Schoenberg's music.)

In pairing these four works we have demonstrated the two major and contrasting stylistic trends which emerged during the latter half of the nineteenth and the beginning of the twentieth century. While change takes place within these two groups (as the examples themselves demonstrate), the differences which we have observed here remain to distinguish German and Russian music throughout the period. We will continue our discussion, then, by pursuing these two trends individually and then bring them back together to consider them both in the context of the total period from 1860 to 1913.

From Wagner to Schoenberg

As we narrow our discussion to the Austro-German composers, differences (which may appear small in a larger context) emerge even between two composers who were writing contemporaneously. In the case of Brahms and Wagner, these differences became a *cause célèbre.*[2]

Wagner (1813–1883) and Brahms (1833–1897)

Listen to the first movement of Brahms's *Symphony 3* and compare it with the "Liebestod" ("Love-Death") from Wagner's *Tristan and Isolde.*

---

[2] See Donald F. Tovey, *The Forms of Music* (New York: New American Library, Meridian Books, 1957), pp. 128–132; and Gerald Abraham, *A Hundred Years of Music,* 3rd ed. (Chicago: Aldine, 1964), pp. 129–132.

Johannes Brahms
(at about age 33)

Brahms, *Symphony 3*, first movement, 1883
Wagner, *Tristan and Isolde,* "Liebestod," 1857–1859 (Example
3.21)

Brahms wrote no operas, Wagner no symphonies. Inherent
in this fact is a fundamental difference in approach. For example,
the Brahms *Symphony 3* falls into the traditional four movements,
each of which in some way embodies a traditional organizing principle (such as sonata form or ABA). On a more detailed level, you
will remember from our discussion of the Brahms first movement
(Chapter 6) that its structure was realized through contrasts in the
functions of sections: statements (generally in one key with a relatively clear melodic shape), transitions (modulatory and more
fragmented melodically), elaborations and development, and cadential passages. In addition, the statement passages differ in
character, providing another kind of contrast. In short, while
Brahms's harmonic, instrumental, and rhythmic means may be

different from, for instance, Beethoven's, you still respond to those structural functions which generate drama in purely musical terms.

Wagner, on the other hand, developed means of organization which derived, to a large extent, from the drama of his text. In the "Liebestod," for example, we are swept along both musically and dramatically in a process of transformation. Even the traditional divisions of opera (aria, recitative, and such) are no longer heard in this music.

Wagner writes continuous music—"endless melody"—in which there is sequential development of "significant motives" (each one usually associated with a character or idea) in a complex, often highly active texture characterized by continuous modulation and avoidance of cadences. In addition to the constant shifting and merging of tonal centers, the harmonic implications of chords are often diverted or left unfulfilled. Specifically, the dominant seventh chord (the crux of the tension-building waiting passages of Beethoven and Bach; see Demonstration 5-1) is frequently heard as stable. It resolves more ambiguous harmonic movement by momentarily defining or pointing to a specific key. The result is music that is continuously searching, building, and surging toward a climax. How different from the carefully contrasted passages, each with its own function, that we hear in Brahms!

Brahms, *Alto Rhapsody,* Op. 53, 1869

Listening to the *Alto Rhapsody,* however, one recognizes that Brahms and Wagner are contemporaneous. Given a text describing an unhappy youth wandering through a desolate, wintry landscape, Brahms explores broader expressive means in his music. In this piece, the harmony, like Wagner's, is more chromatic. Cadences are avoided, and sectionalism is therefore abandoned. The mood is unified; and, in a sense, we are asked to listen in a different way. This is dramatic music, but without the charged intensity of the Wagner excerpt—and with the singer playing a more predominant role.

In short, it is the *genre* rather than the date of composition that brings these two composers stylistically closer together. In Chapter 6 we suggested that traditional forms became more dramatic in the nineteenth century. But set alongside Wagner Brahms now appears rather closer to tradition in his instrumental works. It is when Brahms turns to music inspired by and expressive of a text that we hear him exploring other musical dimensions. What, then, constitutes drama in Brahms's symphonic movements as compared with drama in his vocal works?

Mahler (1860–1911)

Mahler, *The Song of the Earth,* "Autumn Loneliness," 1908

This song for voice and orchestra, written 39 years after Brahms's *Alto Rhapsody,* at first sounds almost like a continuation of that piece. The affinity between the two songs lies in:

1. Their clear, largely diatonic melody lines, which soar above a relatively thin orchestral texture.
2. The rich harmony of the accompaniments with their elusive cadences.
3. The single, poignant mood of the texts, from which the continuous musical structure of each piece derives.

Gustav Mahler, Auguste Rodin
(The Rodin Museum, Philadelphia)

Paradoxically Mahler, who considered himself in the Wagner camp, was not fond of Brahms's music: "All I can say of him is that he's a puny little dwarf with a rather narrow chest. . . . It is very seldom he can make anything whatever of his themes, beautiful as they often are. Only Beethoven and Wagner, after all, could do that."[3] (Of course, it should be remembered that Mahler was speaking here primarily of Brahms's symphonies rather than of his dramatic vocal music.)

But despite Mahler's devotion to the music of Wagner, his style differs from Wagner's in that he does not create a "competition" between voice and orchestra. Mahler's orchestra lacks Wagner's thick, active texture in which the instruments merge into a mass of sound; and in Mahler we do not hear Wagner's constant surging toward an ever-bigger climax.

Mahler, *Symphony 1*, 1888 (Examples 1.6, 6.5)

Similarity of genre, however, need not result in similarity of style. Mahler's *Symphony 1* was written only five years after Brahms's *Symphony 3*, yet the differences between them are striking. Mahler, unlike Brahms, tended to be influenced by extramusical associations even in his symphonies. For example, his *Symphony 1* is subtitled "The Titan." Many of his later symphonies also have programmatic associations, and often a text and voice are introduced even in symphonic works. Traditional forms appear in a freer guise; they are greatly expanded and do not have the same sense of classical tradition which pervades the symphonies of Brahms.

In listening to the movements of Mahler's *Symphony 1*, notice particularly:

1. The large orchestra and extensive use of horns, trumpets, and even woodwinds at the top of their ranges.

---

[3] Letter to his wife, written June 23, 1904; quoted in Irving Kolodin, ed., *The Composer as Listener* (New York: Collier, 1958), p. 51.

2. The very active texture, which is yet so transparent that you seem to be able to hear through it, with each instrumental color standing out clearly.
3. The folklike and strongly diatonic melodies contrasted with more chromatic, almost Wagnerian melodies.
4. The strong pulse, often emphasized by tympani.

The jubilant mood of this movement is created in part by Mahler's virtuoso ability to toss these contrasting melodies through the orchestra, combining them, fragmenting them, and opposing them with abandon. Mahler himself described this process in terms of his use of

> . . . *themes*—clear and *plastic,* so that they are distinctly recognizable in every transformation and further unfolding; then a working out, full of variety, and, above all, gripping because of the *development* of the inner idea and also because of the *genuine opposition* of the motifs placed in contrast to each other."[4]

Richard Strauss (1864–1949)

Richard Strauss, *Don Juan,* 1888

Mahler described Richard Strauss as a "literary man." Indeed, the majority of Strauss's works are programmatic in some sense. In the same year that Mahler wrote his *Symphony 1,* Strauss composed a *tone poem*—an orchestral work in one movement inspired by the poem *Don Juan* by the Hungarian poet Nikolaus Lenau. The character of the Don "on a gallant hunt for womanly perfection" is immediately portrayed in the music by its huge melodic range (so different from Mahler's folklike melodies), its martial rhythmic patterns, the use of brass in a characteristic fanfare manner, and the massive orchestra and thick texture out of which melodies and instruments seem to struggle for individual existence.

---

[4] Gustav Mahler, *Briefe,* p. 191, quoted in William A. Austin, *Music in the 20th Century* (New York; Norton, 1966), p.129.

Richard Strauss

As the tone poem progresses, notice how themes of strongly contrasting character rapidly succeed one another (for example, a momentary dance melody, the Don's theme, and eventually a "feminine" solo violin melody). The structure is generated largely by *extramusical* events and characters with which particular themes, instruments, and rhythms are associated. The music is more chromatic than Mahler's, full of contrast and yet nonsectional in the classical sense. We hear it freely evolving through the transformation, juxtaposition, and intertwining of thematic material.

Richard Strauss, *Elektra,* 1909

We turn now to an opera by Strauss. Listen to Elektra's soliloquy on the death of her murdered father.

Strauss, like Brahms, pushes his musical vocabulary to its extremes in the service of his text. *Elektra,* written 21 years after *Don Juan,* reveals a considerably extended chromaticism (a single tonal center is never maintained). The melodic line is often sharply disjunct, with a range that puts the most extreme demands on the singer. The relationship between singer and orchestra varies from a kind of accompanied recitative to an almost Wagnerian struggle between voice and instruments. All this is designed to express the intense, nearly insane emotion of Elektra. Imagine Mahler's choosing the story of Elektra as a subject for a piece of music!

Schoenberg (1874–1951)

Schoenberg, *Transfigured Night,* 1899

Schoenberg's *Transfigured Night* was written ten years before *Elektra* and goes back still further to Wagner for its musical ancestry. The surging climaxes, thick, turbulent texture, chromatic harmony, motivic manipulation, unified mood, and even the motives themselves are particularly reminiscent of *Tristan and Isolde*. A jury that reviewed the piece for possible performance declared: "It sounds as if one had smeared over the still moist *Tristan* score."[5]

With this early work of Schoenberg we approach the last phase in our study of Austro-German works up to World War I.

[5] The Vienna *Tonkünstlerverein* jury (which refused performance of the work); in Sam Morgenstern, ed., *Composers on Music* (New York: Pantheon, 1956), p. 377.

Self-portrait, Arnold Schoenberg.
(Used by permission of Belmont Music Publishers, Los Angeles, California 90049)

It has provided only a tourist's view; the traveler needs to spend more time to understand fully where one has been. The remaining works, all by Schoenberg, take us through 1912, allowing us to focus on the style of a single composer. This closer look at the works of only one composer might seem to make issues of stylistic change less problematic. But Schoenberg's stylistic transformation is nevertheless quite remarkable over this period of 13 years. While his essays and letters describe his personal struggle for what he considered "necessary" means of expression,[6] his works themselves are equally—perhaps more—revealing.

Schoenberg, *Chamber Symphony 1 in E Major,* Op. 9, 1906

This symphony, written seven years after *Transfigured Night,* is scored for 15 solo instruments. The charged atmosphere, reminiscent of the earlier work, requires the utmost from each instrument in the unique ensemble. The two pieces are also similar in their extensive use of a few motives—rather than clear, palpable melodies—and in their constant manipulation of them. The music is continuously developmental. In the following extract Schoenberg discusses the composition of this work.

> There was at hand from the start a sufficient amount of motival forms and their derivatives, rather too much than too little. The task, therefore, was to retard the progress of development in order to enable the average good listener to keep in mind what preceded so as to understand the consequences. To keep within bounds and to balance a theme whose character, tempo, expression, harmonic progression, and motival contents displayed a centrifugal tendency: this was the task here.[7]

The striking difference between this work and *Transfigured Night* is the curious mixture of new and old found in the later work. In his chamber symphony, tonality is still operative (notice the full cadence at the end of the brief introductory passage) but

---

[6] See especially Schoenberg's essay "Composition with 12 Tones," in Arnold Schoenberg, *Style and Idea,* trans. and ed. Dika Newlin (New York: Philosophical Library, 1950).

[7] Schoenberg, "Heart and Brain," *Style and Idea,* p.162.

almost as if it were struggling for existence under an attack of extreme chromaticism. Coupled with this is a wildly active texture in which angular, even jagged, motives overlap, interrupt, and intrude on one another.

Rhythm depends on the length of motives, pace of attack, and harmonic change rather than on pulse or meter, which are often submerged. The ascending chain of fourths in the horn near the beginning of the piece is used as a basis for new chord formations built on the interval of the fourth rather than the third. The use of solo instruments creates a complex but transparent texture, which becomes increasingly significant in Schoenberg's music.

The dramatic intensity of the piece lies not in a program but in more purely musical processes—for example, the transformations of a few motives, the movement from solo statement to increasing textural density and activity, and the dissolution to solo statement again. The strangely anguished quality of the piece seems to lie partly in its struggle with past means of comprehensibility—with past assumptions which are being pushed to their limits. What emerges is music that is simultaneously decadent and explosive!

Schoenberg, *Five Pieces for Orchestra,* Op. 16, no. 1, 1909.

Three years later, Schoenberg had created a new musical world—a world that has had its effect on every subsequent composer. This "new" music was characterized by its extreme brevity, and its sense of condensed action. Schoenberg says of the works of this period:

> The first compositions in this new style were written by me around 1908 and, soon afterwards, by my pupils Anton von Webern and Alban Berg. From the very beginning such compositions differed from all preceding music, not only harmonically but also melodically, thematically and motivally. But the foremost characteristics of those pieces *in statu nascendi* were their extreme expressiveness and their extraordinary brevity. At that time, neither I nor my pupils were conscious of the reasons for these features. Later I discovered that our sense of form was right when it forced us to counterbalance extreme emotionality with extraordinary shortness.

Thus, subconsciously consequences were drawn from an innovation which, like every innovation, destroys while it produces. New colorful harmony was offered; but much was lost.[8]

Harmonically, this work seems to have burst the limits which we were so acutely aware of in the chamber symphony. Schoenberg ascribes the difference to the "emancipation of the dissonance":

> The term *emancipation of the dissonance* refers to its comprehensibility, which is considered equivalent to the consonance's comprehensibility. A style based on this premise treats dissonances like consonances and renounces a tonal center. By avoiding the establishment of a key, modulation is excluded, since modulation means leaving an established tonality and establishing *another* tonality.[9]

In this music, melody and harmony, as previously understood, are highly fragmented—almost shattered. Here your awareness of specific melodic and rhythmic motives becomes crucial to grasping the logic of the piece. In the midst of a complex counterpoint we hear strong, terse, constantly evolving melodic fragments, sometimes sounding against a repeated figure in the bass and occurring in a vast array of slightly varied, interconnected shapes and instrumental colors. The large orchestra is treated almost like a group of solo instruments, as in the chamber symphony, and this singular treatment allows a highly intricate detail to emerge. Through manipulation and contrast of rhythmic and textural activity, the structure seems to develop out of itself with the "logic" of free association. The overall effect is one of tremendous energy and vitality. The work seems alive and fresh rather than decadent —self-contained rather than explosive.

Schoenberg, *Quartet 2 in F-Sharp Minor,* third movement, 1910

In this composition Schoenberg introduces the voice into the string quartet—another invasion of the instrumental realm. Schoenberg writes:

---

[8] Schoenberg, "Composition with 12 Tones," *Style and Idea,* p.105.

[9] Ibid.

. . . it seemed at first impossible to compose pieces of complicated organization or of great length. A little later I discovered how to construct larger forms by following a text or poem. The differences in size and shape of its parts and the change in character and mood were mirrored in the shape and size of the composition, in its dynamics and tempo, figuration and accentuation, instrumentation and orchestration. Thus the parts were differentiated as clearly as they had formerly been by the tonal and structural functions of harmony.[10]

The third movement from the *Quartet 2* is somewhat reminiscent of *Elektra* in the great demands made on the singer, the wide range, the very disjunct melody, and the quest for climaxes. But unlike Strauss, Schoenberg uses a limited number of instruments. He exploits their possibilities in new ways, creating a texture which is relatively thin and transparent but rich in coloristic effect. Throughout we hear Schoenberg reaching for the extremes to create an effect of intense emotional expression.

Schoenberg, *Pierrot lunaire,* "Mondestrunken," 1912

We arrive at the end of our study of German and Austrian music with one of the masterpieces of the twentieth century. In *Pierrot lunaire* Schoenberg brings together in the most concentrated form all the aspects of his music that we have heard emerging in his earlier works. The bizarre, almost frightening atmosphere of the text (by the Belgian poet Albert Giraud) is reflected in every detail of the music. Combining singing and speaking (*sprechstimme*), the singer penetrates the atmosphere, portraying the madness of a moonstruck clown.

Despite the effect of hysteria, the music unfolds with an intense, tight logic. Scored for only five players and eight instruments (piano, flute and piccolo, clarinet and bass clarinet, violin and viola, and cello), the song develops, with an extreme concentration of detail, out of initial motives which the composer transforms to reflect the text.

Notice, for example, the "waves" created by a sequentially re-

---

[10] Ibid., p. 106.

peated motive played transparently by the flute, violin pizzicato, and the upper register of the piano. The motive "pours from the moon in waves at nightfall." This passage is in immediate contrast to a thick, active texture in which the cello enters and the motive moves within the predominant sound of percussive low piano chords: "The poet by his ardor driven."

Historically, perhaps the most remarkable aspect of this piece is that in it Schoenberg, incorporating many of the characteristics of his earlier style (so clearly influenced by the Austro-German composers of the late nineteenth century), has spawned something entirely new. Schoenberg's stylistic change over this period of 13 years includes both what he termed the "dissolution of tonality" and the creation of fresh bases for organizing pitch, the full implications of which were realized only in the years following 1914. The particular means which Schoenberg found are inextricably bound with the stylistic characteristics of the Austro-German tradition—as will become even clearer when we consider the quite different style of Stravinsky and his predecessors. You may find it interesting now to go back to the first Wagner examples and listen to them in the light of your awareness of later developments in German and Austrian music.

From Moussorgsky to Stravinsky

In our earlier discussion we noticed a rather striking similarity between the two Russian composers who delimit our time period: Moussorgsky (1839–1881) and Stravinsky (1882–1971). Indeed, there seemed to be more in common between them than between the two Austro-German composers. Their similarities suggest a clear stylistic tradition in the Russian music of this period.

The fact that the similarity between the two Russian works is more striking than that between the German works (*Tristan and Isolde* and *Pierrot lunaire*) tells us something about the stylistic traditions of each country. We might say that the "surface," or the "face," of German music changed radically during these 50 years, while certain less immediately accessible characteristics (such as structural process) remained to define the tradition. In Russian music the surface remains recognizable, and it is this more obvious quality that is crucial in defining the style.

Another body of music, that of France, relates closely to the Russian music of this period. There was a great cultural affinity between Russia and France during the late nineteenth century. Members of the Russian aristocracy spoke French as a second language. The intellectual, artistic, and social elite traveled frequently between the two countries (Debussy, for example, worked for some months in Moscow in his early years). Both Russian and French intellectuals shared a certain revolutionary spirit. This relationship comes alive in the novels of Tolstoi, Dostoevski, and Turgenev and in the plays of Chekhov.

A Characteristic Surface

Musically, this affinity is immediately evident. Listen to the openings of the following works:

> Moussorgsky, *Khovantchina,* prelude, 1873–1881 (Example 3.18)
> Debussy, *Prélude à l'après-midi d'un faune,* 1894
> Debussy, *Iberia,* "Parfums de la nuit," 1906–1909
> Stravinsky, *Le Sacre du printemps,* 1913 (Examples 1.1, 4.23)

What contributes to the characteristic sound of these works? They are rhythmically amorphous, haunted by the changing color of solo instruments (particularly winds) set against a background texture which is mobile—often shimmering and nebulous. We are drawn into a musical world in which the play of sounds itself is the prime source of pleasure. Although differences will emerge as we study the period and the individual works of Russian and French composers, these qualities persist. They make it possible to speak of a Russian-French tradition.

Modest Moussorgsky,
Il'ya Yefimovich Repin.
(Sovfoto, New York)

Our approach to this music will be somewhat different from that used in examining the music of Germany and Austria. Instead of treating the period strictly chronologically, we will focus on its recurring common threads. We will make a series of temporal sweeps rather than temporal steps—first within Russian and then within French music.

Russia: Nationalism and The Folk Song

Moussorgsky, *Khovantchina,* prelude, 1873–1881 (Example 3.18)
Moussorgsky, *Boris Godunov,* prologue, 1868–1872
Moussorgsky, *Pictures at an Exhibition,* "Promenade" (Example 1.16), "Polish Oxcart," "Great Gate of Kiev," 1874
Borodin, *Prince Igor,* Polovtsian Dances, 1869–1887
Stravinsky, *Firebird Suite,* finale, 1910 (Example 1.10)
Stravinsky, *Petrouchka,* Part I, 1911

In these examples a new element appears: a pervasive sense of Russia. Nationalism was a powerful factor guiding and inspiring a group of Russian composers known as the Mighty Five—Moussorgsky, Borodin, Rimsky-Korsakov, Cui, and Balakirev. Seeking out Russian history, myth, and folk song, they tried to free themselves from foreign (especially German) influence to create a music that was truly Russian. Their aggressive, almost violent anti-German feelings are expressed by Moussorgsky in the following remarks, written to two young ladies requesting information about German songs:

> Of the German things sing the ones you like, because it's better for you to make the choice *accidentally,* than for me—at a distance: *accidentally,* for I am very doubtful about German vocal music in particular. German men and women sing like roosters, imagining that the more their mouths gape and the longer they hold their notes, the more feeling they show. To speak harshly, *Kartoffel, Kirschensuppe, Milch* and *Tchernickensuppe* do not have an especially good influence on the power of feeling and particularly on artistic feeling, and for my taste the Germans, moving from their leather fried in pork-fat to the seven-hour operas of Wagner, offer nothing attractive for me.[11]

The Mighty Five used Russian folk melodies or composed folklike melodies extensively. Cesar Cui describes the attributes of the Russian folk song as follows:

> One of the principal elements in the structure of Russian song is the complete freedom of rhythm, carried to the point of caprice. Not only may the musical phrase be composed of an unequal number of measures, but even in the same song the rhythm of the measures may change several times. These changing rhythms are, above all, *right,* since they are supremely expressive. At the same time, they utterly exclude the impression of banality and monotony which sometimes results from the prolonged use of a uniform and overworked rhythm.
>
> But their very variety is such that an unpracticed ear does not grasp certain Russian songs clearly, as long as the musical phrases

---

[11] Letter to Alexandra and Nadezhda Purgeld, written June 20, 1870 in Petrograd; in Jay Leyda and Sergei Bertensson, eds. and trans., *The Musorgsky Reader,* (New York: Norton, 1947), p. 138.

are not divided and established into precise measures. Another notable fact is . . . that very often, the theme is not constructed on the current European scale, but on old Greek modes, the origin of church music. . . . The use of the Greek modes . . . has the further advantage of a great diversity because, in Greek music, the position of steps varies with each mode, while in European music it is fixed.

The Russian folk song imperiously demands an original harmonization and a very special art of modulation. First, it is rare to come on a song the melody of which can be treated entirely in one of the two modes, major or minor; most often, even if it spans but a few measures, it passes from the minor to its relative major and vice versa.

It also happens that the harmony of a single chord remains stationary throughout an entire song, which lends it an overall quality of vague melancholy, a complexion of deliberate monotony.

Russian folk tunes are ordinarily confined within a very restricted note-span, only rarely exceeding the interval of a fifth or sixth. . . . The theme is always short; some are limited to two measures, but these measures are repeated as many times as the scope of the text demands.[12]

Cui's comments quite accurately describe the unique qualities of the melodies we heard in the previous examples.

These works are all characterized by a process of organization which stems in part from the use of folk song. Sectional in the larger sense, they proceed from one part to another by juxtaposition rather than by transition. (Notice the difference in this respect between the excerpts from *Boris Godunov* and *Tristan and Isolde,* or between *Pictures at an Exhibition* and the movement from Brahms's *Symphony 3.*) Within the parts we hear clear smaller sections. These sections are often created by the repetition of whole melodies which are varied largely by orchestration and texture rather than by transformation or motivic elaboration.

Indeed, one of the crucial differences between Russian and German compositions of this period lies precisely in the concept of

---

[12] Cesar Cui, from *La Musique en Russie,* quoted in Morgenstern, pp. 220–225.

development. In the German music we noticed an emphasis on what we called "organic growth": the manipulation of a motivic germ to create passages of varying structural functions, climax, dissolution, and so forth. In Russian music, melodies tend to remain intact. Development then consists of exploiting a variety of coloristic and textural possibilities while melodic and harmonic relationships remain relatively constant within any one section.

On the other hand, the fluid and elusive structure of the melodies themselves, as described by Cui, generates a kind of mobility within stasis. For example, the *Khovantchina* melody (which is stated after the introduction), especially the ordering of its various phrases, is difficult to remember. The wandering quality of this melody contributes to the prelude's sense of mobility in spite of the many repetitions.

Perhaps most important to the sense of contained mobility in these pieces is their remarkable variety and richness of texture and, even more striking, the use of strange and wonderful instrumental colors. Listen to these works again, along with those listed below, and pay particular attention to how the composers change the character of a melody or a chord by altering its instrumentation and its sonorous surroundings.

Rimsky-Korsakov, *Capriccio espagnol,* variations, 1887
Moussorgsky, *Boris Godunov,* Coronation Scene, 1868–1872
Stravinsky, *Le Sacre du printemps,* "Dance of the Adolescents,"
    1913 (Example 1.1)

Harmony (chord relationships) is tied very closely to color and sonority in these examples. A particular combination of tones (a chord) is often used to imitate the sound of an object (bells or a circus) or to evoke an image (dancing adolescents). Consider specifically the opening of the coronation scene in *Boris Godunov* and the "Dance of the Adolescents" from *Le Sacre du printemps.* Both make use of a particular and unique chordal sonority rather than functional syntax (a framework in which tension, resolution, direction, or goal is implicit).

In the coronation scene, two chords move only by alternating with one another. Each is in itself a familiar combination of tones. But juxtaposed, they neither imply a particular tonal center nor create harmonic direction or even tonal ambiguity. Harmonically, the passage is static.

Compare this opening, for example, with the opening of the *Tristan* prelude. The situation is almost the opposite. In the prelude there is directed harmonic motion. Goals are implied; tension is created because the direction shifts and the goals are avoided. In *Le Sacre du printemps,* as in *Boris Godunov,* a particular sonority is used, but it is different in nature—it is not a triad. To this factor and its historical significance we will return shortly.

There is a crucial connection here between harmonic and structural style, just as there was between melodic style and structure. The fact that we feel little sense of built-in directed harmonic movement is inextricably related to our sense of an additive structure. Each section is contained by its relatively static harmony; motion within it derives primarily from coloristic and textural variation. Chords, then, become a part of the dimension of color. They are sensuous entities to be embellished and enjoyed rather than elements in a complex of interrelated functions.

This harmonic stasis is animated rhythmically as well as melodically and texturally. The *Godunov* coronation scene, for example, moves (within its limits) through an increase in rhythmic activity. While the beat remains regular (the tempo does not change), the number of notes per beat continuously increases as the texture thickens and more instruments are introduced. In *Le Sacre du printemps,* rhythm is considerably more complex from the outset. It grows increasingly more so as new melodic-rhythmic fragments are superimposed on its static harmony and as the texture becomes thicker, more active, and more varied in color.

The emphasis on color and texture in Russian music is not confined to works for large orchestras. In Moussorgsky's *Pictures at an Exhibition,* which he wrote originally for piano (you heard an excerpt from Ravel's orchestration of the Promenade as Example 1.16), the sound possibilities of the piano alone are exploited

Project for the City Gate of Kiev,
Victor Hartmann.
(Pictures at an Exhibition)

*Bronze Clock in the Form
of Baba Yaga's Hut,*
Victor Hartmann.
(Pictures at an Exhibition)

seemingly without limits. How does Moussorgsky make the piano sound like, for example, chickens, an oxcart, an old witch, and even the great gate of Kiev? This wonderfully imaginative and unfettered use of the instrument for creating "sound pictures" stems from the following devices:

1. Exploiting the suggestiveness of the various registers of the piano (high and low).
2. Using at some times a small, pinched range and at other times a large, sweeping range.
3. Contrasting all kinds of textures—thick chords, unison, thin linear textures.
4. Demanding legato, staccato, or an almost percussive touch.
5. Using rhythm to imitate, at times almost to mimic, the movement of what is being depicted—for example, two Jews or children playing.
6. Using particular combinations of tones (chords) that do not operate functionally but, like the rhythm, imitate, evoking images of people or things.

We have attributed the special quality of Russian music in part to the nationalistic loyalties of its composers. But to the folk-like melodies and the harmonic and structural characteristics which follow from them must be added a particular kind of originality, stemming perhaps from the fact that all but one of the Mighty Five were amateurs who had had little formal musical training. Moussorgsky in particular was proud of being a self-taught composer. Undoubtedly this was a crucial factor in his own peculiarly original style. All of Moussorgsky's music is in some way motivated by extramusical considerations (he wrote no symphonies, no chamber music, and no sonata forms). Yet how different his music is from that of Mahler, Strauss, or Wagner! The following comments written in a letter to a friend express Moussorgsky's attitude toward academic music and learned musicians:

> In one [music school] Z . . and T . . , in their professorial, antimusical togas, stuff the heads of their students with various abominations and infect them in advance. The poor pupils see before them not human beings but two fixed pillars to which are nailed some silly scrawls said to contain the laws of music. . . . Being raised to the rank of a doctor of music—*a cobbler in an academic fool's cap*—he [Z . .] is not so childish as to base his opinions and advice on esthetics and musical logic—oh no! He has learned the rules and uses this as a smallpox antitoxin to inoculate against free learning anyone who longs to study art.[13]

Moussorgsky was often criticized for his lack of "technique." Of this he says:

> Why do I, *do not tell me,* when I listen to our musical brethren, seldom hear a vital idea, but mostly stuff from a school-room bench —technique and musical ABC's? . . . Maybe I'm afraid of technique, because I'm poor at it? However, there are some who will stand up for me in art. . . .
> Leave aside the boundaries of art—I believe in them only very relatively, because *boundaries of art* in the religion of the artist, means *standing still.* . . . I've taken up the cross and with lifted head,

---

[13] Letter to Mili Balakirev, written April 28, 1862, in the village of Volok; in Leyda and Bertensson, p. 44.

bravely and happily, I shall go forth against *all sorts of things,* towards bright, strong and righteous aims, towards a genuine art that loves man, lives his joys, his grief and his sufferings.[14]

Finally here is what Debussy writes about Moussorgsky:

> He is unique and will remain so because his art is spontaneous and free from arid formulas. Never has a more refined sensibility been conveyed by such simple means; it is like the art of an enquiring savage discovering music step by step through his emotions. Nor is there ever a question of any particular form; at all events the form is so varied that by no possibility whatsoever can it be related to any established, one might say official, form since it depends on and is made up of successive, minute touches mysteriously linked together by means of an instinctive clairvoyance.[15]

France: Debussy (1862 –1918) and Ravel (1875 –1937)

These comments provide a convenient link to the French music of this period. Debussy's admiration and sympathy for Moussorgsky's music is reflected in his own music—perhaps not so much by "influence" (although he knew the Russian's music well) as by "elective affinity." The importance given to color and texture and the immersion in direct, sensuous sound relationships, together with the organizing processes we have observed, identify the fundamental similarity between Russian and French music. Let us consider this similarity, as well as the differences between the two bodies of music more carefully now. Listen to the following works:

Debussy, *Rondes de printemps,* 1906–1909 (Example 1.7)
Debussy, *Iberia,* "Parfums de la nuit," 1906–1909
Ravel, *Rhapsodie espagnole,* "Prélude à la nuit," 1907
Debussy, *Préludes,* Book II, no. 1, 1910–1913
Ravel, *Orchestration of Moussorgsky's Pictures at an Exhibition,* 1922

---

[14] Letter to Vladimir Stasov, written July 13, 1872, in Petrograd; in Leyda and Bertensson, pp. 192–194.

[15] Claude Debussy, *Monsieur Croche the Dilettante Hater* (London: N. Douglas, 1927), p. 35.

Claude Debussy

In the first four examples we can hear again music character-ized by a kind of animated, ebullient stasis. The means of anima-tion, however, are different, more subtle, and perhaps more re-fined: perfume rather than a coronation or a great gate. In "Parfums de la nuit" from *Iberia* the stasis is quite literal—a single note is sustained while melodic fragments hover above and below it. We relish the sound of each instrument (often a solo woodwind) as it appears and disappears. The melodic fragments are wispy (in contrast to the folk melodies of Russian music), defined neither by clear tonal relationships nor by phrase structure. Rhythmically, events take place extremely slowly. Pulse seems nonexistent, and we are encouraged to surround ourselves with the sonorities with-out concern for their extension in time. Contrast and movement are created by the introduction of new sounds (new chords, a thicker or more active texture, different instruments). But instead of a juxtaposition of events as in Russian music, there is a merging of one sound into the next.

Harmonically, this music does not obstruct or negate tonality (as does the music of Wagner and Schoenberg). Instead, it seems to absorb it, replacing it with a chordal sonority which is often repeated up or down a series of whole steps. Unlike Moussorgsky's, Debussy's chordal sonorities are sometimes nontriadic combinations of pitches. Thus they are less defined—more amorphous.

In Ravel's *Rhapsodie espagnole,* "Prélude à la nuit," a single *melodic* motive generates the sense of stasis. The varieties of sounds it acquires seem endless. The varieties of *surroundings* it assumes give the listener full opportunity to revel in sensory delight. It is like watching the reflection of a branch in the water. It never moves but is moving all the time; motion is contained within the limits of its confining shape.

In his piano prelude we hear Debussy exploiting the sonorous qualities of a single instrument. Like Moussorgsky in *Pictures at an Exhibition,* Debussy seems able to work magic in creating unique piano sounds. But his purpose is less literal, or perhaps less pictorial, than Moussorgsky's. Debussy makes more of sounds for their own sake; their associations are secondary and somehow more private.

In all these works we have little feeling of directed motion. Instead of a German walking tour punctuated by arrival at certain destinations, our experience is one of sitting quietly, deeply absorbing a single vista. Debussy wrote of his *Images:*

> The music of this piece has this about it: it is elusive, and consequently cannot be handled like a robust symphony which walks on all fours (sometimes on threes, but walks nevertheless).
>
> Besides, I am more and more convinced that music is not, in essence, a thing which can be cast into a traditional and fixed form. It is made up of colors and rhythms.[16]

Finally, listen to Ravel's orchestration of Moussorgsky's *Pictures at an Exhibition.* (The work is the result of a fascinating inter-

---

[16] Letter to Jacques Durand, September 3, 1907; quoted in Morgenstern, *op. cit.,* p. 329.

twining of personalities and media. An exhibition of watercolors and drawings of architecture by Victor Hartmann, Moussorgsky's friend, inspired a set of pieces for the piano; Ravel, inspired in turn by these pieces, composed an orchestral version.)

As you listen to it, consider why Ravel was drawn to the possibilities of orchestrating this work. In what ways does the orchestration change the effect? Do you think Ravel has improved it? Which piece do you like better? Which more effectively evokes the intended images? Does Ravel's style intrude on Moussorgsky's?

> Debussy, *String Quartet in G Minor,* 1893
> Ravel, *String Quartet in F Major,* 1902–1903

Debussy and Ravel each wrote one string quartet. Both are rather early works, Debussy's dating from his thirty-first year. It is difficult to describe this piece adequately in the terms we have been using. Consider the second movement, for example, marked *Scherzo* ("*assez vif et bien rythmé*"). Its relationship to traditional scherzos is tenuous though revealing. In form the movement can be described as ABA′, but this fact seems unimportant in the light of its unique inner processes.

Harmonically the movement could again be described as static—one bass note is maintained throughout a large part of the A section. Yet it seems inappropriate to describe the harmony negatively as "without motion." In the context of tonal harmony the implications of the term *static* (as used in Demonstration 5-1) are quite different; harmony plays a different role in that style, where syntax is largely defined or generated by harmonic functions.

Listening to this movement, we perceive the bass note as a *dynamic* element—a constant against which all the events of the piece take place but which (like any background) is itself affected by them. For example, there is a passage near the middle of the A section (*b* in the *a b + a′* structure within A) in which the bass note is not played. This is a moment of tension—of climax; resolution occurs with the return of the bass note. Another point of tension occurs at the end of A, when the cello, carrier of the constant, takes up the predominant melody and goes on to form a transition to the B section.

Equally "static" is the melody—a single two-measure figure which is also repeated almost continuously throughout the A section. But like the bass, it is not heard as unchanging. It does, in fact, move about. In the beginning it is played by the viola. The violin takes it up in the second half (*a'*), and finally it is given to the cello. But more important, its surroundings vary so much that it is only after listening analytically that we realize it remains literally unchanged for long stretches.

Coming now to the surface of the Debussy work, we focus on what is most immediately perceived: the sparkling pizzicato upper strings. Moving through a large range, they enliven the piece by creating marvelous rhythmic shifts from the prevailing three-beat to two-beat groups, teasing the regularity of the repeated motive, the beat, and the phrase grouping. Toward the middle (*b*) of the first section, the pizzicato "ingredient" takes over. The sparkling surface seems to absorb the rest at this moment of tension. The two constants (bass note and motive) cease, and we are left suspended, to return to an altered norm in which the sound fabric is tipped over—the motive appearing on top, the pizzicato underneath.

To describe this as *a b + a'* is certainly correct, but does this place the work in the tradition of eighteenth- and nineteenth-century German composition? Does it significantly contribute to an understanding of its style? How does form function in this work? This last question is a crucial one in our consideration of stylistic character.

What of the B section, whose themes (related to A) are elusive enough to make it difficult to say whether they are one or several? What of the passages which we hear as "waiting," but not so much because of their dominant harmonic implications as because of their thinner texture and relative cessation of activity? What *does* articulate structure in this work? What means does Debussy use to create stability, tension, and climax? Is there a sense of directed motion?

These are some of the questions that must be answered if we are to define or describe the style of this music. Debussy warned against this kind of analysis, however, in a letter to a musician who had tried to describe his harmonic style:

> Think of all the inexpert hands that will utilize your study without discrimination, for the sole purpose of annihilating those charming butterflies which are already somewhat crumpled by your analysis.[17]

Listen now to the Ravel quartet, written 10 years later. Compare the second movement (marked, similarly to Debussy's *assez vif—très rythmé*) with that in Debussy's quartet. Notice that the ABA′ structure is much more clearly articulated. The B section is much slower and has a distinctly contrasting character. The return of A is prepared for by a long passage where the motives of A appear in fragmentary fashion, finally emerging full-blown in the return (A′). The return here is closer to the original A section than it is in the Debussy movement.

Harmonically Ravel depends more on functional chord relationships. We hear, for example, clear tonic-dominant and tonic-subdominant progressions. The melodies are more diatonic (although they have modal aspects, like the lowered seventh degree in the otherwise A-minor opening melody). There is a stronger sense of pulse and a clearer articulation of the phrase rhythm in Ravel's work. The feeling of static structure is not a pervasive one. While color and texture are certainly a source of variety and contrast, they seem to reinforce the other structural elements rather than to be themselves the means of structural articulation.

For all these reasons Ravel is often said to be more in the "classical tradition" than Debussy. But what does this mean in the light of Ravel's use of that characteristic French shimmer, his cascading of sounds and rhythms in the final movement of the quar-

---

[17] Letter to René Lenormand; quoted in Austin, *op. cit.,* p. 19.

tet, his own way of "teasing" functional harmony, which makes that harmonic framework really quite different from what it is in the hands of Brahms or Strauss?

Opera and Ballet

Let us leave these questions and turn for a moment first to opera and then to another group of pieces which unites Russian and French forces, namely, music of the ballet.

Debussy wrote one opera, *Pelléas and Mélisande,* using Maeterlinck's symbolist play as his literary source. Like *Tristan and Isolde,* this is essentially a love story, but at no point does it approach the heavy, hyperemotional atmosphere characteristic of Wagner's opera. Even at the moment of greatest emotional inten-

Wagner, *Tristan und Isolde* (photograph taken at first performance, 1865)

A scene from the New York City Opera production of *Pelléas et Mélisande*. (Photo by Beth Bergman)

sity—when Pelléas and Mélisande finally declare their love for one another—the atmosphere is one of understatement, of a tender, quiet, make-believe world of unreal children. Compare this scene which you heard in Chapter 7 with the lengthy and passionate scene in which Tristan and Isolde first meet as lovers (they still have two more hours to consummate their love).

Wagner, *Tristan and Isolde,* Act II, sc. 2, 1857–1859
Debussy, *Pelléas and Mélisande,* Act IV, sc. 4, 1902 (example 7.5)

As you listen, notice the difference in the relationship between the voices and the orchestra. In the Debussy opera the orchestra rarely impinges on the vocal line. The orchestra is once again often static, sustaining one sonority while the voice hovers above it in recitative-like song. We can hardly speak of motives or development of motives or even phrases. The texture is characteristically shimmering but inactive in the Wagnerian sense.

Harmonically too we feel little sense of directed tension, avoided cadences, or ambiguous chromaticism. Tension is created coloristically—by instrumentation, range, contrasts in density of texture, increase in rhythmic motion. Notice particularly the beautiful moment when Pelléas says, "Je t'aime" and Mélisande answers, after a breath of silence, "Je t'aime aussi," on one, unaccompanied note. We are gently led into a world that seems ephemeral, refined, dreamy, and sensuous.

Turning finally to the ballet, we come once again to Stravinsky, in whom our rather rapid sweeps through Russia and France converge. Stravinsky's three early ballets were commissioned by Sergei Diaghilev, whose Ballets Russes had its first season in Paris in 1909. This company was a vital force in Parisian artistic life for 20 years. Diaghilev, the director, Fokine, his choreographer, and Nijinsky, his principal male dancer, all played a part in the inception and realization of Stravinsky's early ballets. (Diaghilev also commissioned Ravel's *Daphnis and Chloé,* as well as other works by Debussy, Stravinsky, Satie, and Prokofiev.)

> *Firebird Suite,* Introduction, "Dance of King Kastchei," finale, 1910 (Example 1.10)
> *Petrouchka,* Part I, Part III, 1911 (Examples 2.27, 4.7)
> *Le Sacre du printemps,* Introduction, "Dance of the Adolescents," 1913 (Example 1.1)

These three ballets are all based on Russian folklore. Listen carefully to the excerpts (some of which you have heard before), noting particularly the changes in style between the earlier and the later works, the reflections of earlier Russian composers (Stravinsky had studied with Rimsky-Korsakov), and the effect of Stravinsky's wider international musical experiences.

Stravinsky wrote *Firebird* in Paris, working closely with Fokine. He gave Fokine the music bit by bit as he wrote it and attended all the rehearsals of the company. The effect of this close association is hard to estimate, but surely the very special character of the work derives in some measure from the immediacy and excitement of performance and from the interactions between choreographer, dancers, and composer.

In *Firebird* and *Petrouchka* we hear the beginnings of the style that came to fruition in *Le Sacre du printemps.* In all three works we hear the sectionalism of the earlier Russian composers, the use of folk song, the strong pulse, and the coloristic use of instruments to activate the "static" harmony. But these characteristics are already becoming transformed in *Firebird*. There is greater variety within the sections, made possible by the materials themselves. The pulse cannot be taken for granted. It is alive, shifting, grouped, and regrouped. Rhythmic patterns are established only to be extended or broken apart, fragmented and put back together; and the folk-like melodic fragments are treated similarly.

The orchestra is larger and is used with all the imagination and skill of the earlier Russian and French composers. But Stravinsky adds new sounds (instruments played in unusual ways), along with a new kind of "layered" effect in which instrumental colors are heard intertwining with one another to create a more complex texture. Harmonically, sections are static, yet tonal implications remain. For instance, we hear a repeated bass figure (*ostinato*) composed of fifths, and also a relatively tonal melody from which the harmonic sonority seems to derive (the opening of Kastchei's dance, for example).

In *Petrouchka* the ostinato becomes more important as an organizing, stabilizing factor in an atmosphere in which sonorities have become more complex (less triadic), and the texture thicker and more active. Notice how the ostinato functions in the opening of Part I. It is not simply a bass figure, but rather a kind of bubbling sound in which it is difficult to pick out individual instruments or even specific durations. It forms an animated color over which melodic fragments, solo instruments, and rhythms are superimposed like flashes. Often stopping abruptly as if used up, one ostinato yields to another, creating strong contrast and sectional articulation. How does Stravinsky's use of a "background" differ from Debussy's in his quartet or in *Iberia*? Why is an ostinato rare in the works of Schoenberg?

Melodic repetition also has a new life in *Petrouchka* because the recurrence of a motive is unpredictable and rarely literal. Stravinsky constantly alters the length of the melodic fragment. The static quality of repetition is both there and not there at the same time. The first bubbling ostinato stops suddenly, yielding to a chordal texture—a kind of congealing of the whole sonority—

which then becomes the norm to be unpredictably manipulated. One thinks of the painter Matisse and his myriad textures, juxtaposed to form a design in which the viewer continuously discovers new relationships.

In *Le Sacre du printemps* Stravinsky created a work equaled in importance only by *Pierrot lunaire* as a disruption of the musical status quo. The ballet generated an equally new but quite different world of musical possibility. Indeed, the works symbolize the two approaches to music which, in the years that followed, often divided composers into opposing camps. Stravinsky himself was more understanding and appreciative of *Pierrot lunaire* than many of his followers:

> Whatever opinion one may hold about the music of Arnold Schoenberg (to take as an example a composer evolving along lines essentially different from mine, both aesthetically and technically), whose works have frequently given rise to violent reactions or ironic smiles—it is impossible for a self-respecting mind equipped with genuine musical culture not to feel that the composer of *Pierrot lunaire* is fully aware of what he is doing and that he not trying to deceive anyone. He adopted the musical system that suited his needs and, within this system, he is perfectly consistent with himself, perfectly coherent.[18]

Yet at the same time Stravinsky viewed the piece from his own vantage point, in terms of his concern with instrumentation and texture, as these create design:

> The instrumental substance of *Pierrot lunaire* impressed me immensely. And by saying "instrumental" I mean not simply instrumentation of this music but the whole contrapuntal and polyphonic structure of this brilliant instrumental masterpiece.[19]

Why is *Le Sacre* considered a revolutionary work? (This was, incidentally, a reaction Stravinsky did not appreciate—"I confess

---

[18] Igor Stravinsky, *Poetics of Music* (New York: Random House, Vintage Books, 1956), p. 14.

[19] Igor Stravinsky and Robert Craft, *Conversations with Igor Stravinsky* (Garden City, N.Y.: Doubleday, 1959), p. 79.

Stravinsky rehearsing *Le Sacre du printemps,* Jean Cocteau. (Permission S.P.A.D.E.M. 1974 by French Reproduction Rights, Inc.)

that I am completely insensitive to the prestige of revolution.") Consider the opening. The bassoon plays alone at the top of its range, sounding to some listeners marvelously new and strange, while sounding to others badly distorted. The melody, based on a Lithuanian folk song, is characteristically repetitive—a small collection of pitches varied by a completely flexible rhythm. As instruments are added, they combine to form sonorities that are no longer triadic but are the result of layers of fragmented melody superimposed—held together and made comprehensible—either by an ostinato or by the flashes of repeated melody. Juxtaposition of textures and melodic fragments still characterizes the structural motion. But now the juxtaposition is more abrupt, episodes are shorter, and motives appear, disappear, reappear unpredictably—recognizable but often in new garb.

In the "Dance of the Adolescents" the unique sound is created by Stravinsky's superimposing two functionally unrelated triadic chords. It is as if he had compressed Moussorgsky's juxtaposed chords into one sound which is neither of them. The unifying sonority is all-pervasive here—more so than in Stravinsky's earlier work because the sound itself siezes and haunts the listener. We feel a strong pulse. But the beats are grouped so irregularly (through sudden accents) that they form not a background but an active ingredient in the compositional fabric—a vital force in the effect of earthy sensuousness. Stravinsky said of the work: "I saw in imagination a solemn pagan rite: sage elders, seated in a circle, watching a young girl dance herself to death. They were sacrificing her to propitiate the god of Spring."

While the composer breaks up the sonority in various ways to create, at times, a linear ostinato, the sonority seems never to disappear. And to it he adds such a variety of elements that it is small wonder that the piece left its first-night audience reeling—from the flashes of coloristic sound, fragments of folklike tunes, instruments playing at the extremes of their ranges, rhythms clashing and abruptly shifting. Can you imagine the dance itself? Certainly it was far different from the toe dancing, arabesques, and tutus of nineteenth-century ballet.

Pagan rites, the unusual Nijinsky dancing in Paris, while the moonstruck Pierrot sang in Vienna and Berlin! Go back now and listen to *Pierrot lunaire* with its concentration of detail; its thin, polyphonic texture; and its brief, closed, organic forms in which development means evolution of a seminal motive. How different from Stravinsky's static structure, within which melodic fragments and fixed sonority undulate and revolve, but somehow create, in themselves, definition and limits. And how very different in mood!

Stravinsky once said:

> The creator's function is to sift the elements he receives from her [imagination or fantasy], for human activity must impose limits upon itself. The more art is controlled, limited, worked over, the more it is free. . . . My freedom thus consists in my moving about within the narrow frame that I have assigned myself for each one of my undertakings. I shall go even farther: my freedom will be so much the greater and more meaningful the more narrowly I limit my field of action and the more I surround myself with obstacles. Whatever diminishes constraint diminishes strength. The more constraints one imposes, the more one frees one's self of the chains that shackle the spirit.[20]

---

[20] Stravinsky, *Poetics of Music,* pp. 66, 68.

As you stand back and consider the period from 1860 to 1913 –from Wagner and Moussorgsky to Schoenberg and Stravinsky– you could view it in terms of the changing notions of limits and freedom and their relative importance. In a crucial sense, composers' styles are defined by the personal and often unconscious limits they impose on possibility and within which they find the freedom to express what is relevant to them.

Historically, too, you can watch and listen to the ebb and flow of this relationship between freedom and limits: Wagner and Moussorgsky living by and espousing the concept of expansive freedom, each in a different way; Schoenberg and Stravinsky each searching for his own limits to contain and at the same time intensify expressiveness.

Can we conclude, then, that to view a work historically is to grasp in it the interplay of innovation and tradition? Perhaps. But more important is this: Ultimately it is an expanded awareness— both of historical context and unique process—that liberates and frees the listener to choose and to listen to any work with a sense of direct personal involvement. This is truly practicing the art of listening.

Suggested Reading

Abraham, Gerald, *A Hundred Years of Music,* 3rd ed., Chicago: Aldine, 1964.

Austin, William A., *Music in the 20th Century,* New York: Norton, 1966.

Boretz, Benjamin, and Cone, Edward T., *Perspectives on Schoenberg and Stravinsky,* New York: Norton, 1972.

Debussy, Claude, *Monsieur Croche the Dilettante Hater,* London: N. Douglas, 1927.

Del Mar, Norman, *Richard Strauss,* London: Free Press, 1962.

Hanslick, E., *The Beautiful in Music,* New York: Liberal Arts Press, 1957. A contemporary discussion of the Brahms-Wagner argument, heavily weighted toward Brahms.

Leyda, Jay, and Sergei Bertensson, eds. and trans., *The Musorgsky Reader,* New York: Norton, 1947.

Lockspeiser, Edward, *Debussy,* New York: Pellegrini & Cudahy, 1951.

Mahler, Alma, *Gustave Mahler: Memories and Letters,* rev. ed., Mitchell and Martner, Seattle: University of Washington Press, 1971. A rather personal account of the composer's life and work, by his wife.

Mellers, Wilfred, *Man and His Music: Romanticism and the Twentieth Century,* New York: Schocken Books, 1969. A good overview of the period from the mid-nineteenth to the mid-twentieth century; available in paperback.

Newlin, Dika, *Bruckner, Mahler and Schoenberg,* New York: King's Crown Press, 1947.

Orenstein, Arbie, *Ravel: Man and Musician,* New York: Columbia University Press, 1975.

Rimsky-Korsakov, N. A., *My Musical Life,* New York: Knopf, 1942.

Schoenberg, Arnold, *Style and Idea,* ed. Leonard Stein, New York: St. Martin's Press, 1975.

Slonimsky, Nicholas, *Music Since 1900,* 4th ed., New York, Scribner, 1971.

Stein, J. M., *Richard Wagner and the Synthesis of the Arts,* Detroit: Wayne University Press, 1960.

Stravinsky, Igor, *Poetics of Music,* New York: Random House (Vintage Books), 1956.

Stravinsky, Igor, and Robert Craft, *Conversations with Igor Stravinsky,* Garden City, N.Y.: Doubleday, 1959.

Stravinsky, Igor, and Robert Craft, *Dialogues and a Diary,* Garden City, N.Y.: Doubleday, 1963.

Stravinsky, Igor, and Robert Craft, *Expositions and Developments,* Garden City, N.Y.: Doubleday, 1962.

Stravinsky, Igor, and Robert Craft, *Memories and Commentaries,* London: Faber, 1960.

Stuckenschmidt, H. H., *Arnold Schoenberg,* trans. E. T. Roberts and H. Searle, New York: Grove Press, 1959. A biography by a close friend of the composer.

Wagner, Richard, *My Life,* London: Constable, 1911.

White, Eric W., *Stravinsky: The Composer and His Works,* Berkeley: University of California Press, 1966.

GLOSSARY

A cappella   Without instrumental accompaniment.

Accelerando   A gradual increase in tempo.

Antecedent-consequent   Two complementary phrases; in the most limited sense, the phrases begin alike but end differently —the first (antecedent) ending with a half cadence, the second (consequent) ending with a full cadence.

Arco   With the bow—a direction for players of stringed instruments. (Compare with *Pizzicato*).

Aria   A song of some complexity, usually for one voice, with instrumental accompaniment. It occurs in operas, oratorios, and cantatas.

Arpeggio   A broken chord; the successive sounding of the notes of a chord.

Atonality   Without tonality; that is, without a tonal center; characteristic of much twentieth-century music.

Augmented interval   A major or perfect interval raised by a half step (e.g., C–E♯ is an augmented 3rd, F–B♮ is an augmented 4th; G–D♯ is an augmented 5th).

Augmented Triad   A three-note chord which, going up from its root, includes a major third and an augmented 5th, or two major thirds (e.g., C–E–G♯).

Bar line   Musical symbol indicating the regular grouping of beats, or meter.

Baroque   The period in music history encompassing the seventeenth and half of the eighteenth centuries.

Basso continuo   Literally, "continuous bass," the lowest part in a composition of the Baroque era, played by a bass instrument and a keyboard instrument that plays chords.

Bransle, also Branle   A popular sixteenth-century dance.

Cadence   The ending of a phrase or longer section (see also *Full cadence; Half cadence*).

Cadenza An improvisatory solo passage usually occurring near the end of a movement of a concerto where it serves to delay the conclusion and gives the soloist a chance to display technical brilliance.

Caesura Moment of arrested motion often articulating phrase structure within a piece; a breathing pause.

Canon A composition in two or more parts in which the melody is imitated exactly and completely by the successively entering voices though not always at the same pitch.

Cantata Literally, a piece that is sung (*cantare,* Italian, "to sing"), in contrast to *sonata,* a piece that is played (*sonare,* Italian, "to sound"). It is an extended work for chorus and/or solo voices, usually with orchestral accompaniment.

Catch English round of the seventeenth and eighteenth centuries. Catches were often based on rather "indecent" texts.

Chorale A hymn tune of the German Protestant church. Chorale melodies are best known today through their harmonizations by J. S. Bach.

Chorus (1) A group of singers; (2) refrain; (3) in jazz, a structural unit, e.g., a twelve- or thirty-two-bar section of a piece.

Chromatic In tonal harmony, use of pitches in addition to those found in a given major or minor scale—therefore, a "mixing of families of pitches."

Chromatic scale Scale consisting of all twelve pitches available in Western music.

Classical The period in music history roughly between 1750 and 1827.

Coda Literally, "tail" (Italian); a passage at the end of a piece or movement that extends the ideas previously presented, bringing the work to a satisfying conclusion.

Codetta A small coda, often occurring at the end of a section rather than at the end of a complete work.

Concerto A work in several movements that exploits the contrast between a solo instrument and the full orchestra. A *violin concerto,* for example, is a work for solo violin and orchestra; a *horn concerto* is a work for solo French horn and orchestra.

Concerto grosso   A work in several movements that exploits the contrast between a small group of solo instruments (called the *concertino*) and the full orchestra (called *tutti*).

Conjunct   Refers to melodies in which the movement is predominantly stepwise.

Consonance   In tonal harmony, a classification of intervals such as the octave and the perfect fifth. Also, moments of relatively stable, or even conclusive, harmony.

Counterpoint   Except for some minor differences in emphasis, synonymous with *polyphony*. (See *Polyphonic.*)

Countersubject   A melody designed as a counterpoint to the subject of a fugue; it usually occurs for the first time above or below the second entrance of the subject.

Crescendo   A continuous increase in loudness.

Da capo   Literally, "from the head" or "top" (Italian); an indication to the performer to go back to the beginning.

Deceptive cadence   A cadence that sounds as if it were going to be conclusive, until its final chord, at which point the conclusion is interrupted (and the motion extended), usually by the substitution of the VI chord for I.

Degree   The numbers (1–7) assigned to the pitches of the diatonic scale; for example, C is the first degree (tonic) of the C-Major scale, B is the 7th degree of the C-Major scale.

Development   The section of a movement in sonata form between the exposition and the recapitulation in which the musical material from the exposition is developed, that is, "analyzed," broken apart, its potential explored. In a more general sense, the elaboration, manipulation, or transformation of musical material in the course of a composition.

Diatonic   Using almost exclusively the seven whole- and half-steps of the major and minor scales, as opposed to chromatic.

Diminished interval   A minor or perfect interval lowered by a half step (e.g., C–E$\flat\flat$ is a diminished 3rd; C–G$\flat$ is a diminished 5th).

Diminished Triad   A three-note chord which, going up from its root, includes a minor third and a diminished 5th or two minor thirds (e.g., C–E♭–G♭).

Disjunct   Refers to melodies in which the movement is predominantly by leap rather than by step.

Dissonance   In tonal harmony, a classification of intervals such as the major seventh, major second, or diminished fifth. Also, moments of relatively unstable or unresolved harmony.

Dodecaphonic   Twelve tones; used in reference to music written in "twelve-tone technique" (after Schoenberg); or, more generally, serial music.

Dominant   The fifth degree of a diatonic scale; the chord built on that tone.

Double   To play in unison with another instrument.

Duo   A piece for two instruments.

Episode   In the fugue, a phase in which the subject is absent or is present only in a fragmentary fashion.

Étude   Literally, "a study" (French); a piece written to help the student in developing technique. Some études (e.g., Chopin's) have become concert pieces in their own right.

Exposition   The first large section of a movement in sonata form; the first section of a fugue in which each of the voices enters with a fugue subject.

Fantasy, Fantasia   A composition in which the composer "exercises his fancy"; thus, a work that tends to be freer in structure than one following a conventional form.

Figure   See *Motive*.

Finale   The last movement of an instrumental work written after about 1750, or the concluding section of an operatic act.

First-movement form   See *Sonata form*.

Flamenco   Folk music of southern Spain (Andalusia).

Fugato   Usually a fugal exposition occurring in the development section of a movement in sonata form.

Fugue   A polyphonic work for two or more voices or instruments built on a subject (theme) that is introduced in imitation and recurs frequently throughout the composition.

Full cadence A phrase ending with a sense of completion—i.e., on the tonic.

Gavotte A French dance originating in the seventeenth century. It is in a moderate to fairly quick tempo and in duple meter (usually $\frac{4}{4}$) and often begins on the third beat of the measure.

Gigue One of the four traditional dance movements in suites written around 1700, usually the last (standard movements being *allemande, courante, sarabande,* and *gigue*). It is characterized by compound meter and dotted rhythm, and frequently by imitative polyphony.

Gregorian chant The liturgical chant of the Roman Catholic church, named after Pope Gregory I (590–604).

Half cadence Unresolved ending of a phrase, usually with dominant harmony.

Harmonic rhythm The rate of change, the rhythm, of the chords in a composition or a part of a composition.

Homophony A texture in which one instrument (or voice) plays a dominant role while the other instruments play a clearly subordinate accompaniment.

Imitation One instrument or voice "imitating" another; that is, successive statements of a motive in different strands of the texture.

Impromptu A title given to a one-movement piece for piano in the early Romantic Period.

Improvisation Spontaneously performed composition usually with reference to some given progression or structure but without reference to written music.

Instrumentation The assignment of specific instruments to play specific parts in a given composition; composers indicate the precise instrumentation in the score.

Interval The distance between two tones.

Invention A term most commonly associated with a set of fifteen keyboard pieces by J. S. Bach that are written in two parts and are highly polyphonic.

Inversion Literally, a change of direction; refers to melodies in which the direction of the successive intervals is reversed.

Also, a rearrangement of the notes in a chord so that the root is no longer the lowest.

Key Tonal center or tonality of a piece.

Ländler An Austrian dance in triple meter, forerunner of the waltz.

Leap See *Disjunct.*

Legato The smooth connection of the successive tones of a melody in performance. (Compare with *Staccato.*)

Madrigal In the sixteenth century, a choral work, usually unaccompanied, with a text which the music follows rather closely. It is often imitative and polyphonic and tends to have a stronger sense of beat than its sacred counterpart, the motet.

Major See *Mode.*

March A piece in duple meter with a strongly marked beat.

Mass The central Roman Catholic religious service and also a musical setting of that service. Its major sections are *Kyrie, Gloria, Credo, Sanctus,* and *Agnus Dei.*

Mazurka Originally, a Polish folk dance, later a stylized piano piece.

Mbira African thumb piano.

Measure The unit formed by the regular grouping of beats, sometimes called a bar, and indicated in the score by bar lines.

Meter The regular organization of the beats into larger groups.

Metronome A device to indicate the precise tempo of a piece; invented by Mälzel in 1816.

Minor See *Mode.*

Minuet A French dance of peasant origin in triple meter and moderate tempo. It had a great vogue at the court of Louis XIV and continued its existence in the eighteenth century as a stylized dance in instrumental music.

Missa Latin for *Mass.*

Mode The specific scalar arrangement of tones within an octave; e.g., Dorian, Phrygian, major, minor, pentatonic.

Modulation. The process of moving from one tonal area to another, change of key.

Monophonic Unaccompanied melody such as chant.

Motet A type of choral work, most often with a Latin sacred text, which had a long history in the Middle Ages and the Renaissance.

Motive A small melodic-rhythmic pattern; smallest meaningful structural unit.

Movement The various self-contained sections of an extended instrumental composition such as a symphony, sonata, or string quartet.

Note The written symbol for a tone.

Obbligato An added part; literally, "required," but it sometimes has taken on the opposite meaning.

Octave An interval of 12 half steps; the octave(s) separates pitches of like names but different register, such as low *C*– high *C*.

Opus Literally, "work" (Latin); a musical composition; Opus 1 would be a composer's first published work.

Ostinato A figure repeated persistently, often in the bass, while other elements of the texture change.

Overture A term that most commonly refers to the instrumental music composed as an introduction to an opera, but also may refer to the first movement of a suite or to an entirely independent work (concert overture).

Partita Originally (in the early seventeenth century) a term signifying a set of variations; later the term was also used to mean a suite.

Passion A musical setting of the gospel accounts of the Passion (sufferings and death of Christ). In the seventeenth century it became a highly dramatic work for chorus and orchestra including recitatives, arias, chorales, and instrumental interludes.

Pedal A sustained or repeated tone, most frequently in the bass, and often the dominant of the key.

Pentatonic A mode of five tones, or a melody based on that mode. In non-western music, a division of the octave into five tones.

Period   A melodic-harmonic unit of two complementary phrases, such as antecedent-consequent.

Phrase   A structurally significant segment of a melody.

Pitch   Frequency, or vibrations per second; the relative highness or lowness of a musical tone.

Pitch-class   The set of pitches described by the same letter name (e.g., all F's or all C's are members of the same pitch class).

Pitch-space   The distance between tones as measured along the chromatic scale.

Pizzicato   A direction to players of bowed stringed instruments (violin, cello, etc.) to pluck the strings with the fingers.

Polyphony   A texture in which instruments or voices move independently of one another and are all of relatively equal importance.

Prelude   Originally, an introductory movement in a suite or an introduction to another piece (as in a prelude and fugue). In the nineteenth century the term was used also as a title for individual piano or orchestral pieces.

Range   The pitch-space between the highest and lowest tones of a melody or instrument.

Recapitulation   The section of a movement in sonata form that follows the development section and parallels the exposition.

Recitative   A style of singing imitating and emphasizing the natural inflections of speech in both pitch and rhythm. It occurs in opera, oratorio, cantata, and passion and tends to serve a narrative function; often coupled with an aria.

Refrain   A phrase or verse which recurs regularly at the end of each large division of a song.

Register   A particular segment of the range of an instrument or voice (e.g., the lower register of the clarinet in contrast to the upper register).

Rhapsody   A title given by composers in the nineteenth and early twentieth centuries to instrumental works of a somewhat heroic or "rhapsodic" character.

Ricercare   A polyphonic instrumental piece, originating in the sixteenth century.

Ritardando A gradual slowing down of tempo.

Romantic The period in music history roughly between 1827 and 1900.

Rondo Most often a movement in a larger work (symphony, sonata, or concerto—of which it is often the last movement) characterized by a highly sectional design which includes a recurring refrain alternating with contrasting material. It may be diagramed as ABACADA . . .

Root The fundamental, or generating, tone of a chord.

Root position Refers to the arrangement of the tones of a chord with the root as the lowest.

Round A circular canon.

Rubato Literally, "rob" (Italian); the subtle give-and-take or flexibility with which the performer treats the rate of the underlying pulse.

Sanctus Literally, "holy" (Latin); a section of the Roman Catholic mass.

Sarabande A dance in slow triple meter which was one of the four dances included in suites around 1700.

Scale Literally, "ladder" (Italian); a series of discrete pitches ordered from low to high.

Scherzo Literally, "joke" (Italian); it is a movement in a symphony (or trio, quartet, or other instrumental work) taking the place of the minuet. Although faster in tempo, it is, like the minuet, in triple meter.

Score The notation of a musical composition.

Sequence Repetition of a melodic pattern or figure at successively higher or lower pitch levels within the same strand of the texture.

Shamisen A Japanese lute, used to accompany singers.

Sitar An Indian lute with many strings.

Sonata Derived from the Italian *sonare* ("to sound"); it is a work in several movements for a small number of instruments.

Sonata form A particular structural design found most frequently in the first movement of a sonata, symphony, or string quartet, but also used in the slow movement and the final movement.

Sonority The sound resulting from a particular combination of instruments, or (in late nineteenth- and twentieth-century music) the sound resulting from a particular combination of pitches.

Staccato A manner of performance in which notes are played quickly, lightly, and detached from one another. (Compare with *Legato*.)

Stepwise See *Conjunct*.

Stress To play louder.

Stretto A phase in a fugue in which each of the voices enters with the subject in rapid succession, that is, before the subject has been stated in its entirety.

String quartet A group of four string instruments—two violins, viola, and cello; also a work in three or four movements for these instruments.

Subdominant The fourth degree of a diatonic scale and the triad built on that tone; the "underdominant" or 5th *below* the tonic.

Subject The opening statement in a fugue; that is, the theme of a fugue.

Suite Before approximately 1750, an instrumental composition consisting of several movements, each of them dancelike and all in the same key. After 1750, a set of movements excerpted from a ballet or opera.

Symphony Essentially a sonata for orchestra; that is, a work in several movements composed for a relatively large group of instruments.

Syncopation A temporary displacement or shifting of the expected accent, often confounding the meter.

Tabla A small Indian drum.

Tamboura A large Indian lute used to play a drone, that is, a repeated or sustained bass tone or tones.

Tempo The rate of speed of the underlying pulse.

Theme The principle musical idea (melody, motive, harmonic progression, sonority, etc.) or subject of a composition.

Theme and variations An independent work or a movement of a larger work (such as a sonata or symphony) in which a musical idea (theme) is presented and then varied so that some aspects of the theme remain constant while others undergo change. The composition is generally highly sectional and "additive" rather than developmental; each variation is often a self-contained unit.

Timbre Tone color; the quality of a tone as played by a particular instrument.

Toccata From the Italian *toccare* ("to touch"); it is a composition for a keyboard instrument characterized by a free style, often with elaborate running passages contrasted with full chords, and occasionally containing fugal sections.

Tone A sound with regularity of vibration and consequently fixed pitch; also refers to timbre.

Tone poem, Symphonic poem A nineteenth-century symphonic composition based on an extramusical idea that is either poetic or descriptive.

Tonic Tonal center; the pitch which functions as the most stable in a collection of pitches within the context of tonal harmony.

Transition The moving from one stable area of thematic statement to another, usually involving change of key.

Transposition In the simplest sense, the playing of a melody in a different key.

Triad A simultaneous sounding of three tones; a chord of only three pitches.

Trio (1) A work for any three instruments. A *piano trio* is a composition for violin, cello, and piano; a *string trio* is usually a work for violin, viola, and cello; a *horn trio* may be a work for French horn, violin, and piano. (2) In the minuet or scherzo movement of a symphony, sonata, or quartet, the middle section played between the minuet or scherzo proper, and its repetition.

Trio Sonata In the Baroque period, a work for two instruments and basso continuo; usually played by four instruments since the continuo includes a keyboard instrument (e.g., harpsichord) and a bass instrument (e.g., cello).

Tritone Literally, "three tones"; the interval of three whole steps, either a diminished fifth or augmented fourth, classified traditionally as the most dissonant interval (for example, C–F#).

Tutti Literally, "all" (Italian); in a concerto grosso, the full ensemble in contrast to the solo group; also a section of a piece played by the full ensemble.

Unison Two or more people playing or singing either the same tones or in octaves.

Variation See *Theme and variations*. In a more general sense variation consists in realizing the implications of any musical material as, for instance, in development.

Waiting passage A passage generating tension through elaboration of dominant harmony and usually preceding a thematic statement.

Waltz A dance in triple meter which may be slow or fast in tempo. It originated in the late eighteenth century in Austria, and stemmed from the Ländler or German dance.

INDEX OF COMPOSERS AND WORKS

INDEX OF SUBJECTS

87 88 89 10